Study Guide: Genesis to Revelation

A Chapter by Chapter Summary of the Entire Bible

by Paul Griffin

First published July 2016

About the Author

Although raised in a religious home, I only really encountered Jesus in a personal way in my late thirties whilst working for an international oil company in Japan. I immediately experienced a great desire to read and understand God's word and shortly thereafter I took early retirement and enrolled in a Bible College back in England.

Since graduating from Bible College in 1991, I have been serving the Lord full time in the healing ministry as part of the Ellel Ministries team at Ellel Grange near Lancaster, England. It has been a great privilege to witness God at work bringing healing and restoration as individuals have understood and appropriated into their own lives the truths revealed in God's word.

Paul Griffin

Table of Contents

About the Author 2

Genesis 7

Exodus 13

Leviticus 19

Numbers 23

Deuteronomy 30

Joshua 36

Judges 40

Ruth 44

1 Samuel 45

2 Samuel 50

1 Kings 54

2 Kings 58

1 Chronicles 63

2 Chronicles 67

Ezra 74

Nehemiah 76

Esther 79

Job 81

Psalms 88

Proverbs 109

Ecclesiastes 127

Song of Songs 130

Isaiah 132

Jeremiah	143
Lamentations	152
Ezekiel	154
Daniel	162
Hosea	165
Joel	168
Amos	169
Obadiah	171
Jonah	172
Micah	173
Nahum	174
Habakkuk	175
Zephaniah	176
Haggai	177
Zechariah	178
Malachi	181
Matthew	182
Mark	190
Luke	196
John	202
Acts	208
Romans	215
1 Corinthians	218
2 Corinthians	221
Galatians	224
Ephesians	226

Philippians 228
Colossians 230
1 Thessalonians 232
2 Thessalonians 234
1 Timothy 235
2 Timothy 237
Titus 238
Philemon 239
Hebrews 240
James 243
1 Peter 245
2 Peter 247
1 John 248
2 John 250
3 John 251
Jude 252
Revelation 253

Genesis 10 records the genealogy of Noah and the lands that they dwelt in. It is interesting to note that Canaan, who was cursed because his father Ham had seen Noah's nakedness, established Sodom and Gomorrah and occupied the land that God was going to give to His chosen people.

In Genesis 11 we read that mankind was scattered throughout the world with different languages, following their attempt to build a tower at Babel and make themselves like God. We also read the genealogy of Shem to Abram. Abram was married to Sarai, who was childless.

Genesis 12 records how Abraham, in obedience to God's call, leaves Ur and travels to Canaan. God promises Abraham that he will become a great nation, through whom the world will be blessed, and that his offspring will be given the land. A famine forces Abraham to go to Egypt, where he is deceptive in saying that Sarai is his sister rather than his wife, in order to gain favour with the Pharaoh.

In Genesis 13 we read how Abraham, who had now become quite wealthy, and his nephew Lot separate. Lot chooses to live near Sodom. Abraham moves to Canaan, and God again repeats His promise that Abraham will have many offspring and that the land will be his for ever.

Genesis 14 records how Abraham rescues Lot and his family. They had been captured by tribes who attacked Sodom and Gomorrah. On his return from battle Abraham gives a tithe (one tenth) of the spoils of victory to Melchizedek, the king of Salem and a priest of God. Abraham refuses to take any reward from the King of Sodom, so that he will not be obligated to him.

In Genesis 15 God repeats for a third time His promise to Abraham, that Abraham will have offspring and will possess the land that will become Israel. God seals this promise with a covenant. God tells Abraham that his descendants will go into captivity for four hundred years before returning to inhabit the land.

Genesis 16 records how Abraham tries to fulfil God's promise of offspring by fathering a child through Hagar, the servant girl of his wife Sarai. The angel of the Lord names the child Ishmael, says he will have many descendants (the Arab nations), and that there will be hostility between him and his brothers.

In Genesis 17, for the fourth time, God repeats His promise that Abraham will have descendants and inherit the land of Canaan. God instructs Abraham to seal this covenant by male circumcision. God promises that Sarai, who is ninety years old and now renamed Sarah, will have a son within a year. This son is to be named Isaac, and God will establish His covenant with him.

In Genesis 18 we read that Abraham meets with the Angel of the Lord, who again promises that Abraham and Sarah will have a son, and two other men (angels) who are on their way to Sodom and Gomorrah to execute God's judgement. In response to Abraham's questions the Angel of the Lord says that, in His mercy, God will not destroy the cities if any righteous inhabitants are found living there.

Genesis 19 records the destruction of Sodom and Gomorrah because of gross immorality and sexual sin. God provides a place of refuge for Lot and his family, but Lot's wife is disobedient to God's instructions and perishes. Lot fathers two sons by his daughters, from whom the Moabites and Ammonites descend.

In Genesis 20 we read how Abraham is again deceptive about his relationship to Sarah. Abimelech takes Sarah into his harem, although he does not sleep with her. When Abimelech learns the truth, he is repentant for what he has done and returns Sarah to Abraham. Abraham prays for Abimelech and his family, and a curse of barrenness because of what Abimelech did is removed.

In Genesis 21 we read that God is faithful to the promise made to Abraham, and Sarah has a son named Isaac. Because of the rivalry between Sarah and Hagar, God instructs Abraham to send Hagar and Ishmael away. God promises that Ishmael will become a great nation and provides water for them in the desert.

In Genesis 22 we read how, in obedience to God, Abraham is willing to sacrifice his beloved son Isaac. He is commended for his fear of the Lord and his desire to be obedient to God whatever the cost. God provides an alternative sacrifice and reaffirms His promises to Abraham.

In Genesis 23 we read how Sarah dies and the arrangements that Abraham makes for her burial. Abraham refuses the gift of a tomb in which to bury his wife, but insists on buying a plot of land. The deal is completed and part of the land of Canaan that God promised to Abraham is now legally his. Abraham did not want his son to marry a Canaanite woman, but someone from his own family.

Genesis 24 records how, with God's leading, Rebekah becomes the wife of Isaac.

Genesis 25 records the death of Abraham and how he was buried in the land he had purchased. The descendants of Ishmael are also listed. Following prayer for her barrenness, Rebekah gives birth to Jacob and Esau. Esau, the first born, 'despises' his birth-right and gives it away to Jacob, in exchange for a bowl of soup.

In Genesis 26 we read that Isaac moves to Gerar and, like his father before him, he deceives Abimelech about the true identity of Rebekah. Isaac becomes wealthy and moves to Beersheba where God meets with him and affirms His covenant with Isaac.

Genesis 27 records how Jacob deceives his father Isaac and receives the blessing that Isaac thought he was bestowing on Esau. Esau has it in his heart to kill Jacob, but Rebekah encourages Isaac to send Jacob away to Haran to find a wife for himself.

In Genesis 28 Jacob meets with God in a dream while he is *en-route* to Haran. God re-affirms that the land will be given to Jacob's descendants. Jacob's response is to set up a memorial stone and name the place Bethel (House of God).

Genesis 29 records how Jacob falls in love with Rachel and agrees to work for Laban for seven years so he can marry her. Laban deceives him and Jacob finds himself married to Leah. He is allowed to marry Rachel on the condition that he works a further seven years for Laban. Rachel is barren, but Leah gives birth to four sons.

Genesis 30 records how Jacob fathers more sons through Leah and the maidservants of Leah and Rachel. Finally, Rachel has a son whom she names Joseph. Jacob becomes very wealthy

Genesis 31 records how God tells Jacob to return to Canaan. Jacob fears Laban will not let him leave, so he departs secretly. Laban follows him, and Laban and Jacob enter into a peace agreement at Gilead.

In Genesis 32 Jacob fears his brother Esau is still angry with him and sends gifts to try and pacify him. Jacob wrestles all night with God, who changes his name to Israel.

In Genesis 33 Jacob and Esau meet again. Jacob insists that Esau keep the gifts he has given him. Jacob finally arrives in Canaan and buys land near Shechem.

In Genesis 34 Shechem falls in love with Dinah, the daughter of Jacob, and rapes her. This angers her brothers. They deceive the men of Shechem into circumcising themselves, and then kill them while they are recovering and still in pain.

Genesis 35 records that Jacob tells his household to get rid of all their foreign gods before they go to Bethel to build an altar to God. God appears to Jacob and re-affirms the promises made to Abraham and Isaac concerning the land of Canaan. Rachel dies giving birth to Jacob's twelfth son Benjamin.

Genesis 36 records the descendants of Esau. After Jacob came back to Canaan, Esau moved away to Seir and became the father of the Edomites. The detailed list of descendants highlights the importance placed on family and identity.

In Genesis 37 Joseph's brothers are jealous of him because he is the favourite of their father Jacob. After Joseph shares a dream of them bowing down to him, they plot to get rid of him, and eventually sell him to an Egyptian slave trader. They deceive their father Jacob into believing that Joseph had been killed by wild animals.

Genesis 38 digresses from the story of Joseph to record incidents in the life of his brother Judah, from whom King David descended. Judah fails to meet the custom of the day by having one of his sons marry Tamar, the childless widow of another son who had died. Tamar pretends to be a shrine prostitute and Judah ends up sleeping with her and fathering twin boys.

Genesis 39 records how Joseph becomes a slave in the house of Potiphar. Because God is with him, he is put in charge of the whole household. When Joseph resists the advances of Potiphar's wife, she accuses him of trying to rape her, and Joseph is thrown into prison. Because God is with him, Joseph is put in charge of all those held in the prison.

In Genesis 40 Joseph correctly interprets the dreams of the Pharaoh's cupbearer and baker. He asks the cupbearer to put in a good word for him with the Pharaoh, but the cupbearer forgets to do that and Joseph remains in prison a further two years.

In Genesis 41 the Pharaoh has a dream, which no one can interpret. The cupbearer remembers Joseph, who interprets the dream to mean there will be seven years of plenty followed by seven years of famine. The Pharaoh appoints him as his second-in-command to store food and manage the distribution of it during the famine. Joseph marries and has two sons, Manasseh and Ephraim.

In Genesis 42 Joseph's brothers come to Egypt to buy grain, but don't recognise Joseph. Joseph holds one of the brothers as a hostage and tells them they must return and bring Benjamin with them. They return home to Jacob, but are amazed and confused to discover that all the money they paid for the grain has been returned to them.

Genesis 43 records how Joseph's brothers return to Egypt, taking Benjamin with them. They are very fearful of how they will be treated. Joseph is overcome with emotion at seeing Benjamin again. He invites them to dinner and the brothers are amazed that they are seated in order of age.

In Genesis 44 Joseph accuses his brothers of stealing his drinking cup which Joseph placed in the grain sack belonging to Benjamin. He tells them that Benjamin must become his slave. Judah (the ringleader many years previously when they sold Joseph to the slave trader) begs Joseph to allow him to take Benjamin's place, because he knows the distress that the loss of Benjamin will cause Jacob, who is still mourning the loss of Joseph.

Genesis 45 records how Joseph, overcome with emotion, reveals himself to his brothers. He tells them that God has orchestrated everything, so that Israel will not perish in the famine. He sends them back to Canaan to fetch his father Jacob, and all their families to come and live in Egypt.

Genesis 46 records how Jacob and all his family leave Canaan and go to live in the land of Goshen. God meets with Jacob (now called Israel), tells him that he will become a great nation, and that God will bring them back out of Egypt. They arrive in Egypt and there is an emotional reunion between Jacob and Joseph.

In Genesis 47 Jacob meets the Pharaoh and is given permission to dwell in Goshen. Joseph continues to manage the food distribution for the Pharaoh and establishes great wealth for him. Jacob makes Joseph swear that when they leave Egypt they will take his body with them back to Canaan.

In Genesis 48 Jacob blesses the two sons of Joseph, Ephraim and Manasseh. They are to be considered as sons of Jacob. (Subsequently in the Bible we do not find Joseph listed as one of the tribes of Israel, but instead find both Ephraim and Manasseh included.) Jacob blesses the younger son Ephraim with the blessing which normally goes to the older son.

Genesis 49 records the blessings that Jacob prayed over each of his sons. Before he dies, he again gives instructions that his body is to be taken back and buried in the land of Canaan.

The Book of Genesis concludes in Chapter 50 with the account of how Joseph and his brothers bury Jacob in the land that Abraham had purchased as a burial ground. They return to Goshen, and Joseph allays his brothers' fears that he might now take revenge on them for the way they had treated him. He tells them *'what you intended to harm me, God intended for good.'*

Exodus

The Book of Exodus records how God delivered the Israelites from captivity in Egypt and dealt with them in the wilderness.

Exodus 1 explains how the family of Jacob multiplied greatly in Egypt, but were ruthlessly used in slave labour. The midwives feared God more than the Pharaoh and did not comply with his order to kill all new born baby males.

Exodus 2 records the early life of Moses. Moses was a Levite who was adopted by the daughter of the Pharaoh, who had found him in a basket floating on the River Nile, where his mother had placed him for fear he would be killed. Moses kills an Egyptian, who was maltreating an Israelite, and has to flee for his life. He becomes a shepherd and marries Zipporah the daughter of Jethro.

In Exodus 3 God appears to Moses in a burning bush and declares that His name is *'I am'*. He has heard the cry of His people in Israel, and is sending Moses to lead them out of captivity. The Pharaoh will not want to let the people go, but God will perform wonders amongst them. The Pharaoh will let them go, and the Egyptians will act favourably towards the Israelites, giving them jewels and clothing as they depart.

In Exodus 4 Moses is fearful that he will be rejected, even though God has given him miraculous signs to perform before the Israelites and the Pharaoh. He asks that God send someone else. God's response is that Moses is to use his brother Aaron as his spokesman. Moses returns to Egypt, and the Israelites rejoice and worship God, because He has heard their cry for help.

In Exodus 5 Moses confronts the Pharaoh and asks him to let the Israelites go, so they can worship God. The Pharaoh refuses, and, instead, puts further burdens on the Israelite slaves.

In Exodus 6 God reaffirms His covenant to Moses and says He will bring the Israelites into the land promised to Abraham, Isaac and Jacob. The Chapter concludes with the family trees of Reuben, Simeon and Levi.

In Exodus 7 God tells Moses that He will harden Pharaoh's heart through many miracles, but will then deliver His people with mighty acts of judgement. Moses and Aaron again confront the Pharaoh. Moses' staff turns into a snake which devours the snakes of the Pharaoh's magicians. Moses strikes the River Nile with his staff and it turns to blood. The Pharaoh, however, refuses to let the Israelites go.

Exodus 8 records the plague of frogs, followed by the plague of gnats. The Egyptian magicians are unable to replicate the plague of gnats, and they acknowledge that this plague is from God. The plague of flies only affects the Egyptians and not the Israelites living in Egypt.

Exodus 9 records the plague which killed off the Egyptians' livestock, the plague of boils and the plague of hailstones. The Pharaoh's heart remains hardened and he refuses to let the Israelites go.

In Exodus 10 the plague of locusts is followed by the plague of darkness, which affects the Egyptians, but not the Israelites. Pharaoh still refuses to let the Israelites depart.

In Exodus 11 Moses tells the Pharaoh that God is about to bring a final plague upon the Egyptians. The first-born son in every family will die.

In Exodus 12 God institutes the festival of Passover. The Israelites are to take a one-year-old lamb without blemish as a sacrifice, and put some of its blood on the door frames of their homes. God will not permit the destroyer to enter any home where the blood has been applied. That night the first-born in each Egyptian family dies. The Pharaoh finally relents and after four hundred and thirty years of captivity the Israelites leave Egypt.

In Exodus 13 God instructs Moses to consecrate the first-born male in each family to God. In memory of how God is bringing them out of slavery, every year, in the future, the Israelites are to eat nothing containing yeast for a seven-day period. As they leave Egypt God guides them in the form of a pillar of cloud by day and a pillar of fire by night.

In Exodus 14 we read that Pharaoh again hardens his heart and pursues the Israelites with his army of chariots. God miraculously divides the Red Sea so the Israelites can cross to safety, before the pursuing Egyptian army is totally destroyed.

Exodus 15 records a deliverance song celebrating how God has rescued the Israelites out of the hands of the Egyptians. They travel to Marah, where the water is bitter and undrinkable. God tells Moses to throw a piece of wood into the water, and the water becomes sweet. God promises the Israelites that He will not bring upon them any of the diseases that He brought upon the Egyptians, if they are obedient to His commands and decrees.

In Exodus 16 the Israelites start to grumble against Aaron and Moses. God provides them with quail and manna. Each day the Israelites are to collect just sufficient manna for that day. (When they collect more and try to store it, it becomes mouldy.) On the sixth day they are to collect sufficient for two days, as there will be no manna on the Sabbath. (The manna collected on this sixth day does not become mouldy.)

In Exodus 17 the Israelites grumble again but God provides water for them at Horeb, after Moses strikes the rock with his staff. The Amalekites attack the Israelites. Moses sends out Joshua to fight them, while himself, Aaron and Hur go to the top of the hill to pray. When Moses raises his hands the Israelites are winning, but, when he lowers them, the Amalekites are winning. Ur and Aaron support the arms of Moses and the Amalekites are defeated.

Exodus 18 records how Moses' father-in-law, Jethro, visits Moses and rejoices in all that the God has done in bringing the Israelites out of Egypt. He advises Moses on how to administer the Israelites so that Moses will not become overworked and burnt out. Moses agrees with his plan and sets up capable men as administrators and judges.

Exodus 19 records how the Israelites reach Mount Sinai, and how God tells them to prepare themselves because He is going to meet with them. Because of God's holiness the people, other than Moses and Aaron, are warned not to approach the mountain.

Exodus 20 records God speaking out the ten commandments. The people are very afraid, but Moses encourages them and tells them that the fear of God should stop them from sinning. God tells the people, through Moses, not to make for themselves any idols of silver or gold.

Exodus 21 records God's instructions to the Israelites. Regulations regarding slavery are given. (The equivalent today would be contracts of employment.) Slaves are to be treated fairly and given back their freedom, unless they voluntarily choose to continue serving their master. Regulations and compensation for personal injuries are specified. The severity of the penalties (loss of one's own life, or an eye for an eye) were to impress upon the Israelites the high value that God places on life.

Exodus 22 continues the regulations given to the Israelites. Laws are given to protect property, and penalties are imposed upon those that steal, or are found in possession of stolen property. Other regulations cover the death penalty for bestiality, witchcraft or idolatry. Widows and orphans are to be protected, and those who borrow money because they are needy are to be treated with compassion.

Exodus 23 records further instructions from God regarding treating others fairly and with compassion. Instructions are given regarding the celebration of special festivals. Good health is promised for worshipping the true God and not entering into idolatry. God tells the Israelites to drive out the inhabitants of the promised land and not to make treaties with them or the inhabitants will become a snare to them.

In Exodus 24 the people agree to follow all of God's instructions. Moses builds an altar and sacrifices to God. The glory of God settles on Mount Sinai and Moses goes up the mountain to meet with God for forty days and nights.

Exodus 25 records the instructions given by God for constructing the sanctuary from offerings of precious metals and materials given by the Israelites. The cover of the tabernacle was to include two cherubim with outstretched wings at either end (symbolically protecting the holiness of God.) God would meet with Moses here and give His instructions to the Israelites.

Exodus 26 records the details of how the tent of the tabernacle was to be made. It was to be 300 feet long and 120 feet wide. Details of the curtains, coverings, frames and support posts are given. Within the tabernacle the Most Holy Place containing the ark of the covenant was to be separated from the Holy Place by a curtain embroidered with cherubim.

In Exodus 27 there are further instructions regarding the construction of the altar and the courtyard of the tabernacle, which was to be 150 feet long and 75 feet wide. The priests were to keep oil lamps burning in the tabernacle throughout the night.

In Exodus 28 detailed instructions are given for making the garments to be worn by the priests. The precious stones adorning the garments symbolise that the priests are representing the people. The details given by God serve to remind and impress upon us something of the holiness of God.

Exodus 29 gives details of how Aaron and his sons are to be ordained and anointed to serve as priests in the tabernacle. The sacrifice of animals and the sprinkling of blood are important parts of the consecration ceremony. The instruction for the daily offering of lambs together with a flour and wine offering reminds us of the perfect sacrifice to be revealed in Jesus.

Exodus 30 has instructions for making the incense altar and the bronze basin for washing. A special anointing oil is to be made, and only used for consecrating or anointing the tabernacle or priests. Instructions are also given for making a special incense, only to be used in the tabernacle. The sacredness of the oil and incense will remind the Israelites of the holiness of God.

In Exodus 31 Bezalel is filled with the Spirit of God and given giftings in all kinds of crafts. This serves as a reminder to us that creativity is a characteristic of God. Because we are made in God's image, we too can be creative. We are reminded of the importance of observing the Sabbath. God writes out the commandments on tablets of stone and gives them to Moses.

Exodus 32 records how the Israelites rebel against God by making a golden calf and worshipping it. This arouses the anger of God, but Moses intercedes on behalf of the people. In his anger at what the people have done Moses throws down the tablets of stone. The Levites rally to Moses' side, and are sent to kill those who are sinning against God.

In Exodus 33 Moses meets with God face to face in the tent of meeting, which was outside the camp. God tells Moses that He will give the Israelites the land He has promised to them, but threatens not to go with them. Moses' response is to ask God not to order them to move unless His presence goes with them.

Exodus 34 records how Moses chiselled out new stone tablets before meeting with God again on Mount Sinai. God renews His covenant with the Israelites. God will drive out the people in the Promised Land. The Israelites are reminded to keep God's commands; not to marry with the people in the land, or to make treaties with them, or the people will be a snare to them. Whenever Moses meets with the Lord his face is radiant.

In Exodus 35 the Israelites bring free will offerings of materials to be used in the making of the tabernacle and the associated utensils and clothing to be worn by the priests.

In Exodus 36 the offerings of materials from the Israelites are in excess of what is needed and they must be restrained from bringing even more. Bezalel and the skilled craftsmen construct all that is needed for the tabernacle in accordance with the instructions that God gave Moses.

In Exodus 37 Bezalel constructs the ark of the covenant, the table of incense and the lampstands, in accordance with God's instructions. They are covered in gold and constructed so that they can be carried from place to place.

Exodus 38 tells us more about the construction of the tabernacle. The craftsmen obediently follow all the design instructions given to Moses by God. Details are given of the quantities of gold, silver and bronze to be used.

In Exodus 39 the craftsmen prepare the sacred clothing to be worn by Aaron and the priests. The Israelites are careful to follow all

God's instructions. They complete the work, and Moses blesses them because everything had been done in obedience to God's plan.

In Exodus 40 the tabernacle is finally assembled and consecrated, along with Aaron and the priests, in accordance with God's instructions. (In this chapter we find the phrase *'as the Lord commanded'* repeated eight times.) When the work is complete the glory of the Lord fills the tabernacle in the form of a cloud and fire, which is visible to all the Israelites.

Leviticus

The Book of Leviticus details moral, ceremonial and dietary laws that stress the holiness of God and how the Israelites are to worship Him.

Leviticus 1 gives general instructions for making burnt animal offerings, with specific instructions regarding the blood of each offering.

Leviticus 2 gives general instructions for the burnt grain offerings. These offerings are to be without yeast (sin) and are to contain salt (cleansing).

Leviticus 3 gives details of the fellowship or peace offering. This type of offering is an act of recognition or renewing of the covenantal relationship existing between God and mankind. The fat, which is considered to be the best part of the animal, is to be given to God by burning it.

Leviticus 4 details the sacrifices to be made as sin offerings. Sacrifices are specified for the cases when the priests, the community as a whole, leaders or commoners have sinned. In all cases sprinkling of the blood is required, symbolising a cleansing from the consequences of the sin. It is stated that these sacrifices relate to 'unintentional' sin. The consequences of sin are not mitigated because the sin was committed in ignorance.

Leviticus 5 records the details of the guilt offerings. These offerings are to be made when people become defiled by touching something unclean, cause an injustice to take place by not speaking up, or carelessly make an oath. The 'sinners' must confess their sin, and different offerings are to be made, (depending upon their wealth).

Leviticus 6 details the sacrifices and restitution to be made when a sin is committed involving someone else's property. Instructions are given for how the priests are to carry out the various sacrifices. The details provided serve as a reminder to us of the holiness of God and how easily we can become defiled by sin.

Leviticus 7 continues the detailed instructions for how the priests are to carry out the various sacrifices. Although offered to God, the sacrifices can be eaten by the priests - effectively the people are supporting the priests, whose full time role is standing in the gap between them and God. The sacrificial offerings are to be considered holy and set apart for God, and will be defiled if not handled correctly.

Leviticus 8 describes how Moses, following the instructions

God gave him, ordains Aaron and his sons to serve as priests in the tabernacle. Anointing the ear lobes, big toe and thumbs of the priests (the physical extremities of the individual) symbolically represents a complete dedication of the individual to God.

In Leviticus 9 Moses instructs Aaron and the priests (who are now ordained for the task) to make sin offerings for themselves and for the people. After they complete the sin offerings, burnt offerings and fellowship offerings, the glory of the Lord appears and fire comes down from heaven and consumes the offerings on the altar.

Leviticus 10 records how two of Aaron's sons are instantly killed by God for being disobedient and offering 'unauthorised' fire. God tells Aaron the importance of separating between the holy and the mundane.

Leviticus 11 lists the animals that are to be considered clean or unclean. A primary reason for this differentiation is to remind the Israelites that they are chosen by God and are different to the other nations.

Leviticus 12 gives the purification ritual after childbirth. It is unclear why the time of purification is twice as long following the birth of a daughter than it is for the birth of a son. (Some commentators consider that this time difference is because the son 'atones' for himself by his own blood shed during his circumcision.)

Leviticus 13 gives detailed instructions concerning skin diseases (leprosy) and mildew. Such conditions are considered 'unclean' and regulations are aimed at preventing further spreading of the condition or defilement of the 'holy'.

Leviticus 14 gives the detailed regulations relating to cleansing and purification after someone has been declared healed of a skin disease, as well as the cleansing of buildings declared free of mildew. In the case of skin diseases, sin offerings, guilt offerings and burnt offerings are to be made, in addition to sprinkling with the 'water of cleansing.'

Leviticus 15 records the regulations concerning ceremonial uncleanness as a result of discharges from the male and female reproductive organs. When considering how to apply Leviticus today we need to distinguish between unchanging moral law (for which a penalty is usually specified in Leviticus) and ceremonial law or hygienic law.

In Leviticus 16 we read the instructions concerning the Day of Atonement. Wearing special garments Aaron is to initially make cleansing sacrifices for himself and the priests. He is then to make burnt and sin offerings for the people, before laying his hands on the scapegoat to signify transferring the guilt and iniquity from the people on to the goat. This chapter reminds us that Jesus has fulfilled the law by becoming the scapegoat for us.

In Leviticus 17 the Israelites are instructed that offerings are only to be made to God at the tent of meeting. In order to impress upon them the significance of the shedding of blood as an important part of the sacrificial system the Israelites are prohibited from following the practices of the other nations. They are not to drink or eat blood indiscriminately.

Leviticus 18 primarily records moral law relating to sexual sin and perversion. Sexual relationships with related family members is prohibited. The practices listed, including homosexuality and child sacrifice, result in the land becoming defiled and are detestable to God.

Leviticus 19 starts with a call to holiness and goes on to stipulate how this was to be practically outworked by the Israelite community. The regulations include moral law and ceremonial law regarding the sacrificial system. The Israelites are not to copy the practices of the pagan nations. Holiness also requires that the Israelites should love and help one another and treat each person fairly.

Leviticus 20 continues to instruct the Israelites in how they are to live in holiness. Worship of Molech, which included child sacrifice, is strictly prohibited. The severe penalties (often a death penalty) is to impress upon the Israelites the seriousness of breaking the law. The authority and power to remove the consequence of sin through deliverance is not yet available and so the death penalty may be seen as a way of protecting future generations.

Leviticus 21 and 22 specifies that the priests must aspire to higher levels of holiness. They must avoid anything that would make them defiled or unclean and disqualify them from being allowed to eat the sacrificial food. Those with physical defects (viewed as an outward consequence of sin) were prohibited from serving as priests. The sacrifices, brought by the Israelites as offerings, had to be without blemish or defect.

In Leviticus 23 the regulations are given for observing the weekly Sabbath and special appointed feasts. The Israelites are to hold sacred assemblies to celebrate the Passover, First Fruits, Feast of Weeks, Feast of Trumpets, Day of Atonement and the Feast of Tabernacles.

In Leviticus 24 the lamps in the temple are to be continually burnt and a weekly offering of loaves made to the Lord. The son of an

Israelite woman and an Egyptian man is stoned to death for blaspheming the name of God. (The Jews were later to try and use this same law to justify crucifying Jesus.) Sanctity of life is stressed, with like for like punishment, including the death penalty for the unlawful killing of another.

Leviticus 25 teaches about the importance of land and records regulations regarding the Jubilee Year, to be celebrated every fifty years, when land is to be returned to its original owner. The Israelites are not to be enslaved by fellow Israelites if they become destitute. They are to be treated as hired men, who could be redeemed at any time by a fair payment, and they are to be completely set free in the year of Jubilee.

In Leviticus 26 the Israelites are told if they follow God's laws and decrees they will prosper in the land, and will enjoy good rainfall and harvests. If they disobey God's commands, they will suffer the consequences. Their crops will fail and their enemies will defeat them. They will experience hardship, be taken into captivity, their cities destroyed and the land will be laid waste. Despite all this God will not forsake them but remember His covenant with them.

Leviticus 27 records the regulations regarding dedications and vows. (These were promises made to give something to God if He would grant some divine favour.) These vows could be monetary amounts, or could be animals, people, houses or land. In some situations, vows could be redeemed by paying the value of the vowed property plus a premium. A tithe of all the produce of the land (including animals) belongs to God.

Numbers

The Book of Numbers (so called because it includes the results of two censuses carried out by Moses) covers the period when the Israelites were in the wilderness before entering the Promised Land.

Numbers 1 records the census of the Israelite men, excluding the priestly tribe of Levi, who were over twenty years old and able to serve in the army. It lists the names of the leaders of each tribe given responsibility for counting their own tribe. The total number of men was just over six hundred thousand.

Numbers 2 describes how the tribes of Israel are to be divided into four groups when they set up camp. Each group is allocated an area to either the north, south, east and west, with the tabernacle in the centre. The order in which they are to set out when they move camp is also prescribed. The tabernacle and the Levis are to be in the centre whenever the Israelites move camp.

Numbers 3 records how the tribe of Levi are to be organised to look after the tabernacle. The names of each leader, the number of Levites in their clan, their specific responsibilities and the place where they are to camp around the tabernacle are listed. Each Levite is to represent a first-born son, who is to be set apart and consecrated to God. This is considered so important that a census is carried out and a redemption fee paid to ensure this requirement is met.

Numbers 4 records the details of the tasks to be performed by the three clans descended from Gershon, Kohath and Merari, the sons of Levi. In all, eight thousand five hundred and eighty men between the ages of thirty and fifty are assigned to look after the tabernacle.

Numbers 5 requires that anyone with an infectious skin disease, or who is ritually unclean through touching a dead body, must be sent outside the camp. If anyone wrongs another they must make restitution. If a woman is suspected of committing adultery she can be brought before the priests by her jealous husband and made to agree to a ritualistic curse coming upon herself, if she has indeed sinned against her husband.

In Numbers 6 we have the instructions concerning the taking of a Nazirite vow. This is when individuals choose to set themselves apart, or consecrate themselves to the Lord for a period of time. They are to abstain from alcohol and all grape products, not cut their hair and not to be defiled in any way by touching a dead body. Details are given of related sacrifices and offerings to be presented before the Lord. Samson, Samuel, John the Baptist and the apostle Paul all undertook Nazarite vows.

In Numbers 7:1-41 the tabernacle is completed, and Moses consecrates it. On successive days the leader of each of the tribes of Israel brings identical dedication offerings. They also bring a gift of carts and oxen, which are given to the Gershonites and Merarites to be used for transporting the tabernacle. The Kohathites are not given any carts however, because the most sacred things from the tabernacle, for which they were responsible, had to be hand carried.

Numbers 7:42-89 continues to record how, on successive days, the leader of each of the tribes of Israel brings identical dedication offerings. The repetition of these identical gifts serves as a reminder that each individual is responsible for their own praise and worship of God. When the tabernacle has been consecrated, Moses enters into the tent of meeting and meets with God

Numbers 8 records how the Levites are to be consecrated for their work in the tabernacle under the supervision of Aaron. The Levites belong to God in the place of the first-born sons of the Israelites. The details of the purification and consecration ceremonies are a reminder to us of the holiness of God and a challenge of whether we desire to be fully committed and set apart for God.

In Numbers 9 the Israelites are told to celebrate the Passover feast each year. It is a very important feast and an alternative date is set for those who are unable to celebrate the feast on the prescribed date. Those who refuse to celebrate the feast are to be excommunicated. A cloud covers the tabernacle. At night this cloud has the appearance of fire. When the cloud lifts the Israelites are to set out, but they are to remain encamped if the cloud does not lift.

In Numbers 10 God commands Moses to make two silver trumpets. These trumpets are to be blown to assemble the people or leaders as a signal for the tribes to move out of the camp during feasts and celebrations, and before the Israelites went into battle. The cloud lifts from above the tabernacle, and the Israelites set out in the order prescribed by God.

In Numbers 11 the Israelites arouse God's anger by craving meat and grumbling. They say it would have been better to have stayed in Egypt. God responds by miraculously providing quail that are blown into the camp, but at the same time a plague breaks out among the people. Moses tells God that he finds the burden of being in leadership too hard to bear. God instructs him to appoint seventy elders to help him and God puts His Spirit upon them.

In Numbers 12 Aaron and Miriam start to undermine Moses' authority, and speak against him because Moses' wife is a Cushite and not an Israelite. God asks them why they are not afraid to speak out against His faithful servant, with whom He speaks face to face. Miriam immediately becomes leprous, but Moses prays to God to heal her. God responds by saying that Miriam has to be put out of the camp for seven days because of her disgrace.

In Numbers 13 Moses sends spies, including Caleb and Joshua, to explore the Promised Land. They return with a good report about the land itself, but are fearful of the people living in the land. Caleb argues that they can certainly take the land, but the negativity of the others and their lack of trust in God, who had promised to give them the land, spreads throughout the encamped Israelites.

In Numbers 14 the people rebel against Moses and refuse to listen to Caleb and Joshua, who argue that the land is good and that the Lord will give them victory. God's glory appears, and He declares that, because of their unbelief, none of that generation except Caleb and Joshua will enter the promised land. The spies who spread the bad report are struck down by a plague. Against Moses' advice, the Israelites try to take the land, but are defeated, because God is not with them.

Numbers 15 documents various laws concerning offerings of animals, flour, oil and wine, to be made after the Israelites enter the Promised Land. These offerings include the first fruits offering, and offerings to be made if it is discovered that someone has sinned unintentionally. The seriousness of intentional sin is shown by the death penalty given to a man who broke the Sabbath. The practice of tying tassels on the hems of garments as a reminder of God's laws is introduced.

In Numbers 16 Korah and others rebel against the authority of Moses and Aaron. God brings judgement by causing the leaders of the rebellion to be swallowed by an earthquake and their followers to be burnt up by fire from heaven. When the Israelites accuse Moses of killing the Lord's people, a plague breaks out among them. It only stops when Aaron makes intercession and atonement for them before the Lord.

Numbers 17 records how God confirms to the people His choice of Aaron and the tribe of Levi to serve Him in the tabernacle. Each tribe has to place a wooden staff in the tent of meeting. Overnight Aaron's staff blossoms and produces fruit. It is decreed that his staff is to be placed before the ark of the covenant as a constant reminder to the people of what God has done.

In Numbers 18 God affirms that He has set apart Aaron and his descendants to be priests, and the tribe of Levi to serve them and do the work in the tabernacle. Aaron and his descendants are not to receive an inheritance in the land, but will receive all the 'non-burnt' offerings from the Israelites. The Levites will receive the tithe given by the Israelites, but they are to give a tithe (tenth) of this to the priests.

Numbers 19 describes the water of cleansing and its use. The water of cleansing is to be prepared from the ashes of a red heifer which has been ritually sacrificed and burnt. This water is to be sprinkled on the third and seventh day on anyone who is unclean because they have touched a dead body. The implication is that the application of the water of cleansing is more than a hygienic regulation. Spiritual cleansing is needed after a person has any contact with a dead body.

In Numbers 20 God provides water in the desert at Meribah when the Israelites grumble against Moses and Aaron. For not following God's commands, and implying that somehow they have provided the water, God decrees that neither Moses nor Aaron will be permitted to enter the Promised Land. The Edomites refuse to allow the Israelites to pass through their territory. (They are later punished for this.) Aaron dies and his son Eleazar takes his place.

Numbers 21 records the journey of the Israelites in the wilderness and how they defeat the Amorites and occupy their land. When the people grumble against God again they are afflicted with venomous snakes. God instructs Moses to make a bronze snake and put it on a pole. When the people look up to the snake they are healed. (A prophetic picture of us looking up to Jesus on the cross carrying our sin and receiving His forgiveness.)

In Numbers 22 the Midianites and Moabites are fearful of the Israelites and send for Balaam to curse them. Balaam initially refuses because God tells him that the Israelites are blessed by God. Later, when offered more reward, he deceives himself that God is allowing him to go. The angel of the Lord confronts Balaam by speaking through a donkey and then opens his eyes to see. Balaam is given permission to go, but instructed only to speak what God tells him to say.

Numbers 23 continues the account of Balaam being asked by the Moabites and Midianites to curse the Israelites. After building altars and sacrificing animals, Balaam twice receives messages of blessing from God and speaks them out in the presence of Balak. Balak protests that he has asked Balaam to curse the Israelites, but Balaam insists that he can only speak out that which God gives him.

Numbers 24 continues the account of Balaam being asked by the Midianites and Moabites to curse the Israelites. For a third time

Balaam speaks out a blessing over the Israelites. This message is not obtained through sorcery but through the Spirit of God, which falls on Balaam. After blessing rather than cursing Israel and thereby arousing the anger of King Balak, Balaam then boldly speaks out a prophecy of destruction to come upon the Moabites and the other nations that oppose Israel.

Numbers 25 records how the Israelites indulge in sexual immorality with Moabite women and worship the Baal of Peor. Phinehas is commended for his zealousness for the Lord when he kills an Israelite and a Moabite woman who blatantly sin in the midst of the Israelite camp. God declares that Phinehas and his descendants will know the blessing of the Lord. His action stops the plague that had come upon the Israelites because of their sexual sin and idolatry and killed twenty-four thousand of them.

Numbers 26 records the results of a second census which was carried out before the Israelites entered into the Promised Land. It records that the total number, excluding the tribe of Levi (separately counted as being twenty-three thousand), was just over six hundred thousand men. This census was to be used as a basis for allocating the land to the different tribes of Israel.

Numbers 27 records how inheritance was to be passed down the family line in the event that there were no male heirs. God tells Moses that Joshua, in whom the Spirit dwells, is to be his successor. Following God's instructions, Moses lays his hands on Joshua in front of the assembled Israelites, and commissions him to take over the leadership when he dies.

Numbers 28 gives details of the regular sacrifices to be offered each day, each Sabbath and on the first day of each month. It also details the timing of the special feasts of Passover, Unleavened Bread and First Fruits, which were to be observed by the Israelites, and the sacrifices to be made at these feasts. Lambs without blemish, flour and oil (bread) and wine are all included in the offerings to be made.

Numbers 29 gives more detail about the sacrifices the Israelites are to offer at the special feasts of Trumpets, Atonement and Tabernacles which are celebrated in the seventh month of the Jewish calendar. We can, however, give thanks to Jesus that He has become the one perfect sacrifice, replacing the need now for all of these individual offerings.

Numbers 30 records the regulations concerning vows and pledges. Such vows and pledges are not to be treated lightly, and a man must fulfil all that he has promised. Single women are under the covering of their fathers, and married women are under the covering of their husbands. A vow or pledge made by a woman could be renounced and nullified by their cover. If their cover knows of the vow or pledge and says nothing, it means that he does not object to what has been spoken out.

In Numbers 31 Phinehas and twelve thousand Israelites go to war against the Midianites and Moabites in revenge for them having tried to curse Israel, and for them leading the Israelites into idolatry and sexual sin. They defeated their enemy without losing any of their own soldiers, and are instructed to kill all of their enemies except any virgin women. All the spoils of war are to be cleansed and purified with fire or the water of cleansing, and part of them given to the priests and the Levites.

In Numbers 32 the tribes of Gad, Reuben and Manasseh come to Moses and say that they would like to take land east of the Jordan as their inheritance. Moses agrees, providing they still send their armed men to cross the Jordan and help the other tribes take possession of their inheritance. They agree to this and build cities east of the Jordan in which their families and flocks will be protected while they fulfil their promise to help the other tribes.

Numbers 33 documents each stage of the journey that the Israelites took in the forty years after leaving Egypt before they crossed the Jordan into the Promised Land. God instructs the Israelites, through Moses, to make sure that they drive out all the inhabitants of the land, and destroy all their idols and places of worship. If they fail to do this the inhabitants will become a problem to them.

Numbers 34 details the boundaries of the land that the Israelites are to establish when they cross over the Jordan into Canaan. The land is to be allocated to the different tribes according to their size. Eleazar and Joshua, together with a representative of each tribe, are assigned the task of distributing the land.

Numbers 35 says the Levites are to be allocated forty-eight cities and grazing land around them. Six of these cities are to be cities of refuge where people who accidently kill someone can go for protection. The sanctity of life is recognised in this chapter, and anyone who kills another person, acting towards them with hostile intent, shall, on the testimony of at least two witnesses, be put to death.

Numbers 36 contains the regulations with regard to land inherited by women. Such women are instructed to marry within their own tribe to ensure that the land will always remain within the tribe to which it was originally allocated, and will not revert to a different tribe at the next year of Jubilee.

Deuteronomy

The Book of Deuteronomy records Moses' instructions to the Israelites as they prepare to enter the Promised Land.

In Chapter 1:1-18 Moses recounts how God instructed him to appoint leaders and judges to help administer the Israelite nation. He reminds the people that God affirmed to them that He was going to give them the land which had been promised to Abraham, Isaac and Jacob.

In Deuteronomy 1:19-46 Moses continues to recount what happened to the Israelites after coming out of Egypt. Instead of believing God's promise that He would give them the land, they choose to be swayed by the report of the spies who had been sent into the land, and they grumbled against God. When God responded by saying none of that generation would enter the land, they tried to take the land in their own strength, but were defeated by the Amorites.

In Deuteronomy 2 Moses continues to recount the history of the Israelites during the wilderness years. They were instructed not to provoke the people of Seir to war. However, the land of Sihon which is east of the River Jordan was given over to the Israelites. They defeated the inhabitants and took possession of it.

In Deuteronomy 3 Moses continues to recount the history of the Israelites during the wilderness years. Following the capture of Sihon, the Israelites defeated King Og and possessed the land of Bashan. The lands taken to the east of the Jordan were to be allocated to the tribes of Reuben, Gad and Manasseh. Because Moses had angered God, he is not to be allowed to enter the Promised Land, but he encourages Joshua that God will give the Israelites the land of Canaan.

In Deuteronomy 4 Moses reminds the Israelites that they are like no other nation, because God spoke to them at Mount Horeb when He gave them the ten commandments. He encourages them to observe the law and to teach it to their children. He reminds the Israelites not to worship false gods, or they will perish from the land. Moses prophesies that they will turn away from God, but will turn back to Him in the latter days.

In Deuteronomy 5 Moses recalls the ten commandments spoken out by God on Mount Horeb and recorded on the tablets of stone. Having heard God's voice, the Israelites are filled with fear and ask Moses to be the intermediary between themselves and God. They want Moses to speak with God, and they promise to listen to and obey all of God's instructions which Moses relays to them.

In Deuteronomy 6 Moses addresses the Israelites declaring the greatness of God and exhorting them to love God with all of their being, and to never forget what He has done for them. If they want to enjoy blessing in the Promised Land they must keep His commandments and impress them upon their children and subsequent generations. Obedience to all of the law will be credited to them as righteousness.

In Deuteronomy 7 the Israelites are instructed to drive out and completely destroy all the inhabitants of the Promised Land. They are not to marry them or make treaties with them. They are to destroy all the idols and places of worship, and not bring them into their homes. Obedience to God's commands will result in blessings and good health. They are encouraged to not be afraid, as God will drive out their enemies little by little, and no one will be able to stand against them.

In Deuteronomy 8 Moses continues to instruct the Israelites before they enter the Promised Land. They must never forget how God brought them out of Egypt and provided for them during their wanderings and time of testing in the desert. If they become proud and forget the Lord and do not obey His law and commandments they, just like the other nations, will bring destruction upon themselves.

In Deuteronomy 9 the Israelites are reminded that they are not being given the Promised Land as a reward for their righteousness, because the truth is that they are stubborn-hearted and not righteous. Moses reminds them how they worshipped the golden calf and rebelled against God and how he had interceded with God not to destroy them. God will give the Israelites victory over their enemies because He is faithful to His promises made to Abraham, Isaac and Jacob.

In Deuteronomy 10 Moses tells how God wrote the ten commandments for a second time on the tablets of stone which are kept in the ark of the covenant. He reminds the Israelites to fear the Lord, love Him, walk in His ways and keep His commandments. Their God is mighty and awesome. He is the God of all gods and the Lord of all lords.

In Deuteronomy 11 Moses reminds the Israelites that they have seen the power of God at work. As they enter the Promised Land, which is a land flowing with milk and honey, they must remember these things. The land they are entering depends upon natural rainfall in spring and autumn. If they rebel against God and do not follow His commands, God will dry up the rains. They are reminded to teach their children that obedience leads to blessings, but disobedience results in curses.

In Deuteronomy 12 the Israelites are instructed to destroy all the places of false worship and to only worship God in the central place of worship (Jerusalem) that He will show them. They are to drain the blood from the meat because the life is in the blood. They must be careful not to be enslaved through imitating the ways in which the pagans worship their false gods (including child sacrifice).

Deuteronomy 13 warns against following false prophets, even if they perform miraculous signs and wonders. Such false prophets are to be put to death for leading rebellion against God. The seriousness of worshipping false gods is stressed, and any of the Israelites enticing others to follow such gods are to be put to death by stoning. Their possessions are to be completely burnt as an offering to God.

Deuteronomy 14 lists the animals which the Israelites are to treat as unclean. Whilst there may be hygienic reasons or cultural reasons for some of the restrictions (for example the milk of a goat in which its kid had been boiled was used in pagan fertility rites), the important thing is that the Israelites, as God's chosen people, are to behave differently to their neighbours. The Israelites are reminded to pay their tithes and not neglect the Levites.

In Deuteronomy 15 the Israelites are instructed to be generous to the poor and needy. All debts are to be cancelled at the end of seven years. Those who have sold themselves as servants are also to be set free at the end of seven years, unless they are willing to become permanent servants of their master. The Israelites are to set aside the first-born of their herds and flocks to be sacrificed and eaten as an offering to the Lord.

Deuteronomy 16 records the instruction given to the Israelites to annually celebrate the Feast of Passover in memory of how God delivered them out of captivity in Egypt. They are also instructed to celebrate the Feasts of Unleavened Bread, Weeks and Tabernacles. They are to appoint officials to fairly administer justice and are reminded not to set up monuments or memorials to false gods.

Deuteronomy 17 instructs the Israelites to not violate God's covenant by worshipping other gods. Those doing this are to be stoned to death, on the testimony of at least two witnesses. The people are to honour the judgements made by the Levites and the appointed judges, and not rebel against them. When they appoint a king, he must be the person whom God chooses. He is to lead a godly life and to meditate on God's law, so he can rule wisely and enjoy a long reign.

Deuteronomy 18 reminds the Israelites that the Levites, who minister to the Lord on their behalf, do not have an inheritance of their own but are to live off the offerings of the people. The Israelites are not to engage in witchcraft, spiritualism, divination or other occultic practices, which are detestable to God. God will raise up prophets to speak His words to the people. A prophet is to be judged by whether what he speaks out actually happens. False prophets are to be put to death.

Deuteronomy 19 gives instructions regarding the cities of refuge to which people could flee for safety if they had accidently killed someone, in order to avoid the shedding of innocent blood in the land. More than one witness is required to convict someone of a crime. If anyone gives false witness, they are to receive the penalty due for the crime about which they have falsely testified.

Deuteronomy 20 gives instructions to the Israelites about going to war. They are not to be fearful of their enemies, because God will be with them. Those who are afraid or have other commitments are to be given the opportunity to be excused from fighting. They are to completely destroy everything which breathes within the cities in the Promised Land, so that they will not be defiled by them. They are permitted to plunder and take captive the people in the cities of other nations.

Deuteronomy 21 documents the sacrificial ritual of atonement to be carried out when the body of someone who has been killed is discovered. Instructions are given with regard to taking a woman captured in battle as a wife. Inheritance laws, when someone has more than one wife, stress the status of the first-born child. The importance of respecting and honouring one's parents is highlighted by the regulation which allowed the death penalty to be applied for a rebellious son.

Deuteronomy 22 records various regulations concerning the responsibility to look after the possessions of others, and prohibitions with regard to mixing two different items. A woman, who is proven to be promiscuous before being married, can be stoned to death. If a husband falsely accuses his wife, however, he has to pay a penalty to her parents and cannot divorce her. The death penalty can be applied to those caught committing adultery.

Deuteronomy 23 continues to record various regulations that the Israelites are to observe when they enter the Promised Land. Certain groups and their descendants (who had involved themselves in pagan and occultic practices) are to be excluded from *'entering the assembly of the Lord'*. The Israelites are to treat their camp as holy and not defile it in any way. They are to be generous towards one another and not even charge interest on money loaned to a fellow Israelite.

Deuteronomy 24 allows divorce under certain circumstances. Remarriage to the same person is prohibited, to prevent the divorce concession being abused. The Israelites are to treat others fairly and justly. Fathers are not to be killed for the sins of their sons, or sons killed for the sins of their fathers. They are not to take pledges which will cause extreme hardship to the borrower. Workers must be paid on time. During harvest time they are to allow the poor to glean the leftovers.

Deuteronomy 25 records various regulations regarding marriage, business and administration of justice. If a crime deserves to be punished by flogging, forty lashes is set as the maximum punishment. To ensure a family maintains its inheritance, a widow's brother-in-law must marry her, if she has no sons. Traders should use honest scales and not defraud their customers.

Deuteronomy 26 reminds the Israelites of the importance of offering the first fruits to the Lord when they enter the Promised Land. They are to do this in remembrance of how God has brought them out of captivity and fulfilled His promises to them. Every third year a tithe of the harvest is to be given to those without land, including the Levites in the local community. Fulfilment of this tithe gives the Israelites the right to ask God to come and bless their land.

In Deuteronomy 27 the Israelites are instructed to set up memorial stones when they enter the Promised Land, and to write the law upon them. The Levites are to proclaim to the people all the sinful actions which will result in them being cursed. The people are to acknowledge their understanding of the law and the consequences of breaking it by responding 'amen' to the words spoken out by the Levites.

Deuteronomy 28 summarises what will happen to the Israelites as a result of their own actions. If they are obedient to God's law they will be blessed. They will enjoy prosperity and good health, they will defeat their enemies and all the nations will look up to them. If they are disobedient to God's law they will be cursed. They will experience poverty, failure and sickness. Their enemies will defeat them, and they will be taken into captivity.

Deuteronomy 29 records the renewal of the covenant with God before entering the Promised Land. Moses recounts what God has done in the past for them, and what He will do in the future, if the Israelites break covenant with Him. If they turn away from God and worship idols, the curses written in this book will come upon them. Calamity will fall upon them and they will be uprooted from the land.

Deuteronomy 30 is a call to the Israelites to choose life and live in obedience to God's word. If the Israelites turn back to God, after they have been uprooted from the land because of their disobedience, God will restore them to the land, and they will again be blessed. What they are being asked to do is not beyond their reach. They can choose between life and prosperity by being obedient, or they can choose death and destruction by being disobedient.

In Deuteronomy 31 Moses encourages the Israelites to be strong and courageous as they enter into the Promised Land. He gives instructions that the book of the law is to be kept besides the ark of the covenant, and read to the assembled Israelites every seven years, at the Feast of Tabernacles. God tells Moses that the people will rebel and break the covenant, and He gives Moses the words of a song to teach the people, which will be a witness against them.

Deuteronomy 32 records the song that God gave to Moses to teach to the Israelites. This song proclaims that God is their creator and rock, and that He chose them as His own. God loves them, provides for them and guides them, but they will rebel against Him and worship other Gods. So they will arouse God's wrath, bring calamity upon themselves, and become subject to a foreign nation. Ultimately God will have compassion upon them and make atonement for them and their land.

In Deuteronomy 33 Moses, at the age of one hundred and twenty, blesses each of the tribes of Israel. He declares that they are a people saved by the Lord, who is their shield and their helper. As they go into the Promised Land, he tells them that their enemies will cower before them, and that the Israelites will trample down their high places.

In Deuteronomy 34 Moses climbs up Mount Nebo and the Lord shows him all the Promised Land which the Israelites are about to enter. Moses dies and is buried by God. No other prophet was like Moses, whom God met with face to face. Joshua, who is filled with the spirit of wisdom, takes over as leader. The Israelites listen to him and are obedient to what God has commanded them to do through Moses.

Joshua

The Book of Joshua records how the Israelites take possession of the Promised Land.

In Joshua 1 God speaks to Joshua and tells him to prepare the people to cross the Jordan and enter the land of Canaan. He tells Joshua to carefully obey the law, and to be strong and courageous. He promises Joshua that He will be with him, just as He was with Moses. The tribes of Gad, Reuben and Manasseh, who have already been allocated land, confirm they will help the other tribes possess Canaan.

Joshua 2 records how two men are sent to spy out the land of Canaan. In Jericho a prostitute named Rahab helps the spies avoid capture. In return they promise that the Israelites will spare her and her family when they invade the land, if she places a scarlet cord in the window of her house. The spies return to Joshua and tell him that the people in the land of Canaan are very fearful and expect to be defeated.

In Joshua 3 we read how Joshua instructs the Israelites to consecrate themselves as they are about to enter the Promised Land. Following God's orders, he tells the priests who carry the ark of the covenant to go ahead of the people. When they enter into the River Jordan the flowing water immediately dries up and the Israelites are all able to cross on dry land.

Joshua 4 continues the account of the crossing of the River Jordan. After all the Israelites have crossed over on dry land Joshua orders that one man from each tribe is to take a stone from the centre of the river. These stones are used to build a memorial at Gilgal, so the people will always remember that God was with them, and dried up the waters, just as He did when they crossed the Red Sea. As soon as the priests carrying the ark come out of the river, the water flows again.

Joshua 5 records that, after crossing over the Jordan, God instructs the Israelite men to be circumcised, because this had not been done during the time of their wanderings in the wilderness. The Israelites celebrate Passover using produce from the Promised Land and the miraculous supply of daily manna now stops. Joshua meets with the commander of the Lord's army (a personification of Jesus), and is told to remove his shoes, because the place where he is standing is holy.

Joshua 6 records how the city of Jericho is defeated. For each of six days the ark of the covenant is carried once around the outside of the city walls, accompanied by the blowing of trumpets. On the seventh day the ark is carried around the outside seven times, before the people give a victory cry, and the walls collapse. The city and all its inhabitants, with the exception of Rahab and her family, are destroyed.

Joshua 7 describes how God's anger is aroused when Achan is disobedient and takes for himself some of the devoted things from Jericho, which they had been ordered to destroy. As a consequence, the Israelites are defeated in battle at Ai, and Joshua fears that this defeat will encourage the Canaanites that the Israelites can be defeated. God exposes that Achan is responsible for the defeat at Ai, because he has violated God's covenant, and so he, his family and possessions are destroyed.

Joshua 8 describes how the city of Ai is defeated. Part of Joshua's army attacks Ai, but then pretends to flee with the army of Ai in pursuit. This allows the other part of Joshua's forces to ambush and capture Ai. The army of Ai now has nowhere to retreat to when the fleeing Israelites turn upon them, and it is defeated. After building an altar and making sacrifices to God, Joshua has a copy of God's law, which was given to Moses, inscribed on stones, and he reads it to all the assembled people.

In Joshua 9 the Gibeonites deceive the Israelites into believing that they come from a distant land. Without enquiring of God, the Israelites enter into a peace treaty with them. When Joshua discovers that the Gibeonites are actually neighbours living in the land of Canaan, he feels honour-bound to uphold the peace agreement (illustrating the seriousness with which covenants and treaties were viewed) and allows them to remain in the land as servants of the Israelites.

Joshua 10 describes how the Amorite kings attack the Gibeonites, who had entered into a peace treaty with the Israelites. Joshua, encouraged by God to not be afraid, responds to the request for help from the Gibeonites and leads his army against the Amorites. He defeats them in miraculous circumstances, when God increases the number of hours of daylight. Joshua kills the Amorite kings, and goes on to capture and destroy their cities, and other cities in the region, in a single military campaign.

In Joshua 11 Joshua defeats King Hazor and all his allies, whom he called together to oppose the Israelites. God gave Joshua complete victory over them. In accordance with the commands Moses received from God, all the defeated foes are put to death (so they will not defile the Israelites because of their idolatrous practices). The chapter concludes by saying that Joshua took the entire land.

Joshua 12 documents all the kings which Moses defeated on the east side of the river Jordan, and all the kings which Joshua defeated on the west side of the Jordan.

Joshua 13 defines the areas of land still to be taken over and possessed by the Israelites, including the lands occupied by the Philistines. The land, which has already been allocated to the tribes of Gad and Rueben and half of the tribe of Manasseh on the east side of the river Jordan, is carefully documented.

Joshua 14 records how Caleb comes to Joshua and asks if he can have the hill country as his inheritance, as promised to him by Moses. Although eighty-five years old, Caleb declares that he is as full of energy as he was forty-five years earlier, when he and Joshua wanted to enter the land but were opposed by the leaders of the other tribes. Joshua grants his request and gives the city of Hebron to Caleb.

Joshua 15 documents the land assigned to the tribe of Judah. The extent of the borders is clearly laid out, as well as a list of all the towns and cities within these borders. Although Caleb drives out the Anakites living in Hebron, Judah fails to drive out the Jebusites living in Jerusalem.

Joshua 16 documents the land assigned to the tribe of Joseph, which was further divided between the tribes of his two sons Manasseh and Ephraim. The Ephraimites fail to dislodge the Canaanites living in Gezer.

Joshua 17 documents the borders of the land assigned to the tribe of Manasseh. It notes that some land is to be allocated to the daughters of one of Manasseh's descendants, because he has no sons. The tribes of Manasseh and Ephraim ask for a larger inheritance of land, complaining that the Canaanites living in their land are well armed. Joshua encourages them and says they are powerful and able to drive out the Canaanites, and that they can also clear and occupy the forested hill country.

Joshua 18 describes how Joshua sends out three men, from each of the seven tribes who have not yet been allocated land, to survey the land and divide it into seven parts. It is to be assigned to the tribes by lot. The borders of the land assigned to Benjamin, and the towns and cities within this land, are documented.

Joshua 19 documents the land assigned to the tribes of Simeon, Zebulun, Issachar, Asher, Naphtali and Dan. This is done by sacred lot in the presence of the Lord at Shiloh. The borders of the land allocations and the towns and villages within these borders are recorded.

Joshua 20 describes how a number of cities are designated as cities of refuge, in accordance with God's instructions to Moses. Anyone, who has killed someone accidentally and unintentionally, can flee to these cities and be protected from the avenger of blood (usually a close relative of the one who had been killed), whilst awaiting trial.

Joshua 21 documents how forty-eight towns and their surrounding pasture lands are allocated to the Levites. (The tribe of Levi is not allocated a portion of land, but is to live in towns distributed among all the Israelite tribes.) The chapter concludes by declaring that God has fulfilled all His promises in bringing them into the Promised Land and handing their enemies over to them.

Joshua 22 records how Joshua releases the fighting men from the tribes of Reuben, Gad and the half tribe of Manasseh to return to the land allocated them in Gilead on the east side of the river Jordan. The returning men build an imposing altar, which almost incites war between them and the other Israelites. Peace is restored when they explain that the altar is not for making sacrifices to another god, but only as a reminder that they are one with their brothers on the other side of the Jordan.

In Joshua 23 Joshua addresses the leaders of the Israelites, shortly before he dies. He reminds them how God has helped them and fought for them. He reminds them to obey all of God's laws, and not to associate with, or intermarry with, the pagan nations who worship false gods. He warns them that, if they violate the covenants of God, and serve other gods, they will quickly perish from the land God has given them.

In Joshua 24 Joshua recounts to the assembled Israelites their history, and how God helped them and gave them victory over their enemies. He calls on them to make a choice and decide to follow God and serve Him. The Israelites respond by acknowledging that God has helped them and declaring that they will serve Him. Joshua 24 concludes by recording the deaths of Joshua and Eleazar the priest, but how that generation of Israelites continue to serve the Lord.

Judges

The Book of Judges covers a three-hundred-year period, ending in about 1025 BC, during which the Israelites frequently backslide and become prey for their enemies, until God raises up a leader (judge) to deliver them.

Chapter 1 records the early conquests of the tribe of Judah, including the capture of Jerusalem and Hebron. The Israelites fail to drive out the Canaanites completely, as they have been instructed, but instead use some of them as slave labour.

In Chapter 2 of Judges we read of the death of Joshua and how the Israelites disobey God by not driving out the Canaanites from the land. Instead they join in the worship of Baal and other Canaanite gods and arouse the Lord's anger. In His compassion, God raises up judges to deliver the Israelites when they are in distress and under attack from raiders. However, when a judge dies, the Israelites quickly return to their idolatrous ways.

In Judges 3 the Israelites inter-marry with the pagan tribes and worship their gods. They eventually become subject to the Aramites, until God raises up Othniel (Caleb's younger brother) to deliver them and establish forty years of peace. The Israelites again turn to idolatry and became subject to the Moabite King Eglon. When they cry out to God, God raises up Ehud, who kills King Eglon, defeats the Moabites and establishes an eighty-year period of peace.

Judges 4 records how God raises up Deborah to lead the Israelites against the Canaanite King Jabin and his army commander, named Sisera. Because God is with them, the Israelite army, under the command of Barak (who had refused to fight unless Deborah went with him), completely destroys the well-armed Canaanite army. Sisera escapes, but, whilst he is sleeping, he is killed by Jael (the wife of Heber the Kenite).

Judges 5 records the song of Deborah, written to celebrate and praise God for the victory He gave the Israelites (led by Deborah) over the Canaanite army (led by Sisera). In this song there is praise for the tribes of Israel who supported Deborah, but a rebuke for the tribes who did not send men to fight alongside her. Following the defeat of Sisera, the Israelites enjoy forty years of peace.

In Judges 6 the 'Angel of the Lord' appears to Gideon at a time when the Israelites are being oppressed by the Midianites. He tells Gideon that he is a mighty warrior and that he is to lead the Israelites against the Midianites. Gideon, in obedience to the Lord, destroys the Asherah pole and the altar his father has built to worship Baal. God confirms that He will give Gideon victory, by responding to the 'fleece' Gideon puts out.

In Judges 7 we read how God instructs Gideon to reduce the size of his army from thirty-two thousand to just three hundred men, before attacking the Midianites. He then spies out the Midianite camp and overhears that they are afraid they will be defeated by Gideon. His men surround the Midianite camp at night, and, when they blow their trumpets and show their torches, the Midianites panic, and start attacking each other. Gideon then calls upon the Ephraimites to attack the fleeing Midianites.

In Judges 8 we read how Gideon and his three hundred men pursue the fleeing Midianites. The towns of Succoth and Peniel refuse to support Gideon, when he asks for food for his army. (Gideon later punishes them for their disloyalty.) Gideon captures the Midian leaders Zebah and Zalmunna, and executes them when he discovers they had killed his brothers and not shown them mercy. Peace reigns for forty years, until Gideon dies, and the Israelites again turn to Baal worship.

In Judges 9 we read how Abimelech (Gideon's son by a slave woman), supported by the citizens of Shechem, and financed by money from the temple of Baal, kills seventy of Gideon's sons, and is made king of Shechem. Jotham, Gideon's youngest son, curses Abimelech and the Shechemites for what they have done. Eventually the Shechemites rebel against Abimelech, and many of them are killed when Abimelech sets the town on fire. Abimelech himself dies when he is struck by a millstone.

Judges 10 records that, after Abimelech was killed, Tola, and then Jair, led Israel. The Israelites continue to do evil and worship Baal and the gods of the pagan nations. The Philistines and the Ammonites oppress Israel so severely that the Israelites cry out to God, confess that they have sinned against Him, and begin to serve Him again.

Judges 11 and 12 records how the Gileadites (tribe of Manasseh) invite the outlawed Jephthah to lead them against the Ammonites. Jephthah refutes their false claims to the land of the Amorites and defeats them in battle. The importance given to fulfilling vows made to God is demonstrated when Jephthah sacrifices his own daughter. Civil war subsequently breaks out with the Ephraimites, who claim that Jephthah had not asked them to fight against the Ammonites.

In Judges 13 a stranger appears to Manoah and his wife, who is infertile, and announces that they are going to have a son (Samson), who will deliver the Israelites from the Philistines (who were now oppressing them). They are told to bring this son up as a Nazarite, and that he is not to eat grapes, drink fermented wine or cut his hair. When they see the stranger ascending in the flames of their sacrifice to God, they realise that the stranger is the 'Angel of the Lord'.

In Judges 14 Samson marries a young Philistine woman. He promises a reward of clothing to thirty men of her town if they can answer a riddle relating to one of his previous exploits when he killed a lion with his bare hands. Samson's new wife betrays him by disclosing the answer to the riddle. Samson kills thirty Philistines and gives their clothing to fulfil his promises, before abandoning his wife and returning to his father's home.

In Judges 15 Samson takes revenge on the Philistines by destroying their crops and vineyards, when he discovers that they have given his wife in marriage to someone else. Samson agrees to be handed over to the Philistines who come to arrest him. However, as soon as he is handed over, the power of the Lord comes upon him, and he breaks free from the ropes binding him, and kills a thousand of the Philistines, using the jaw bone of a donkey as a weapon.

In Judges 16 Samson is delivered into the hands of the Philistines by Delilah. After persistent nagging by Delilah, Samson tells her that he has strength because he is a Nazarite, and his hair has never been cut. While he is asleep she cuts his hair, and the Philistines capture him and blind him. Samson takes his final revenge on the Philistines when God answers his prayer for strength, and he causes the temple of Dagon to collapse, killing himself and over three thousand Philistines.

In Judges 17 we read that the people in Israel did as they saw fit. Micah (from the tribe of Ephraim) stole silver from his mother. When he returns the silver she has some of it made into an idol, which Micah places in the shrine in his house. Micah later hires a young Levite to come and live in his house and become his priest.

In Judges 18 spies from the tribe of Dan visit Micah's house. When the army of Dan returns to attack the land of Laisha they steal the idols from Micah's shrine, and persuade his priest to come with them. After the Danites have burnt down the city of Laish, they rebuild it and rename it Dan. At Dan they set up their own shrine, in which they place the idols stolen from Micah.

Judges 19 records the horrific story of how the concubine of an un-named Levite is raped and dies at the hands of wicked men from the tribe of Benjamin. (This crime highlights the moral degradation now existing in Israel. That the Levite was willing to hand over his concubine to these wicked men illustrates the very low place and value accorded to women in society at this time). The Levite divides up the body of his dead concubine and sends a part of it to each of the tribes of Israel.

In Judges 20 the tribes of Israel respond to the horrific crime committed by the Benjamites. Gathering a large army, they demand that the Benjamites hand over those responsible for the atrocity. When the Benjamites refuse, war is declared. Initially the Benjamites appear successful, but they are led into an ambush and, with the exception of six hundred men who escape into the desert, are completely defeated, and their towns and cities burnt to the ground.

Judges 21 records how the Israelites grieve over what has happened to the tribe of Benjamin. In order that the tribe is not wiped out completely, they give the remaining Benjamites all the virgins from Jabesh Gilead (where they had failed to support the outcry against the crime committed by the Benjamites), and allow them to capture wives for themselves at the annual feast in Shiloh. The book of Judges concludes with the sad statement that '*at that time everyone in Israel did as he saw fit*'.

Ruth

The Book of Ruth records the story of the Moabite woman Ruth, who become the great-grandmother of King David.

In Chapter 1 we read how Naomi decides to return from Moab to her original home town of Bethlehem following the death of her husband and two sons. Her daughter-in-law Ruth, who is a Moabite, chooses to go with her, declaring that Naomi's people would be her people and Naomi's God would be her God.

In Ruth 2 Ruth finds favour with Boaz, who is a relative of her late father-in-law. He is appreciative of all that Ruth has done in leaving her own country in order to help and support Naomi. He allows Ruth to glean in his fields during the harvest season, instructs his men to protect her from harm, and to even leave some of the harvest for her to collect.

In Ruth 3 Naomi instructs Ruth to go and sleep at the feet of Boaz. When he awakes she asks him if he will be her kinsman-redeemer, and thus expresses her willingness to become his wife if he chooses to have her. Boaz is honoured that she has approached him in this way, and not sought after younger men, or the relative who is a closer kinsman-redeemer than himself.

In Ruth 4 the closest kinsman-redeemer to Naomi and Ruth gives up his rights to redeem them because of the consequences this may have on his own children's inheritance. This clears the way for Boaz to take Ruth as his wife, and for their offspring to inherit the land formerly belonging to Naomi's deceased husband. Boaz and Ruth conceive a child whom they name Obed and who was to become the grandfather of King David.

1 Samuel

The Book of 1 Samuel is an account of the life of Samuel, the establishment of Saul as the first king of Israel, and the emergence of his successor King David.

Chapter 1 records how Hannah, who is childless, cries out to God in her anguish and promises to dedicate her child to God if He answers her prayer. Her prayers are answered and she has a son, whom she names Samuel. After he is weaned, Hannah takes Samuel to serve in the house of the Lord under the guidance of Eli the priest.

1 Samuel 2 records Hannah's prayer declaring that God involves Himself in the affairs of mankind, and that He is the judge of all things. The sons of Eli the priest are treating the sacrifices made to God with contempt and are taking the best portions for themselves. Through a prophet of God, Eli is rebuked for not correcting and disciplining his sons, and is told that they will both die on the same day. God declares that He will raise up a faithful priest who will serve Him for ever.

In 1 Samuel 3 the Lord begins to speak to Samuel. Initially Samuel thinks it is Eli who is calling him, but he learns to recognise the voice of God. God reveals to him that He is going to bring judgement upon Eli and his sons, because they have treated the sacrifices with contempt and Eli has failed to restrain them. The Lord is with Samuel, and the people of Israel recognise him as a prophet of God.

In 1 Samuel 4 the Israelites, following a battle defeat, decide to take the ark of the covenant into battle with them. Although this initially brings fear to the Philistines, they determine not to submit to their enemy. The Philistines win the battle and capture the ark of the covenant. On hearing that both his sons had been killed, Eli collapses and dies. Eli's daughter-in-law also dies in labour, giving birth to a son whom she names Ichabod, meaning the glory has departed from Israel.

In 1 Samuel 5 the Philistines take the ark of the covenant and place it in the temple of Dagon at Ashdod. However, during the night, the statue of Dagon falls down and breaks into pieces. Outbreaks of tumours start to inflict the inhabitants of Ashdod. The Philistines move the ark to the city of Gath, and then to Ekron, but in each place outbreaks of tumours inflict the inhabitants. The people ask their leaders to send the ark back to Israel.

1 Samuel 6 records how the Philistines send the ark of the covenant back to Israel. They make gold models of tumours and rats

as guilt offerings to accompany the ark . As a test, their priests instruct them to yoke two cows, who have just calved, to the cart carrying the ark . Ignoring their calves, the cows immediately set out and return the ark to the Israelites in Beth Shemesh. The Israelites are overjoyed with the return of the ark , but a number are struck dead when they look inside the ark .

In 1 Samuel 7, following the return of the ark , Samuel encourages the Israelites to recommit themselves to God, and not to worship the Baals or Ashtoreths. When the Philistines attack them at Mizpah, God gives the Israelites victory, and the towns of Gath and Ekron, previously captured by the Philistines, are returned to them. For the remainder of Samuel's life there is peace in Israel.

1 Samuel 8 records how the Israelites come to Samuel and say they want to be like the other nations and have a king to lead them. God tells Samuel that the people are not rejecting Samuel and his family, but are rejecting God. The people ignore God's solemn warning about how a king will rule over them, and will take the best of their produce and demand a tithe to support himself, his officials and his army. God instructs Samuel to listen to the people and give them a king.

In 1 Samuel 9 Saul, a Benjamite, described as a young man without equal amongst the Israelites, is searching for his father's lost donkeys. He seeks out Samuel, to whom God has already revealed that the man he is to appoint as king will be from the tribe of Benjamin. When Saul meets Samuel, God confirms that Saul is the person who will rule Israel.

1 Samuel 10 records how Samuel privately anoints Saul and prophesies what will happen to Saul on his way home, including the fact that the Holy Spirit will come upon Saul. These prophecies are all fulfilled. Samuel summons the people of Israel to Mizpah, where it is revealed that Saul is the one chosen to be king. Before dismissing the people, Samuel explains to them the regulations regarding kingship.

In 1 Samuel 11 the Ammonites besiege Jabesh Gilead. When Saul hears of this he cuts two oxen into pieces and proclaims that a similar thing will happen to all who do not join him to attack the Ammonites. Over three hundred and thirty thousand men join Saul, and the Ammonites are totally defeated. Samuel and the Israelites take Saul to Gilgal, where he is reaffirmed as king in the presence of God.

In 1 Samuel 12 Samuel addresses the Israelites at Gilgal and declares that they now have a king as they requested. He recounts the history of Israel, proclaiming how God has always answered their prayers when they sought Him. By asking for a king they have rejected God as their king. If they and the king obey God all will be well, but if they rebel and persist in sin, they and their king will be swept away.

In 1 Samuel 13 Saul's son, Jonathan, attacks a Philistine outpost, and as a result the Philistine army assembles to attack Israel. Saul gathers an army at Gilgal, but they have few weapons and begin to scatter in fear. Instead of waiting for Samuel, King Saul breaks the law by performing the priestly function of offering sacrifices before the Lord. Samuel rebukes Saul and tells him his kingdom will not endure, and that God will appoint another king after his own heart.

In 1 Samuel 14 Jonathan and his sword bearer, knowing that God is with them, overcome a Philistine outpost, causing panic within the Philistine army, who begin to fight among themselves. The Israelites attack and the Philistine army is routed. Jonathan eats some wild honey, unknowingly breaking an oath that Saul had bound the men with, to fast that day under penalty of a curse if they don't. His men protect Jonathan and insist that he should not be put to death.

In 1 Samuel 15 God instructs Samuel to tell Saul to attack the Amalekites and to completely destroy them and all their belongings. Saul defeats the Amalekites, but spares their king and the best of their livestock, which he later claims was to be sacrificed to the Lord. Samuel rebukes Saul for what he has done, declaring that God delights in obedience rather than sacrifice. The kingdom will be taken from Saul and given to another.

In 1 Samuel 16 God instructs Samuel to anoint one of Jesse's sons to be king. God does not choose the son that Samuel thought He would, but instead chooses David, declaring that God looks at the heart rather than the outward appearance. The Spirit of God leaves Saul, and he becomes tormented by an evil spirit. David enters into the service of Saul as an armour-bearer, and plays his harp to bring relief to Saul when he is being tormented.

In 1 Samuel 17 the Philistine giant, Goliath, taunts the armies of Israel, and everyone is afraid of him. Saul declares that he will give great wealth, and his daughter in marriage, to anyone who kills Goliath. David, who has killed bears and lions while protecting his father's sheep, is unafraid and, refusing the offer of Saul's armour, faces Goliath in battle. David strikes him down with a single sling shot, and kills him. The Philistine army flee when they see that Goliath is dead.

In 1 Samuel 18 David becomes a successful officer in Saul's army, because the Lord is with him. He becomes a close friend of Saul's son Jonathan. Saul is very jealous of David and his popularity with the people, and even tries to kill him. He tells David that he can marry his daughter Michal if he kills a hundred Philistines, but secretly hopes the Philistines will kill David. David, however, is successful in the task, and Saul now sees David as his enemy.

1 Samuel 19 records how Saul wanted to kill David, but Jonathan persuades him to change his mind. However, after David has further military success against the Philistines, Saul again tries to kill him. Michal deceives the men sent to capture David, thus enabling David to escape and join Samuel at Ramah. Three times Saul sends soldiers to capture David at Ramah, but each time the Spirit of the Lord falls upon them and they start prophesying. He eventually goes himself.

In 1 Samuel 20 David and Jonathan make a covenant of friendship together. Jonathan warns David that Saul is still planning to kill him, and to not attend the festival meal with Saul. Saul is greatly angered by Jonathan's actions, and even tries to kill him by throwing a spear at him.

In 1 Samuel 21 the priest Ahimelech helps David by allowing David and his men to eat the sacred bread set before the Lord. He also arms David with Goliath's sword. (Ahimelech's actions in helping David are witnessed by Doeg the Edomite.) David then flees to the town of Gath where he feigns insanity before king Achish.

In 1 Samuel 22 Doeg the Edomite tells Saul how Ahimelech the priest has helped David escape. Saul orders that Ahimelech, and the priests who have sided with David, be killed, but Saul's officials are not prepared to carry out his orders. Doeg, however, strikes down the priests and their families, and only Ahimelech's son, Abiathar, is able to escape and join up with David's men.

In 1 Samuel 23 David and his 600 followers attack and defeat the Philistines at Keilah. Warned by God that the citizens of Keilah will hand him over to Saul, David goes to the desert of Ziph. Jonathan visits David and encourages him that one day he will be king over Israel. The Ziphites agree to betray David into Saul's hands, but Saul has to break off his pursuit of David to deal with a Philistine raiding party.

1 Samuel 24 records how Saul and an army of three thousand men search for David in the En Gedi desert. Unbeknown to Saul, David has an opportunity to kill him, but refuses to raise his hand against the anointed king of Israel. He simply cuts off a piece of his robe. When Saul hears that David has spared his life, he declares that David is more righteous than himself, and will surely become king over Israel. Saul asks David to swear that he will not wipe out all his

descendants.

In 1 Samuel 25 Nabal (the husband of Abigail) offends David by refusing to give his men food, even though David has protected them from the Philistines. When Abigail hears what has happened she makes amends by providing food and drink for David's men, who are about to take revenge against Nabal. When Nabal later dies, David asks Abigail to become one of his wives.

In 1 Samuel 26 Saul again sets out to try and capture David. During the night, David and Abishai enter Saul's camp and have the opportunity to kill Saul. David, however, will not allow the king, anointed by God, to be killed, but, instead, they simply take Saul's spear and water jug as evidence of their presence. When Saul realises that David has spared his life for a second time, he repents of his actions and declares he will not try to harm David again.

1 Samuel 27 records how David, fearful that Saul would again try to kill him, settles in the land of the Philistines. Achish, the king of Gath, allows David and his followers to occupy the city of Ziklag. From Ziklag David and his men raided and plundered neighbouring territories occupied by the Geshurites, Girzites and Amalekites, but tell King Achish that the raids have been against the Israelites.

In 1 Samuel 28 the Philistines again assemble to attack Israel, following the death of Samuel. Saul, who is unable to find guidance from God, violates God's commandments by visiting a spiritist medium (the witch of Endor) in order to obtain guidance. She contacts the spirit of Samuel, who declares that the kingdom of Israel has been taken from Saul and given to David. He tells Saul that he and his sons will be killed in battle by the Philistines.

In 1 Samuel 29-30 the Philistine rulers refuse to allow David and his men to be part of their army. They return to Ziklag, but discover that it has been destroyed by the Amalekites and their families taken captive. David and his men pursue and defeat the Amalekites, recovering all that has been stolen. David insists that the recovered plunder be shared, even among those men who have been unable to fight through exhaustion, and sends some of the plunder as gifts to the Israelites.

In 1 Samuel 31 the Philistines defeat the Israelites in battle. Saul's sons, including Jonathan, are killed. Saul is critically wounded and, in order to avoid falling into the hands of his enemies, commits suicide by falling upon his own sword, when his armour bearer refuses to kill him. The men of Jabesh Gilead recover the bodies of Saul and his sons, which have been put on public display by the Philistines, and bury them at Jabesh.

2 Samuel

The Book of 2 Samuel records how David is established as king over all of Israel and survives the rebellion of his son Absalom.

In chapter 1 we read how David hears of the death of Saul and Jonathan and is filled with grief. Hoping to win favour with David, the young Amalekite bringing the news claims that he killed Saul, who had been critically wounded in the battle. David declares that the young man should have been afraid of killing God's anointed king, and has him put to death.

In 2 Samuel 2 David leaves Ziklag and goes to Hebron, where he is anointed king over Judah. Meanwhile Abner makes Saul's son, Ishbosheth, king over the rest of Israel. Fighting breaks out between David's men, led by Joab and Abner, and his men. During the fighting Abner kills Joab's brother Asahel.

In 2 Samuel 3 Abner, who holds the power in the house of Saul, decides to betray Ishbosheth, and help David become king over all Israel. David agrees to meet with Abner, after he arranges for David's wife Michal to be returned to him. Joab, however, meets with Abner and kills him in revenge for the death of his brother Asahel. David is distressed by what Joab has done and leads the mourning for Abner, to demonstrate to the people that he had no part in his death.

2 Samuel 4 records how Baanah and Recab, from the tribe of Benjamin, kill Ishbosheth and take his head to David at Hebron, expecting to be rewarded for what they have done. David, however, is angry towards them for killing an innocent man and has them both put to death.

2 Samuel 5 records how the elders of all the tribes of Israel come to David at Hebron and anoint him as king. David captures the city of Jerusalem and develops it as his stronghold. When the Philistines hear that David has been anointed king they came to attack him, but God is with David, and he defeats them at Baal-Perizim (the place of breakthrough). The Philistines attack a second time, but God gives David a new strategy before going ahead of him, and giving David the victory.

2 Samuel 6 records how the ark of the covenant was brought to Jerusalem. Fear of the Lord and the seriousness of what he is doing comes upon David when Uzzah is struck down dead for treating the ark with irreverence. David dances before the Lord as the ark reaches Jerusalem, but Michal despises David for doing this, and the Bible records that she remains childless.

In 2 Samuel 7 God's covenant with David is spoken through

Nathan. God declares that He will establish an everlasting kingdom through David's descendants. He will be a father to Israel, and Israel will be His son. David responds by declaring the greatness of God, who is faithful to fulfil His promises.

2 Samuel 8 records how David subdued the Philistines and defeated the Moabites, Edomites and Arameans. He ruled over the whole of Israel, and the Lord gave him victory wherever he went.

In 2 Samuel 9 David shows kindness to Mephibosheth, the grandson of King Saul and the son of Jonathan. (He was crippled in both feet as a result of being dropped by his nurse (2 Samuel 2:4.) David invites him to eat at his table, just like one of his own sons. David instructs Ziba to farm the land previously owned by Saul, to provide an income for Mephibosheth.

In 2 Samuel 10 David goes to war against the Ammonites, after they humiliated the men sent by David to express sympathy, following the death of their king. The Ammonites hire Aramean soldiers to help them, but are defeated by the Israelite army, led by Joab and his brother Abishai.

In 2 Samuel 11 David commits adultery with Bathsheba (the wife of Uriah), who becomes pregnant. David unsuccessfully tries to manipulate Uriah, so it will appear that he is the father of the child. David then conspires to have Uriah killed by ordering Joab, the commander of his army, to place Uriah at the front of the army, so he will be exposed to the enemy. Following Uriah's death, David takes Bathsheba as his wife.

In 2 Samuel 12 Nathan the prophet uses a parable to confront David about his sins concerning Bathsheba and Uriah. He prophesies that the conceived child will die, and that someone close to David will publicly sleep with David's wives. (Fulfilled when David's son Absalom did this, 2 Samuel 16:22.) David acknowledges that he has sinned and, although he repents before God, the child dies. Subsequently Bathsheba conceives again and they name the child Solomon.

2 Samuel 13 records the very sad story of how David's son Amnon rapes his half-sister Tamar, and then completely rejects her. David's son Absalom (brother of Tamar) takes his revenge by inviting Amnon to a meal, where he has him killed. He then flees to Geshur, where he stays for three years.

2 Samuel 14 records how Joab tries to bring reconciliation between David and his son Absalom, who fled after killing Amnon. Joab instructs a woman to ask David to save her son from a revenge killing, because he had killed his brother. When David says he will

protect her son, the woman asks David why he does not treat Absalom in the same way. Absalom returns to Jerusalem, but only sees David two years later, after persuading Joab to arrange a meeting between them.

2 Samuel 15 records how Absalom gains favour with the Israelites by undermining King David, and telling them what he would do if he were the king. Eventually he goes to Hebron and declares himself king. David, in fear for his life, has to flee from Jerusalem, but instructs Zadok and Abiathar (the priests) to stay in Jerusalem and send him information about Absalom's plans. David also asks Hushai to stay in Jerusalem and frustrate the advice given Absalom by Ahithophel.

2 Samuel 16 continues the account of David fleeing Jerusalem after Absalom has declared himself king. Ziba brings David donkeys and food, claiming that his master Mephibosheth has sided with Absalom. In response David declares that all he gave Mephibosheth should be given to Ziba. David refuses to retaliate against Shimei when he curses him. Absalom enters Jerusalem and, following advice from Ahithophel, sleeps with David's concubines to demonstrate to the Israelites that he is now king.

In 2 Samuel 17 we read how Hushai counters the advice given Absalom by Anithopel to immediately attack David. Absalom chooses to follow Hushai's advice, which gives David time to escape and gather his supporters to oppose Absalom and his followers. The sons of Zadok and Abiathar evade capture and bring David news of Absalom's plans. Anithopel commits suicide when he discovers that his advice has been rejected.

In 2 Samuel 18 David's army, under the command of Joab, Abishai and Ittai, marches out to fight against Absalom and his supporters. Joab ignores David's instruction to be gentle with his son, and kills Absalom when the latter's hair becomes entangled in a tree. When David hears of the death of Absalom he is grief stricken, and declares it would have been better if he had died in Absalom's place.

2 Samuel 19 records how Joab confronts David and tells him that his mourning for Absalom is discouraging. It demeans the actions of the men who risked their lives to crush the rebellion led by Absalom. The men of Judah go out to welcome David back as king. Shimei repents for cursing David, and Mephibosheth says he was slandered by Ziba, and that he always supported David. The northern tribes of Israel are upset that Judah welcomes David back without consulting them.

2 Samuel 20 records how Sheba encourages the tribes of Israel

to follow him rather than David. Joab murders Amasa (David's nephew who led Absalom's army, and whom David invited to lead his own army), claiming that Amasa was secretly supporting Sheba. Sheba takes refuge in the city of Abel Beth Maacah but, when the city is besieged by Joab's army, the citizens there kill him and hand over his head to Joab.

2 Samuel 21 records that the Israelites experienced a time of famine as a consequence of Saul's attempt to ethnically cleanse Israel by destroying the Gibeonites. David appeases the Gibeonites by sentencing seven of Saul's relatives to death. He later arranges for the bodies of these men to be buried together with those of Saul and Jonathan. In further battles with the Philistines, David's men kill the four brothers of the giant Goliath, whom David had killed with a sling shot.

2 Samuel 22 is essentially a repeat of Psalm 18 in which David gives thanks because he has been delivered from the hands of his enemies. He poetically describes how this happened, because God moved in the heavenly realms in response to his prayer, and because he walked in righteousness before the Lord. He acknowledges that the victory comes about because God showed His faithfulness to him, and strengthened him.

In 2 Samuel 23 we find the names and genealogies of David's mighty men (thirty-seven in all). The exploits and bravery in battle of some of these mighty men are carefully recorded.

In 2 Samuel 24 David displeases God by ordering a census of the fighting men available to him. (In 1 Chronicles 21 it says that Satan incited David to take the census.) David perhaps was operating out of pride so that he could boast about the size of his army, was not trusting in God, or failed to collect, or misused, the redemption tax that should accompany a census (Exodus 30:12). A plague strikes Israel, until David builds an altar and sacrifices offerings before the Lord.

1 Kings

The Book of 1 Kings (possibly written by Jeremiah) records the history of Israel from about 1000 BC to about 850 BC. In Chapter we read how, in the latter part of King David's reign, his son Adonijah, supported by Joab, prepares to succeed him as king. Prompted by Bathsheba, Nathan the prophet, and Zadok the priest, King David instructs Nathan and Zadok to anoint Solomon as the next king. Solomon grants mercy to Adonijah for his treacherous behaviour.

In 1 Kings 2, before his death, David instructs Solomon to walk in God's ways. He warns Solomon not to trust Joab (the commander of David's army), and Shimei, who had cursed David. Following David's death, Solomon firmly establishes his throne by having Adonijah killed for requesting that he be allowed to marry Abishag, having Joab killed in revenge for the murder of Abner and Amasa, and having Shimei killed for violating the terms of his house arrest.

In 1 Kings 3, instead of asking for wealth or the death of his enemies, Solomon asks for the gift of wisdom, when God appears to him in a dream. This response pleases God, who promises Solomon riches and honour as well as the wisdom he had asked for. Solomon demonstrates this wisdom in settling a dispute between two women who both claim to be the mother of a baby. The true mother is willing to give up the baby rather than see it harmed in any way.

1 Kings 4 documents the names of King Solomon's administrators. Under his rule Israel enjoyed a time of peace and prosperity. King Solomon was known for his knowledge and wisdom, and people from all the nations came to listen to his words.

1 Kings 5 records how Solomon makes preparations for the building of the temple at Jerusalem. He enters into an agreement with King Hiram of Tyre to supply timber in exchange for wheat and olive oil. He conscripts a labour force to go to Lebanon to help in cutting down trees and shipping them to Israel. He conscripts another work force to work in the quarries and prepare stones for the temple.

1 King 6 describes how Solomon builds the temple in Jerusalem over a period of seven years. The main hall is about 90 feet long, 30 feet wide and 45 feet high, constructed of stone, and lined with timber. A three-storied building of side rooms is built around the main hall. An inner sanctuary, lined with gold, is constructed to house the ark of the covenant. Statues of cherubim with outstretched wings form a protective cover over the ark .

1 Kings 7 describes the palaces that Solomon builds for himself and one of his wives. They are constructed of stone and cedar wood.

Huram, a skilled craftsman from Tyre, creates furnishings and decorations for the temple out of cast bronze. These furnishings include pillars, water basins, moveable stands and the utensils used by the priests.

1 Kings 8 records how the presence of God fills the temple when the ark of the covenant is placed in the inner sanctuary. Solomon dedicates the temple, declaring that God has been faithful to His promises. He entreats God to respond to the prayers of the people when they ask Him to forgive their sins or bring their needs before Him in prayer. He prays that the hearts of the people may always be turned to God, and that they may know that God is with them.

1 Kings 9 records how God appears to Solomon a second time and declares that He will uphold all of His promises to David. However, if the people forsake Him, they will be cut off from the land and become an object of ridicule among the nations. We also read how Solomon rebuilds Gezer and constructs other cities to house his chariots, using conscripted labour from the Canaanite tribes still living in the land of Israel.

1 Kings 10 describes the wealth and prosperity of Israel during the reign of King Solomon. Israel had a fleet of trading ships importing wood and treasures, and there was a plentiful supply of gold. Solomon used some of the gold to produce shields, drinking goblets and a magnificent golden throne. Visitors from all over the world visited Solomon, including the Queen of Sheba, who was overwhelmed by his wealth and wisdom.

In 1 Kings 11 Solomon has many wives and concubines who turn his heart after other gods. God's anger is aroused, and He tells Solomon that, after his death, the kingdom will be divided, and part given to one of his subordinates. Ahijah the prophet tears up his new cloak into twelve pieces and gives Jeroboam (who was in charge of Solomon's labour force) ten of the pieces, declaring that he will rule over ten of the tribes of Israel. When Solomon dies Rehoboam his son becomes king.

In 1 Kings 12 Rehoboam ignores the Israelites' request that the burdens put on them by Solomon be lifted, and says he will treat them even more harshly. As a consequence, ten of the tribes rebel and make Jeroboam their king, and only the tribes of Judah and Benjamin remain loyal to Rehoboam. Jeroboam makes two golden calves and altars, which he sets up at Bethel and Dan, and tells the people they can worship there, rather than go to the temple in Jerusalem.

In 1 Kings 13 a prophet of God rebukes Jeroboam as he is offering sacrifices on the altar at Bethel. He declares that a descendant of David, named Josiah, will sacrifice the false priests on this altar. Jeroboam's hand becomes shrivelled when he threatens to seize the prophet, but is healed when the prophet prays for him. The prophet later ignores God's command not to accept hospitality from the people of Bethel, and is killed by a lion as he is leaving the region.

In 1 Kings 14 Jeroboam's wife disguises herself and consults Ahijah the prophet in Shiloh, concerning their son who is ill. However, God reveals to Ahijah who she is, and he declares that Jeroboam and all his family will be destroyed because of idolatry, and that his son will die as soon as she returns home. Judah (ruled by King Rehoboam) also sins by setting up Asherah poles and engaging in shrine prostitution. Egypt attacks Jerusalem and carry off treasures from the temple.

1 Kings 15 records that Abijah succeeds Rehoboam and rules as King of Judah for three years. He continues to sin as his father did, but is succeeded by his son Asa, a godly king, who removes the Asherah poles set up by Abijah. In Israel Jeroboam is succeeded by his son Nadab, but he and all Jeroboam's family are killed by Baasha, who makes himself king. War rages between Israel and Judah, and King Asa enters a treaty with Syria to help Judah in the battle against Baasha.

In 1 Kings 16 God uses the prophet Jehu to rebuke King Baasha of Israel and declare that his household will be destroyed. After a reign of twenty-four years, Baasha dies and is succeeded by his son, but Zimri rebels against him and kills him and his family. Zimri himself only reigns seven days, before Omri, the commander of the army, defeats him. Omri rules for twelve years, and is succeeded by his son Ahab, who is more evil than his ancestors. He marries Jezebel and begins to worship Baal.

In 1 Kings 17 Elijah confronts King Ahab of Israel and proclaims a prolonged period of drought in the land. God provides for Elijah by directing him to a source of water, where ravens bring him food every morning and evening. God later directs him to go to Zarephath, where a widow is able to feed him because her oil and flour are miraculously replenished. When the widow's son dies, Elijah prays over him, and his life is restored.

In 1 Kings 18 Elijah meets Ahab (who blames the drought on Elijah), and Elijah confronts the prophets of Baal on Mount Carmel. They are unable to call down fire on their sacrifices, but God responds to Elijah's prayer, and his sacrifices are burnt up, when fire from heaven falls upon them. Elijah has the prophets of Baal killed and declares to Ahab that the drought will now be broken. The appearance of a small cloud in the sky is the prelude to a rain storm.

In 1 Kings 19 Elijah flees when his life is threatened by Jezebel the wife of King Ahab. Angels bring him food and drink, before he hears the quiet, encouraging voice of God on Mount Horeb. God instructs Elijah to anoint Hazael as King of Aram, Jehu as King of Israel and Elisha as his successor. Elisha responds to the call by burning up his plough and sacrificing his oxen, before leaving everything behind to follow Elijah.

1 Kings 20 records how the Arameans, led by King Ben-hadad, attack Israel. They are defeated in the hill country, but return the following spring, declaring that the God of Israel is only a mountain god. They are defeated again on the plains of Israel. Because King Ahab of Israel enters into a treaty with Ben-hadad, rather than killing him, the prophet of God declares that Ahab will forfeit his life instead.

In 1 Kings 21 Ahab desires to obtain for himself the vineyard belonging to Naboth. When Naboth refuses to sell it to him, Queen Jezebel causes false accusations to be brought against Naboth, resulting in his being stoned to death. Elijah confronts Ahab and declares that God will bring disaster upon him and his household, and that dogs will devour Jezebel. Because Ahab humbles himself, God declares that the promised disaster will come in the days of his son.

1 Kings 22 records how King Ahab of Israel, and the godly King Jehoshaphat of Judah, plan to attack the Arameans, encouraged by some false words of the prophets. The prophet Micaiah, however, declares that the prophets are lying, and that Ahab will meet his death in battle. This prophecy is fulfilled when Ahab, who has gone into the battle in disguise, is struck by a random arrow and dies. He is succeeded by his son Ahaziah, who continues in the sinful ways of his parents.

2 Kings

The Book of 2 Kings covers the history of Judah and Israel from about 850 BC to the fall of Jerusalem in about 585 BC.

Chapter 1 records how Elijah confronts King Ahaziah, who has sent messengers to consult the Baal god of Ekron. Ahaziah dispatches soldiers to arrest Elijah, but Elijah calls down fire from heaven and they are consumed. When Elijah finally visits Ahaziah, he tells him that he will die, because he attempted to consult the Baals. Ahaziah is succeeded by his son Joram.

Kings 2 records how Elisha refuses to leave Elijah, and requests that he succeed Elijah, when the latter is taken up into heaven in a whirlwind. Elisha takes up the cloak of Elijah and demonstrates his anointed role as prophet when the waters of the Jordan separate before him, as they did for Elijah. Elisha miraculously cleanses the contaminated water supply at Jericho and calls down a curse on the local youths at Bethel, who were taunting and verbally abusing him.

In 2 Kings 3 King Joram of Israel, King Jehoshaphat of Judah and the King of Edom set out to attack the Moabites, but find themselves without water. Elisha seeks the Lord on their behalf, and declares they will successfully defeat the Moabites. He instructs them to build ditches, which, overnight, become filled with water. The Moabites are defeated, and the invading armies only withdraw when the King of Moab incites his men to action by offering his son as a burnt sacrifice.

In 2 Kings 4 a small quantity of oil is miraculously multiplied when a widow, with two sons to support, follows Elisha's instructions. Elisha declares to a barren Shunammite woman, who had shown him kindness, that she will become pregnant and have a child. Later when the child dies, Elisha raises him back to life. (Possibly deliverance from a spirit of death). We also read how Elisha miraculously feeds a hundred people with twenty small loaves, and makes poisoned stew edible.

In 2 Kings 5 a young Jewish girl encourages Naaman from Syria to seek healing for his leprosy in Israel. Initially angered because Elisha does not personally meet with him, Naaman eventually humbles himself and receives his healing, when he obediently follows Elisha's instructions. Elisha's servant Gehazi, acting deceptively and in disobedience to his master, accepts gifts from Naaman. Elisha confronts Gehazi and declares that leprosy will afflict him and his descendants.

In 2 Kings 6 God reveals to Elisha the plans of the Syrians who are waging war against Israel. When Syrian soldiers try to capture him, Elisha is not afraid, and prays that his own servant's eyes will be open to see the army of God that surrounds them. The soldiers are temporally blinded, and Elisha treats them with kindness, before releasing them to return home. Later the Syrians besiege Samaria and the King of Israel blames Elisha for the resultant severe famine.

In 2 Kings 7 Elisha prophesies that the famine in Samaria will end the next day and that food will be in abundant supply. Overnight the invading Aramean army besieging Samaria flee, because they believe they are being attacked by the Hittites or Egyptians. They leave behind all their belongings and food supplies, thus fulfilling Elisha's prophecy. In fulfilment of Elisha's words, the officer who belittled them dies in the stampede to gather the food supplies.

In 2 Kings 8 the Shunammite woman, whose son Elisha had raised from the dead, finds favour with the King of Israel and has her property restored. Elisha tells Hazael (sent to consult Elisha by the King of Syria), that he will one day become king and inflict cruelty upon the Israelites. On his return home, Hazael murders his master and succeeds him as king of Syria. Jehoram succeeds Jehoshaphat as King of Judea. Both he and his son Ahaziah who succeeds him are ungodly kings.

2 Kings 9 describes how Elisha instructs one of the prophets to go and declare to Jehu that he is to be the next king of Israel, and that he is to take revenge on the household of Ahab. Jehu kills King Joram and throws his body on to Naboth's field. His soldiers attack King Ahaziah of Judah, who later dies of the injuries he sustains. Jehu goes to Jezreel where he orders that Queen Jezebel be thrown down from her tower. Dogs consume her body, as previously prophesied by Elisha.

In 2 Kings 10 Jehu orders the guardians of Ahab's seventy children to kill them, and bring their heads to Jezreel. He also kills all the chief men and close friends who supported Ahab, and thus he destroys the house of Ahab, as prophesied by Elisha. Jehu also calls an assembly of all the priests who worship Baal, but then orders his men to kill them and destroy the temple of Baal. Despite his zeal for the Lord, Jehu continues to worship the golden calves at Bethel and Dan.

2 Kings 11 records how, following the death of King Ahaziah of Judah, his mother Athaliah takes over the throne and orders that all the royal princes be murdered. Joash, however, escapes and remains hidden in the temple for six years. Jehoiada the priest wins the support of the army commanders, and proclaims Joash as king. He orders that

Athaliah be killed, and the temple of Baal destroyed. Jehoiada makes a covenant with the king and the people, that they will follow the Lord.

In 2 Kings 12 Joash is a righteous king in Judah, although he fails to remove the high places where people offer sacrifices. He instructs the priests to use the money collected in the temple to be used for repair and restoration of the temple. When attacked by King Hazael of Aram (Syria), Joash gives him the sacred objects from the temple, so that he will withdraw from Jerusalem. His officials conspire against Joash and assassinate him, and he is succeeded by his son Amaziah.

2 Kings 13 records that Jehoahaz, his son Jehoash and his grandson son Jeroboam reign as kings in Israel. During this time the armies of Israel are almost completely destroyed by Syria. Jehoash visits Elisha and is rebuked for only striking the ground with arrows three times when Elisha is prophesying some future victories for Israel over Syria. Elisha eventually dies and is buried. An un-named Israelite is raised back to life when his body is thrown into Elisha's tomb.

In 2 Kings 14 King Amaziah ruled in Judah for twenty-nine years, before his officials conspired against him and killed him. During his reign, King Jehoash of Israel attacked Jerusalem and took the gold, silver and articles found in the temple, back to Samaria. Following the death of King Jehoash, his son Jeroboam ruled in Israel (Samaria) for forty-one years. Although he was not a godly king, God used him to re-establish the borders of Israel.

2 Kings 15 records that the godly King Azariah, although he has leprosy, rules in Judah for fifty-one years, before he is succeeded by his son Jotham. The kings in Israel continue in their evil ways. King Zechariah and King Shallum have short reigns, before they are assassinated. King Menahem exacts money from the rich to buy protection and support from Assyria. His son Pekahiah reigns for two years, before he is assassinated by Pekah, who himself is assassinated by Hoshea.

2 Kings 16 records that King Ahaz of Judah (the son of Jotham) was ungodly, and even sacrificed his son as a burnt offering. He paid the Assyrians to help him in his war against Israel and Aram. Ahaz had an altar built in the temple at Jerusalem, modelled after a pagan altar he had seen in Damascus, and instructed the priests to use it for the daily offerings. On his death Ahaz was succeeded by his son Hezekiah.

In 2 Kings 17, during the reign of King Hosea, the Assyrians invade Israel and the people are deported. This happens because Israel has failed to heed the warnings of the prophets and has continued in her idolatry. The people from different nations, whom the Assyrians re-settled in Samaria, worship their own gods, even though the Assyrians have sent one of the deported priests from Israel to instruct them how to worship the God of Israel.

In 2 Kings 18 we find King Hezekiah is the most godly king ever to rule in Judah. He removes the high places and cuts down the Asherah poles. He even destroys the bronze snake made by Moses, because the people are treating it as an idol. During his reign, the armies of King Sennacherib of Assyria conquer Israel and invade Judah. Their commander boasts of the power of the Assyrians, and tries to discourage the people from following King Hezekiah and putting their trust in God.

2 Kings 19 records how King Hezekiah prays to God for protection from the invading Assyrian armies led by King Sennacherib, who blasphemes against God. The prophet Isaiah declares that God will deliver them, and that the Assyrian king will be killed in his own country. During the night an angel of the Lord kills 185,000 men in the Assyrian camp, and the Assyrians withdraw back to Assyria, where Sennacherib is struck down and killed by his own sons.

In 2 Kings 20 God responds to King Hezekiah's prayer when he is on the point of death, and extends his life by fifteen years. As a sign that this will happen, the shadow of the sun moves back ten steps on the stairway of Ahaz. Following a visit from envoys from Babylon, Isaiah prophesies that the people of Judah will one day be deported to Babylon. When Hezekiah dies he is succeeded by his son Manasseh.

In 2 Kings 21 we read how Manasseh is an evil king, who again leads Judah into idolatry. He rebuilds the high places and installs altars in the temple, dedicating them to the starry hosts and the Baals. He practises witchcraft and divination, and even sacrifices his own son. God declares through the prophets that Jerusalem and Judah will be plundered, because of Manasseh's wickedness. After a reign of fifty-one years, Amon succeeds Manasseh, but is assassinated after a reign of two years.

In 2 Kings 22 the Book of the law is rediscovered, during the reign of King Josiah. Realising that they have sinned by not following the law, Josiah sends his priests to enquire of the Lord. The prophetess Huldah confirms that the disasters recorded in the Book of law will come upon Judah and Jerusalem, but not during the reign of King Josiah, because he has humbled himself and sought the Lord.

2 Kings 23 records how King Josiah renews the covenant to serve and follow the Lord. He instructs the priests to remove from the temple all the objects relating to the worship of Baal and other false gods. He gets rid of all the spiritists and mediums, and has all the high places, in both Judah and Israel, desecrated, and the pagan priests put to death. Josiah is killed in battle by the Egyptians, who take his son Jehoahaz into captivity and install Jehoiakim as king of Judah.

In 2 Kings 24 the Babylonians, under King Nebuchadnezzar, invade Judah, in fulfilment of the warnings given through the prophets during the reign of King Jehoiakim. King Jehoiachin, together with many of his officials, army officers and craftsmen, are deported to Babylon. The Babylonians also remove all the treasures from the temple. Zedekiah is made king in Judah, but he rebels against the Babylonians.

In 2 Kings 25 King Nebuchadnezzar of Babylon again invades Judah and lays siege to Jerusalem. Following a severe famine, the walls of Jerusalem are broken down and the temple destroyed, after all the bronze articles have been taken to Babylon. Many of the Israelites are either killed or taken into exile in Babylon. The Babylonians appoint Gedaliah as governor, but after he is assassinated by Ishmael, the other officials and army officers flee to Egypt.

1 Chronicles

The Book of 1 Chronicles documents the genealogies of the tribes of Israel, the emergence of the Davidic Kingdom, and the preparations for the building of the temple in Jerusalem.

Chapter 1 records the genealogies, starting with Adam, and gives the origins of many of the tribes and nations that we read about in the Old Testament.

1 Chronicles 2 records the genealogies of the tribe of Judah up until the time of King David. We come across a number of the names given in these genealogies as we read the events in the Bible relating to King David. From these records we see that some of David's fighting men such as Joab, Amasa and Abishai were his cousins.

1 Chronicles 3 records the genealogies of the descendants of King David. All the children born to King David are recorded. The record includes all the Kings of Judah to the time of the exile, as well as the family records of some of the returning exiles descended from King Jehoiachin.

1 Chronicles 4 is a continuation of the genealogies of the tribe of Judah. Included in this list is Jabez, who prayed that God would bless him, protect him and keep him from pain.

1 Chronicles 5 records some of the history of the tribes of Reuben, Gad and Manasseh. Although Reuben was Jacob's first son, the rights of the first-born were given to Joseph's sons, because Reuben had defiled his father's marriage bed (Genesis 35:22; Genesis 49:4).

I Chronicles 6 records the genealogies of the tribe of Levi who serve as priests and musicians. Also documented are the various towns which are assigned to the clans of Levi.

In 1 Chronicles 7 we find partial genealogies of the tribes of Issachar, Benjamin, Naphtali, Manasseh, Ephraim and Asher.

1 Chronicles 8 records a number of genealogies relating to the tribe of Benjamin.

1 Chronicles 9 concludes the genealogical section of this book by documenting the names of some of the exiles returning to Israel and Jerusalem from Babylon. Various duties of the priests, Levites and temple servants are also recorded.

In 1 Chronicles 10 Saul is wounded and his sons are killed in battle against the Philistines. When his armour bearer refuses to kill him, Saul falls upon his own sword. The men of Jabesh Gilead recover the bodies of Saul and his sons, which have been put on public display, and bury them. Saul died because he was unfaithful to God, failed to keep God's Word and even consulted a spiritist medium for guidance.

In 1 Chronicles 11 David is anointed King at Hebron, defeats the Jebusites, and captures the city of Jerusalem and fortress of Zion, which became known as the city of David. We also read the names and some of the exploits of the mighty men who supported David.

1 Chronicles 12 documents the names of the Benjamites, Gadites and men of Manasseh, who defected from Saul and joined David at Ziklag. Also listed are the number of fighting men from the different tribes of Israel who came to Hebron to turn over Saul's kingdom to David. The men of Issachar understood the times and knew what they should do.

In 1 Chronicles 13 David, after conferring with his army commanders, gives instructions for the ark of the covenant to be brought to them. The ark is loaded on a new cart (contrary to the instructions originally given Moses that it should only be carried by the Levites, Numbers 4:15 & 7:9). Uzzah dies when he puts his hand on the ark to steady it, after the oxen pulling the cart stumble. David, now in fear of the Lord, leaves the ark in the care of Obed-Edom.

In 1 Chronicles 14 David defeats the Philistines at Baal Perazim (which means God of the breakthrough). When the Philistines invade a second time, God gives David a different strategy, and tells him not to attack them until he hears the sound of marching in the balsam trees, signifying that God has gone out ahead of him. The Philistines are again defeated and all the nations fear Israel.

In 1 Chronicles 15 David instructs the Levites to consecrate themselves and prepare to bring the ark of the covenant to Jerusalem. Musicians and singers are appointed to accompany it in joyful celebration. David himself dances before the Lord with joy, but his wife Michal, the daughter of Saul, sees him and despises him in her heart.

In 1 Chronicles 16 David makes sacrifices and blesses the people, after the ark is placed in the tent prepared for it. David assigns various duties to the priests, and those who will minister before the tabernacle of the Lord. David also delivers a new psalm of thanksgiving, declaring the glory of God, and encouraging the people to always praise and thank God.

In 1 Chronicles 17 David determines to build a temple for the Lord. God, however, declares through Nathan the prophet, that David is not to build the temple, but that his son will perform this task. God further declares that His covenant with David is an everlasting covenant, extending to his descendants. David responds by proclaiming that there is no other god who has chosen a nation for Himself, and redeemed them.

In 1 Chronicles 18 David overcomes the Philistines, Edomites, Moabites and the Arameans, because God gives him victory wherever he goes. The gold, silver and bronze taken from these nations are dedicated to the Lord. David rules over all Israel, doing what is right and just.

In 1 Chronicles 19 the Ammonites offend David by treating a delegation sent to them with disrespect. In the ensuing war the Ammonites hire the Arameans to help them, but David and his army, led by Joab and Abishai, put both of these armies to flight.

1 Chronicles 20 records how the Israelites continue to have military successes. Joab lays waste to some of the towns in Ammon. The captured Ammonites are consigned to manual labour. In battles with the Philistines some of the giant-like descendants of Rapha are killed, as is Lahmi, the brother of Goliath.

In 1 Chronicles 21 Satan incites David to sin by taking a census of his fighting men, despite opposition from Joab. (This is possibly pride, lack of trust in God or not conducting the census in accordance with the instructions given to Moses.) As a consequence, Israel suffers a plague in which seventy thousand people die. The plague only stops when David takes responsibility for what he has done, and makes sacrifices to the Lord on an altar, building it on a threshing floor which he purchases from Araunah.

In 1 Chronicles 22 David begins to make preparations for the building of the temple, which Solomon his son will oversee. He tells Solomon that God has declared that he, Solomon, will build the temple. He encourages Solomon to be bold and courageous, and to keep the laws of God.

1 Chronicles 23 documents the genealogies of the Levites who are assigned various duties associated with the temple. In total there are 38,000 Levites. Some are to supervise the work of the temple, some are to be judges and officials, some are to be gatekeepers, and others are to be musicians. The descendants of Aaron are set apart as priests to offer sacrifices and proclaim blessings in the name of God.

1 Chronicles 24 records how David divides the descendants of Aaron into twenty-four divisions. Lots are drawn to determine the order in which they will minister in the house of the Lord.

In 1 Chronicles 25 the sons of Asaph, Heman and Jeduthun are set apart for the ministry of prophecy. The skilled musicians are divided into twenty-four divisions.

1 Chronicles 26 documents how the gatekeepers are divided into groups and allocated different areas of responsibility. Some of the Levites are allocated to be in charge of the treasuries and the gifts and offerings dedicated to the temple. Other Levites are assigned duties away from the temple as officials and judges over the different geographical regions of Israel.

1 Chronicles 27 records the names of the commanders of the twelve divisions of the army (each consisting of 24,000 men) who are on duty month by month. Also recorded are the officers over each of the tribes of Israel, and the names of individuals put in charge of King David's livestock and properties.

In 1 Chronicles 28 David calls together all the leading officials and army commanders from throughout Israel. He declares to them that his son Solomon is to succeed him and is to build the temple for the Lord, in accordance with all the plans that God has given him. He charges them to carefully follow all the commands of the Lord.

In 1 Chronicles 29 David concludes his address to the assembled leaders of Israel by telling them how much has already been given for the building of the temple. The leaders respond by also donating gold, silver, bronze and precious stones. David declares that all wealth and honour come from God and that they have given back freely to Him. The leaders and all David's sons pledge their allegiance to Solomon.

2 Chronicles

The Book of 2 Chronicles records the history of the united kingdom under King Solomon, and the history of Judah following the division with the northern kingdom.

Chapter 1 records how Solomon asks God for wisdom and knowledge to lead and govern the people. This request pleases God because Solomon has not asked for wealth or victories over his enemies. God declares that he will give Solomon wisdom and knowledge as well as wealth. This promise is duly fulfilled.

In 2 Chronicles 2 Solomon gives orders for the building of the temple. He assigns over 150,000 men to this project. Solomon requests help from King Hiram of Tyre to supply timber, and agrees to pay him with wheat, wine and olive oil. King Hiram sends a skilled craftsman named Hurum-Abi to oversee the work of building the temple.

2 Chronicles 3 describes the temple built by Solomon. The sanctuary is about 90 feet long by 30 feet wide. It is panelled with cedar wood and overlaid with gold. The inner sanctuary measuring 30 feet long by 30 feet wide is separated from the sanctuary by a curtain. Within the inner sanctuary are two carved cherubim also overlaid with gold. They each have a wingspan of about 15 feet, and their wings touch, thus making a covering over the tabernacle.

In 2 Chronicles 4 the craftsman Hurum-Abi produces all the articles made of bronze and gold to be placed in the temple area. These include the 15-foot diameter Sea of cast bronze, two pillars, washing bowls, lampstands and the pots, bowls, shovels and other utensils used by the priests in performing the sacrificial ceremonies.

2 Chronicles 5 records that when the work of building the temple is completed all the leaders, priests and elders assemble in Jerusalem. They carry the ark of the covenant into the temple with much praise and sacrifice, and place it beneath the wings of the cherubim in the Most Holy Place. As they praise and worship God singing 'He is good and His love endures forever', the presence of God fills the temple, and the priests are unable to perform their services.

2 Chronicles 6 records the prayer of Solomon when he dedicates the temple. He praises and thanks God for His faithfulness. He asks that God will always be attentive to the prayers made to Him. He asks that, even when individuals sin, or the nation sins, against Him, God will hear and answer their prayers, as they repent of sin and seek His face. He prays that God will deal with each person according

to what is in his or her heart.

In 2 Chronicles 7 fire comes down from heaven and consumes the sacrifices, as Solomon is dedicating the temple. Many sacrifices are offered over a period of fourteen days, as the people celebrate the completion of the work. God appears to Solomon and declares that He will respond in the future if the people repent of their backsliding and turn back to Him. If the people, however, forsake God and His commands, they will be uprooted from the land and the temple destroyed.

2 Chronicles 8 records some of the building projects undertaken by Solomon, using conscripted labour from the non-Israelites who lived in the land. He did not use the Israelites for this work, who were his fighting men and administrators. Following the instructions of David, Solomon appointed divisions of priests and Levites to carry out all the functions associated with the temple.

In 2 Chronicles 9 Solomon and Israel both grow in prosperity, as leaders from the nations donate gifts of gold and silver. Solomon makes large shields of gold and a splendid throne covered with gold, unlike anything made by any other kingdom. He imports horses and chariots from Egypt and other countries. His trading ships bring back rich cargoes of gold and precious materials. The Queen of Sheba visits Solomon and is overwhelmed by his wisdom and wealth.

2 Chronicles 10 records how Rehoboam, who had succeeded Solomon as king, responds to the Israelites led by Jeroboam who ask that the burdens placed upon them be lightened. Ignoring the advice of his elders, Rehoboam declares he will treat the people even more harshly than his father. This response leads to the division between the tribes of Judah and Benjamin led by Rehoboam, and the other tribes of Israel led by Jeroboam.

In 2 Chronicles 11 God tells Rehoboam, through the prophet Shemaiah, not to attack Jeroboam and the other tribes of Israel. Instead he fortifies Jerusalem and the other cities in Judah. He disperses some of his sons throughout the region to govern the people. Many of the Levites support Rehoboam and abandon their land and come to live in Jerusalem and Judah.

In 2 Chronicles 12 we read that, once Rehoboam has established his kingdom, the Israelites abandon the law. They are invaded by King Shishak of Egypt who carries off all the treasures from the temple and the royal palaces. Because the Israelites humble themselves and turn back to God, God declares through the prophet Shemaiah that He will not destroy them but deliver them.

2 Chronicles 12 records that Rehoboam's son Abijah succeeds

him as king in Judah. When he goes into battle with Jeroboam, Abijah declares that Jeroboam is in rebellion against the Lord who promised the throne to David's descendants. The sacrifices that Jeroboam and the Israelites are making are to false gods. Despite being greatly outnumbered and ambushed from behind, Judah triumphs over Jeroboam, because they rely on God, and Israel suffers many casualties.

2 Chronicles 14 records that King Asa succeeds Abijah as king in Judah. He was a righteous king commanding the people to seek the Lord and follow God's commandments. He destroys all the places of false worship and cuts down all the Asherah poles. When Judah is attacked by a large army of Cushites, Asa calls on the Lord for help, and the invading army is completely crushed.

In 2 Chronicles 15 we read how Asa is encouraged when Azariah prophesies over him and declares that God is with him. He repairs the altar of the Lord and removes all the idols in the land. He calls all the people to Jerusalem (including those from the other tribes who have settled in Judah) and they enter into a covenant to seek the Lord wholeheartedly. Because they sought the Lord, Judah enjoys a time of peace and prosperity during the reign of King Asa.

2 Chronicles 16 records how King Baasha of Israel goes to war against Judah and fortifies the city of Ramah. King Asa uses silver and gold from the temple treasuries to pay King Ben-Hadad of Aram to attack King Baasha. The prophet Hanani is imprisoned when he rebukes King Asa for not trusting in God to give him victory. At the end of his life, Asa is afflicted by a disease in his feet, but does not seek healing from God, and dies after ruling Judah for forty-one years.

In 2 Chronicles 17 Jehoshaphat succeeds his father Asa as king of Judah. His heart is devoted to the ways of the Lord and he sends officials and priests to all the towns in Judah to teach them from the book of the law. Jehoshaphat builds forts and store cities throughout Judah and becomes very powerful, with over one million fighting men under his control.

2 Chronicles 18 records how King Jehoshaphat allies himself with King Ahab of Israel, who invites him to join in battle against the Arameans. The false prophets of Israel, operating under the power of lying spirits, declare that God will give them victory. The prophet Micaiah is imprisoned by King Ahab when he rebukes the lying prophets and declares that Israel will become leaderless. Ahab enters the battle in disguise but is struck down by an arrow, shot randomly by the Arameans, and dies.

2 Chronicles 19 describes how the prophet Jehu rebukes

Jehoshaphat for allying himself with the wicked King Ahab of Israel, but does commend him for setting his heart on seeking God. King Jehoshaphat appoints judges in all the fortified cities of the land, instructing them to serve faithfully and wholeheartedly, in the fear of the Lord, whom they represent.

In 2 Chronicles 20 the Ammonites and Moabites come to attack Judah. When Jehoshaphat and the people seek God's help, the prophet Jahaziel declares that the battle is not theirs, but belongs to the Lord. Jehoshaphat sends out worshippers ahead of his army, and his enemies turn against each other and destroy themselves. Towards the end of his life Jehoshaphat is rebuked by Eliezer for entering into a trading alliance with Israel, which fails when their ships are wrecked.

2 Chronicles 21 records that Jehoram succeeds his father Jehoshaphat as king of Judah. He kills all his brothers and does evil in the sight of the Lord by leading the people into false worship. Elijah the prophet rebukes him and prophesies that his family will be taken away, and that he will die a painful death. This prophecy is duly fulfilled when the Philistines attack Judah, and Jehoram eventually dies because of an incurable bowel disease.

2 Chronicles 22 describes how Ahaziah succeeds Jehoram as king of Judah. His mother Athaliah encourages him to act unrighteously and follow the ways of Ahab and the kings of Israel. Whilst visiting King Joram of Israel, with whom he had gone to war against the Arameans, he is killed by Jehu. When Athaliah hears of his death she takes the throne for herself, murdering all of her grandchildren except Joash, who is hidden by his aunt Jehosheba, the wife of Jehoiada the priest.

In 2 Chronicles 23 Jehoiada the priest makes a covenant with the army commanders, leading officials and the Levites to overthrow Queen Athaliah and make Joash king of Judah. After arming his supporters, he publicly proclaims Joash as king and Athaliah is put to death. Jehoiada declares that he, the people and the king will follow the Lord. The people respond by destroying the temple of Baal and rejoicing because Athaliah had been overthrown.

In 2 Chronicles 24 King Joash places a large chest at the gate of the temple in which to collect the offerings of the people, to be used to restore the temple. After the priest Jehoiada dies, the people return to the false worship of Asherah poles and idols. Jehoida's son Zechariah rebukes them, but is put to death on the orders of Joash. The Arameans invade Judah, and Joash, who is wounded in battle, is killed by his own officials in retaliation for the death of Zechariah.

In 2 Chronicles 25 Amaziah succeeds Joash as king in Judah.

When he hires fighting men from Israel, the man of God rebukes him for not trusting in God. When he dismisses these foreign soldiers his army is still able to defeat the Edomites. Amaziah, however, captures their idols and worships them. As a result, King Joash of Israel defeats Judah in battle and plunders Jerusalem. Amaziah eventually dies when his officials conspire against him, because of his apostasy.

2 Chronicles 26 describes how Uzziah succeeds his father Amaziah and rules for fifty-two years as king in Judah. He follows the way of the Lord, and Judah prospers during his reign. Uzziah becomes very powerful, but this leads to pride and his downfall, when he wrongly enters the temple to offer incense, (a task that only the high priests were permitted to do). As he argues with the priests, who confront him, leprosy breaks put on his face, and he spends the rest of his life living in isolation.

2 Chronicles 27 records that Jotham succeeds his father Uzziah as king of Judah and reigns for sixteen years. Because he walks steadfastly before the Lord, Judah prospers during his reign and he is given victory over the Ammonites. Sadly, it is recorded that the people of Judah themselves continue in their corrupt practices.

In 2 Chronicles 28 the unrighteous Ahaz succeeds Jotham as king in Judah. He worships the false gods of Damascus, sacrifices his sons in the fire, sets up altars and shrines in the streets of Jerusalem and closes the door of the temple. As a consequence, Judah is oppressed by her enemies, including Edom, Syria and Israel, who take many prisoners. Oded the prophet, however, rebukes the Israelites for taking the Judeans as slaves and so they release them and they return to Judah.

2 Chronicles 29 describes how the righteous Hezekiah succeeds Ahaz as king and sets about restoring the temple. He orders the priests and Levites to consecrate themselves before removing all the defilement from the temple. They spend sixteen days removing all the unclean objects found, and cleansing and preparing the temple. Many sacrifices are offered, accompanied by much praise and worship, as the temple is rededicated to the Lord and temple services are re-established.

In 2 Chronicles 30 Hezekiah invites all the people in Judah and Israel to celebrate the Passover in Jerusalem. Many of the Israelites in the northern kingdom scorn and ridicule the couriers sent to proclaim the invitation. Those who do attend have not purified themselves, but God answers Hezekiah's prayer that He would pardon them and heal them. Many of the priests and Levites consecrate themselves and there is great joy as they celebrate the Passover for fourteen days.

2 Chronicles 31 records that, after celebrating the Passover in Jerusalem, the Israelites go throughout the land of Judah destroying all the high places and altars, and cutting down the Asherah poles. Hezekiah assigns the priests and Levites in divisions to carry out their work in the temple and orders the people to bring their tithes and offerings to the temple to support and feed them. The people generously respond and there is more than enough to distribute to all the priests and Levites.

In 2 Chronicles 32 King Sennacherib of Assyria invades Judah. Hezekiah fortifies Jerusalem and encourages the people to be bold and courageous, because God is with them. Sennacherib boasts that none of the gods of the nations that he has invaded have been able to save their people, and claims that the same will be true of Judah. Hezekiah and Isaiah, however, cry out to God who responds by sending an angel to destroy the Assyrian army.

2 Chronicles 33 records that Manasseh, who succeeds his father Hezekiah as king, is very evil. He worships the Baals, engages in witchcraft and sacrifices his own sons by fire. When God brings the Assyrians against Judah they capture him and take him in chains to Babylon. Manasseh humbles himself and repents of his actions and God restores the throne to him. Amnon, his son, who succeeds Manasseh, acts unrighteously, and is assassinated by his own officials after a reign of only two years.

2 Chronicles 34 describes how Josiah, who succeeds Amnon as king, destroys the places of false worship in Jerusalem and Judah and restores the temple that has been allowed to fall into ruin. When the book of the law is discovered, Josiah assembles all the people and reads it to them. They determine to follow God wholeheartedly and obey Him. Because they have turned back to Him, God declares that they will not experience the disasters that will come upon Judah and Jerusalem.

In 2 Chronicles 35 King Josiah instructs the priests and Levites to celebrate the Passover in Jerusalem. He and his officials provide a great number of animals for the prescribed sacrifices. The priests and Levites work together to serve the people, whilst the musicians worship God. Josiah eventually dies in battle at Megiddo (the plain of Armageddon), when he engages the Egyptian army, led by King Neco, despite the latter's insistence that he is not invading Judah.

In 2 Chronicles 36 Josiah's son Jehoahaz is taken captive by King Neco of Egypt, who appoints Jehoiakim as king. Jehoiakim is taken captive to Babylon by King Nebuchadnezzar, as is his son Jehoiachin. When Zedekiah, who was appointed king by

Nebuchadnezzar, rebels against him, the Babylonians invade Judah, destroy the temple and take the remnant of Judah into captivity, where they remain for seventy years, until King Cyrus issues a decree allowing their descendants to return to Jerusalem.

Ezra

The Book of Ezra documents the return of the exiles from Babylon which took place in the period 540-450 BC.

In Chapter 1 Cyrus, King of Persia, issues a proclamation authorising the Israelites (taken captive seventy years earlier) to return to Jerusalem and rebuild the temple. (This proclamation fulfils the prophecy of Jeremiah 29:10). He gives back all the articles previously removed from Jerusalem to the returning exiles and requests that the Persians give gifts to the exiles.

Ezra 2 lists, by family name, the exiles who returned to the land of Israel with Jeshua and Zerubbabel. In total there were 42,360 people together with about 7,500 servants. After giving offerings for the rebuilding of the temple they settled in their original towns.

In Ezra 3 we read how the returning exiles build an altar in Jerusalem and reinstate the daily sacrifices and offerings in accordance with the law of Moses. They begin to gather the materials for rebuilding the temple. In the second year following their return they begin the work of rebuilding the temple under the supervision of the Levites. When the foundations are completed they hold a dedication ceremony with great rejoicing and many tears.

In Ezra 4 the work of rebuilding the temple is opposed by the enemies of Israel who are living in the land. They discourage and frustrate the work of rebuilding and eventually appeal to Artaxerxes, King of Persia, to stop the work. They argue that, if the rebuilding continues, Jerusalem will again become rebellious and remind Artaxerxes that Jerusalem was destroyed because the Israelites were rebellious. Artaxerxes issues a decree to stop the rebuilding work.

Ezra 5 records how Tattenai, the governor of Trans-Euphrates, challenges the work of rebuilding of the temple. The Israelites recount to him their history and how Cyrus had authorised the rebuilding work. Tattenai writes to King Darius asking him to search the court records and verify that the Israelites have really been authorised to reconstruct the temple.

In Ezra 6 we read how King Darius searches the court records and discovers the proclamation previously made by King Cyrus. He replies to Tattenai that he must not hinder the rebuilding work but, in fact, must pay for it out of the royal treasury. In the sixth year of Darius' reign the temple is completed. The Israelites rejoice that the work is completed and praise God for the way in which He has moved King Darius to show them favour.

In Ezra 7 Ezra, a descendant of Aaron, and well versed in the law of Moses, comes to Jerusalem in the seventh year of the reign of the Babylonian King Artaxerxes. He has found favour with King Artaxerxes who has given him gifts of silver and gold in order to buy animals, to be sacrificed at the altar in Jerusalem. Artaxerxes declares that those who work in the temple are to be free of paying taxes, and he authorises Ezra to administer justice and appoint magistrates.

Ezra 8 records the family names of those who return to Jerusalem with Ezra. Before setting out on their journey they fast and pray for protection. The gifts of silver and gold are carefully recorded and distributed for safe keeping. On arrival in Jerusalem the gifts of silver and gold are fully accounted for and deposited in the temple, after which the returning exiles sacrifice burnt offerings to the Lord.

In Ezra 9 it is reported to Ezra that the Israelites, including some of the Levites, have been disobedient to God's commands and have taken non-Jewish wives for themselves from among the pagan nations. Ezra prays and confesses their sin before God. He acknowledges that Israel's captivity and exile was a result of their failure to follow God's commandments. God had shown them favour in bringing them back to the land, but now they are again sinning against Him.

In Ezra 10 Ezra prays and mourns before God over the faithlessness of the exiles. An assembly of all the Israelites is commanded. At this assembly the Israelites covenant that they will put away their foreign wives, and that those concerned will individually present themselves before the elders and judges and make atonement before the Lord. The names of the Israelites who have broken God's commands by taking foreign wives are all recorded.

Nehemiah

The Book of Nehemiah, written in about 450 BC, records the rebuilding of the walls of Jerusalem and the rededication of the city and its people to follow God's laws.

Chapter 1 relates how Nehemiah, who was living in exile in Susa (present day Iran), hears that the walls of Jerusalem are broken down. His response is to confess that his sins and the sins of his ancestors have brought this calamity upon Israel. He reminds God of His promise to restore the Israelites if they turn back to Him.

Nehemiah 2 records how Nehemiah receives favour from King Artaxerxes and is given permission and letters of authority to go to Jerusalem to rebuild the walls. After secretly surveying the state of the walls, Nehemiah meets with the local officials and initiates a rebuilding programme. He immediately encounters verbal opposition and mockery from Sanballat, Tobiah and Geshem, but Nehemiah declares that God will help them and give them success.

Nehemiah 3 records how the work of rebuilding the walls and gates of Jerusalem begins. Different families take responsibility for rebuilding a section of the walls. They are from all sorts of different backgrounds and professions, but they begin to work in unity to restore the walls.

Nehemiah 4 records how opposition to the work of rebuilding the wall increases. Sanballat and Tobiah plan to attack the Israelites, and those building the walls become discouraged. Nehemiah encourages them that God will fight for them. He organises the workers so that half of them are armed, and act as guards for the others. If they are attacked at any one point everyone will rally to that point to defend it.

In Nehemiah 5 we read how Nehemiah, motivated by his righteous anger, introduces social reform. The Israelites are being exploited by the nobles and officials, and are having to mortgage their properties, and even sell themselves and their family members into slavery. The nobles and officials promise on oath to no longer oppress the people and to return their lands. Nehemiah himself leads by example and does not exact taxes from the people, as previous governors did.

In Nehemiah 6 Sanballat, Tobiah and Geshem continue to oppose the work, and intimidate Nehemiah by spreading false rumours that he is about to rebel and proclaim himself king. They even bribe one of the Israelites to discourage Nehemiah by giving him a false prophecy, and try to get him to be afraid and go into hiding.

Despite the opposition, the work continues, and, after fifty-two days, the work is completed, and Nehemiah's enemies lose their confidence.

Nehemiah 7 records that when the walls are rebuilt Nehemiah turns his attention to other administration matters. He organises a registration of all the Israelites who have returned from captivity back to Jerusalem and Judah. In all there are over 42,000 people together with over 7,000 servants. Some of the heads of the returning families give financial support for the rebuilding of the walls.

In Nehemiah 8 the Israelites celebrate the Feast of Tabernacles in Jerusalem. Each day they assemble before Ezra and the priests, who read from the book of the law, and then explain it to the people in a way that they can understand it. They then enjoy choice food together and celebrate with great joy, because they understand the words that have been made known to them.

Nehemiah 9 records how the Israelites gather again before the Lord to worship Him and confess their sins. The priests recite their history from the calling of Abraham until the present day. They praise God for providing for them, even though they rebelled against Him in the wilderness. They acknowledge that they turned away from God and hardships came upon them. God was faithful, but they sinned. They now want to re-dedicate themselves to God.

Nehemiah 10 records the names of those who sign the re-dedication covenant on behalf of the Israelites. They promise to follow God's law and to obey His commandments. They promise not to inter-marry with people from other nations, to keep the Sabbath regulations, and to bring tithes and offerings to support the Levites who do the work of the Lord. They declare that they will not neglect the house of God.

Nehemiah 11 lists the names, job roles and genealogies of the Israelites who settle in Jerusalem. (Some were volunteers and some were elected by lot.) Also listed in this chapter are the names of the villages in which some of the returning exiles settle.

Nehemiah 12 records the names and genealogies of the priests and Levites who returned with Zerubbabel. After purifying themselves they dedicate the walls of Jerusalem which have been rebuilt. Two choirs lead the praise and thanksgiving with great joy, and march around the top of the walls in opposite directions. Men are appointed to be in charge of the storerooms and the Israelites bring their tithes and contributions to them.

Nehemiah 13 records how Nehemiah is horrified to find that Tobiah has been given a room in the temple. He has him expelled, and the room purified. He also sends away one of the priests who married the daughter of Sanballat. He appoints trustworthy men over the storerooms, because the Levites are not receiving any support. He puts a stop to the trading that is taking place on the Sabbath, and rebukes the Israelites for being disobedient and marrying foreign wives.

Esther

The Book of Esther records how the Jews in Susa (Persia) are delivered from anti-Semitic persecution in about 475 BC.

Chapter 1 records how Queen Vashti refuses to submit to an order given by her husband King Xerxes. Concerned that such rebellion will be imitated throughout his Kingdom, Xerxes confers with his advisers and issues a royal decree declaring that every man should rule over his household, and that Queen Vashti is to be banished for ever from the King's presence.

Esther 2 records how Esther, a beautiful young Jewish girl, who is the adopted daughter of her cousin Mordecai, wins the favour of King Xerxes and is appointed Queen in the place of Vashti. (Mordecai is a direct descendant of one of the Jews taken into exile by King Nebuchadnezzar, but King Xerxes is unaware of Esther's background and ancestry.) Mordecai learns of a conspiracy to assassinate King Xerxes and Esther is able to report this to the King, and thus save his life.

In Esther 3 and 4 Haman is appointed as a high official by King Xerxes. Because Mordecai will not bow down and worship him, Haman determines to kill all the Jews in Persia, and persuades King Xerxes to issue a decree declaring a date on which this should happen. Mordecai asks Esther to intervene with the king, even at the risk of losing her own life. Esther agrees to try and help, and requests that the Jews fast and pray to God on her behalf.

Esther 5 records how Esther goes into the king's presence and finds favour with him. She invites King Xerxes and Haman to a banquet and subsequently to a second banquet on the following day. Haman, full of self-importance, is angry that Mordecai still refuses to bow down to him. He plans to kill him and orders that a gallows be built for his execution.

Esther 6 records how King Xerxes reads the court records and discovers that Mordecai has never been honoured for saving the king's life. Without mentioning Mordecai's name, the king asks Haman how someone who pleases the king should be honoured. Thinking the king wants to honour him, Haman suggests that the person should be paraded around the streets with great pomp and ceremony. He is mortified when he is ordered to do this for Mordecai.

Esther 7 records how Esther, at the second banquet with King Xerxes and Haman, petitions the king to spare the Jewish people from Haman's plot to have them all destroyed. King Xerxes is angry when he realises how Haman has used his authority to try and destroy the

Jews. When he perceives that Haman is trying to molest Esther, he orders that Haman be hanged on the very gallows that Haman has had built for the execution of Mordecai.

In Esther 8 King Xerxes appoints Mordecai to the position previously held by Haman. (Haman's estates are given to Esther, and she puts Mordecai in charge of them.) Because Haman's decree permitting the destruction of the Jews cannot be revoked, Mordecai is allowed to write a second decree, in the name of King Xerxes, giving the Jewish people the right to assemble and protect themselves from their enemies.

Esther 9 and 10 record how the Jews in exile receive help from the Persian authorities, and are able to overthrow the enemies who plotted to destroy them. Haman's ten sons, together with many of their enemies are killed. In celebration of this great deliverance from their enemies, the annual two-day feast of Purim, still celebrated today, is established. Mordecai is held in high esteem by the Jews because he has worked for the good of the people, and spoken up for their welfare.

Job

The Book of Job records the trials of Job at the hands of Satan and provides helpful insights about human suffering.

In chapter 1 we read that Job was a wealthy man who was upright, blameless and shunned evil. God allows Satan to bring calamity upon Job's family, but is not allowed to touch Job himself. Job's sons and daughters are killed and Job's livestock is destroyed. Job does not accuse God of wrong doing, but declares that God gives, and God has the right to take away.

In Job 2 the reader is given insights into what is happening in the heavenly realm with regard to Job's suffering. To refute Satan's claim that Job will curse God if he experiences loss and suffering, God allows Satan to bring physical suffering to Job. Although afflicted with sores, Job still refuses to curse God. Job's four friends Eliphaz, Bildad, Zophar and Elihu come to comfort him. They are shocked by his appearance and for seven days sit with him and say nothing.

Job 3 records how Job, in the depth of his suffering and turmoil, questions why he had been born. He feels it would have been better if he had never been born, rather than to have to endure the sufferings he is now going through. Job finally declares that what he had feared (and presumably tried to avoid through his righteous lifestyle) had come upon him.

In Job 4 Eliphaz declares that, in his experience, those who plough evil or sow trouble reap the consequences of their actions. He believes that God does not allow the righteous or innocent to perish. If Job is as righteous as he claims, then he should not be feeling dismayed. In a vision an angel had said to Eliphaz that mortal man cannot be as righteous as God, or even as righteous as the angels whom God had to confront regarding their errors.

In Job 5 Eliphaz continues his first speech by proclaiming that God directs the affairs of man, and He performs miracles that cannot be counted. He tells Job not to despise the discipline of God, thus implying that he considers Job's difficulties are of his own making. He says God is able to rescue and bless those who turn to Him in their distress.

In Job 6, Job declares that his desire to die comes out of the deep anguish and misery of the suffering he is experiencing. If he were to die, he would have the comfort of knowing he had not denied or turned against God. He rebukes his comforters and says that they are not dependable. They do not understand his suffering and are challenging his integrity by accusing him of some wrongdoing.

Job 7 records Job arguing that life does involve hardships, and he likens it to a slave, or a hired man, looking forward to the end of the working day. In his case, however, there is no relief from his suffering. He can look forward to sleep, but his sleep is restless, and he is tormented with terrifying dreams. Job asks that God show him why He is treating him this way. If he has sinned, he asks God to reveal his sin, so that he can seek forgiveness and receive God's pardon.

Job 8 records the first speech of Bildad. He argues that God does not pervert justice. He claims that Job's children have been destroyed because they sinned. If someone turns from God, they will perish. He likens such a person's life to trying to grow plants without adequate water, or trusting in a spider's web to support their weight. He concludes that God does not abandon the righteous and that Job can be restored if he turns back to God.

Job 9 records Job's response to Bildad's first speech. Job agrees that God does not abandon the righteous, but questions whether any mortal person can be completely righteous. Because God is all powerful and His wisdom beyond understanding, how can he argue his case before God? Even though Job considers himself blameless, he realises that God would always be able to find some fault in him. Job concludes that he needs an arbitrator to stand in the gap between himself and God.

Job 10 is a continuation of Job's response to Bildad's first speech. Job acknowledges that God created him and sustains him, but does not understand why he is experiencing so much suffering. Job declares that he loathes his life and that it would have been better if he had died at birth.

Job 11 records the first speech of Zophar. He rebukes Job for trying to present himself as blameless. He argues that Job is experiencing the judgement of God, and that Job should not be questioning this. If Job would only repent of his sins and turn back to God, he will be restored and again know God's blessings in his life.

In Job 12 we read Job's response to Zophar's first speech. Job declares that he has become the laughing stock of his friends, because he has tried to lead a righteous and blameless life, for which God has rewarded him with suffering. (Job sees God as being completely in control of everything that happens in an individual's life, and therefore concludes that God must be the source of his problems.)

In Job 13 we read the continuation of Job's response to Zophar's first speech. Job has witnessed how God directs the affairs of man, but expresses his desire to be given an opportunity to argue his case before God. Job again insists that he is innocent of any wrongdoing, and no one can bring any charges against him. He wants to know why God seems to be treating him as an enemy, and has caused this suffering to come upon him.

In Job 14 we have the conclusion of Job's response to Zophar's first speech. Job's lifespan is only short, so what is the purpose behind the suffering that God has brought upon him? He is not like a tree that can sprout new growth. He cannot understand how his suffering fits into God's overall plans for His creation, so consequently he can only feel his own pain, and feel sorry for himself.

In Job 15 we have the second speech of Eliphaz. He accuses Job of having no wisdom, and that his arguments are worthless. He declares that Job is speaking out of pride, and that no one can claim to be blameless before God. He claims that Job's own words condemn him. He describes the fate of the wicked, including some of the sufferings that Job is experiencing, and declares that the wicked bring these calamities upon themselves.

In Job 16 we have Job's response to Eliphaz's second speech. He argues that it is easy to make accusatory speeches as his friends are doing, but this does not bring any comfort to the one who is suffering. Job again proclaims that God has afflicted suffering upon him. Despite what has happened to him, Job declares that he has not turned to violence, and that his prayers to God are pure.

Job 17 is the continuation of Job's response to Eliphaz's second speech. Job declares that his spirit has been broken by his sufferings, and that all who see him are appalled. If he accepts that he really deserves what has happened to him, his hope will be gone, and he might as well be dead. He challenges his comforters to give him hope.

In Job 18 we read Bildad's second speech. He rebukes Job for not listening to his friends, and again declares that the wicked suffer as a consequence of their unrighteous actions. He describes, in poetic terms, what happens to those who rebel against God, implying that this is happening to Job.

In Job 19 we read Job's response to the second speech of Bildad. He rebukes his friends for only tormenting him and crushing him with their words. He feels he has been wronged by God by being treated as if he were an enemy, and in being afflicted with suffering. Job's servants no longer respect him, and his friends have all turned against him. Job finally declares that, even if he is destroyed and dies, he will not be cut off from God, who is his redeemer.

Job 20 records the second speech of Zophar. He considers that

Job is dishonouring his friends by rejecting their conclusion that he has brought his suffering upon himself. The wicked always suffer and perish because of their pride. They and their children will lose all that they have gained through their sinful actions. Eventually the wicked always experience the judgement and wrath of God.

In Job 21 we read Job's response to Zophar's second speech. Job declares that his friends' argument that he must be suffering because of his own sin is false. He has seen the wicked prosper and not come under the judgement of God in their earthly life. To argue that their children will have to suffer the consequences is no consolation to Job. Because the wicked are self-centred, they are not troubled by the thought of what will happen to others after they die.

Job 22 records Eliphaz's third speech. He declares that, if Job were blameless, his sufferings would bring no pleasure or benefit to God. Therefore, he argues, Job must have sinned by oppressing others and showing no compassion to the poor or to the widows. He is acting like the wicked who reject God and think that God is indifferent to their actions. Job, he says, needs to return to God and submit to Him, and he will be restored.

Job 23 is the start of Job's response to Eliphaz's third speech. He maintains that he has not broken God's commandments, and has treasured God's word. In his suffering he feels separated from God, and his desire is only to present his innocence to God. Can he ever trust and not be fearful of a God who unjustly treats him in the way he believes God is treating him?

Job 24 is the conclusion of Job's response to Eliphaz's third speech. Job identifies himself with the poor and oppressed. He describes their suffering, and asks why God does not bring immediate judgement upon the wicked who oppress them. He lists some of the things that the wicked do, which only come to an end when they die. He considers it unfair that they often do not have to endure suffering during their earthly life, whereas he, who is blameless, does have to.

In Job 25-26 Bildad declares in his third speech that no one can consider themselves righteous and pure before God. Job responds by declaring that God is almighty and powerful and can do anything that He wants to do.

Job 27 is a continuation of Job's response to Bildad's third speech. Job acknowledges that the godless will ultimately know the judgement of God and will lose everything. However, Job continues to declare that he has tried to live a righteous life, and his suffering cannot be as a result of some wrong doing.

Job 28 is a continuation of Job's response to Bildad's third speech. Man, he argues, is able to search for and discover jewels and precious metals, but where can he find wisdom from? It cannot be bought, for only God can reveal true wisdom. True wisdom results in a fear of the Lord and a desire to avoid all evil.

In Job 29 Job looks back and longs for the time before his troubles began. He remembers how he felt the Lord's presence with him, and felt blessed in all that he did. He was respected and looked up to by others, and they all spoke well of him. He helped the poor, the widows and the fatherless to obtain justice, and he expected to live a long and fruitful life.

Job 30 is a continuation of Job's response to Bildad's third speech. Following his troubles, he is no longer respected by others and even the unrighteous now mock and scorn him. He blames God who he feels has taken away all his defences, afflicted him and allowed enemies to attack him. He cries out to God, but receives no answer, and, as a consequence, feels betrayed. In the past he tried to bring hope and comfort to others, but now feels that no one is doing the same for him.

In Job 31 we read the conclusion of Job's response to Bildad's third speech. Job understands that ruin and disaster come upon the unrighteous, but he has led his life in the fear of the Lord. He has not entered into idolatry or adultery. He has helped the poor and sought justice for the widows and orphans. He has not made wealth his security nor rejoiced over the misfortunes of others. In summary Job maintains that he has always tried to live a blameless life.

In Job 32 we have the speech of Elihu, a young man who is angered that Job's three friends have failed to refute Job's arguments, but simply condemned him. He declares that it is not age which gives one wisdom and understanding, but rather the spirit in a man; the breath of Almighty God.

Job 33 continues the speech by Elihu. He has heard Job say that he is completely pure and without sin, but declares that only God can say this about Himself. He rebukes Job for saying that God is not speaking to him, and declares that God speaks in lots of different ways, although we do not always perceive what He is saying. He suggests that, if an angel appeared to Job and showed him his sin, Job would be quick to repent, and tell others how God had delivered him from the pit.

In Job 34 Elihu continues his speech by rebuking Job for saying that God has acted unjustly towards him. He declares that it is unthinkable that God would do wrong or pervert justice and, by saying this, Job is behaving like a wicked man. God does not show partiality, and ultimately everyone receives what he deserves. God knows every deed and cannot be accused, even if we think He has chosen to be silent. He concludes that Job does not have insight or understand God's ways.

In Job 35 Elihu continues his speech by responding to Job's claim that he has not profited by trying to live a sinless life. He argues that we should live righteously in response to God's righteousness, and not as a means of reaping a reward. It is arrogant to complain that God is not responding when we cry out in our distress, if we haven't acknowledged Him, or thanked Him when things were going well. God is all-knowing, and Job insults God by saying that He is unaware of his suffering.

In Job 36 Elihu continues his speech by declaring that, although God is mighty and beyond our understanding, He does not despise mankind. He gives the wicked the opportunity to repent, but those who are hard-hearted, and do not respond to His discipline, will perish. In his suffering Job must be careful that he does not go away from God and turn to evil. God's mighty power and care for mankind is displayed through nature.

In Job 37 Elihu continues to declare that God's might is beyond our understanding, and is displayed through nature. He concludes by declaring that God is righteous and just. Job is wrong to accuse God of being unfair and unjust, and is wrong in demanding that God should explain or justify himself to Job.

In Job 38 God starts to speak and respond to Job. He asks Job a series of questions relating to the creation and sustaining of the universe. Through these questions God declares that His power and understanding are far beyond our own, and that He created and established the universe and the physical laws which govern the way in which it operates.

In Job 39 we have the continuation of God's response to Job. By asking Job a series of questions about the natural world and how it functions, God is humbling Job and showing him how little he really does know. If Job knows so little, what possible right does he have to challenge the wisdom and understanding of God?

In Job 40 and 41 Job is rebuked for discrediting God's justice and trying to justify himself by accusing God of wrongdoing. God tells Job that if he can't tame or subdue the behemoth (hippopotamus?) or leviathan (crocodile or mythical creature), why does he think he can successfully challenge God's authority and His response to events on earth. (Some commentators consider Leviathan represents Satan, who, unbeknown to Job, had been given the right to inflict his sufferings.)

In Job 42 we read that Job acknowledges that he has been wrong to judge and criticise God, and repents humbly before God. God rebukes Eliphaz, Bildad and Zophar because they have not spoken rightly about Him, or portrayed His heart when trying to comfort Job. The Book of Job concludes by stating that Job prayed for his three friends, and that God healed and restored Job, and blessed him with twice as much as he had before his troubles began.

Psalms

Psalm 1 tells us that we will be blessed if we walk in the way of the Lord. Delighting in God's word gives a foundation to our lives which will produce growth and fruit.

Psalm 2 is a prophetic picture of earthly events from God's perspective. Ungodly nations may rise up and oppose God and reject His ways, but ultimately God's kingdom will triumph.

In Psalm 3 David is surrounded by his enemies and calls out to God to deliver him. When we feel spiritually oppressed we too can ask God to be our shield and our deliverer.

In Psalm 4 we are encouraged to put our trust in the Lord, even when He does not seem to be answering our prayers, and not to respond in a sinful way to the circumstances we face. We can have peace in our hearts knowing that God hears our prayer.

In Psalm 5 David contrasts what happens to the righteous and the unrighteous. He declares that he wants to be righteous and enjoy the protection and blessing of God.

In Psalm 6 David pours out all his troubles to the Lord. He asks the Lord to deliver him. He consoles himself that the Lord hears his prayer, and that, one day, all his enemies will be put to shame.

In Psalm 7 David gives thanks that God is a righteous judge, who searches the mind and heart. He declares that he has done nothing that would give his enemies any rights over him, and that God will take action against his unrighteous enemies unless they repent.

In Psalm 8 the writer praises the majesty of God. He marvels that the God of all creation should care so much for mankind, to whom God gave dominion over the earth.

In Psalm 9 David rejoices and gives thanks that his enemies have at last been defeated. When we are facing trials and difficulties we can be encouraged that, if we remain righteous, the Lord will eventually bring us into a place of victory.

In Psalm 10 the psalmist questions why it is that wicked men seem to prosper and take advantage of the weak and helpless, but recognises that God ultimately hears the cry of those who call to Him, and is the defender of the oppressed and the fatherless.

In Psalm 11 we are encouraged to remember that God is on His heavenly throne when everything around us seems to be crumbling. In God's timing justice will be done.

In Psalm 12 David expresses his despair that everyone has abandoned truth and resorted to deception and lies. He recognises that

God's word is without error, and prays for protection from wicked men.

Psalm 13 is an encouragement to all who feel depressed or in despair. Despite his feeling of being abandoned by God, and being heavy in heart, David continues to put his trust in God's unfailing love. Despite the circumstances, he chooses to remember God's past blessings and worships Him.

In Psalm 14, foolishness in ignoring and denying God leads to corruption and wickedness. Those who behave like that oppress the poor, whose refuge is in God. David prays to be saved from such wickedness.

Psalm 15 is a short psalm summarising the qualities of those who can dwell with God. Honesty, righteousness, truthfulness and faithfulness are praised. Slander, usury and bribery are condemned.

In Psalm 16 David praises the Lord for the security and peace he has in this life by trusting in the Lord. He also expresses the certainty he has that he will spend eternity with God.

Psalm 17 is David's prayer to God asking for help and deliverance from his enemies. When reading Psalms, it is helpful to remember Paul's word in Ephesians 6 that our battle is not against flesh and blood, but against powers and principalities in the heavenly realm which work through others.

Psalm 18:1-24 is a prayer of thanks because the psalmist is saved from the hands of the enemy. He poetically describes how this happened because God moved in the heavenly realms in response to his prayer, and because he walked in righteousness before the Lord.

In Psalm 18:25-50 David continues his prayer of thanksgiving to God for his deliverance from his enemies. He acknowledges that the victory comes about because God shows His faithfulness to him and strengthens him.

Psalm 19 is a wonderful song of praise and worship. The psalmist declares that God's glory can be seen in the wonders of His creation. God's laws are for our benefit, and keeping them gives life and joy.

Psalm 20 is a prayer that others may know God's help when they are in distress, and that God will give them their heart's desire. It comes out of David's own experience of trusting God and seeing Him do this in his own life.

Psalm 21 praises God for giving David victory over his enemies in response to his trust in God. It talks prophetically of the Lord's appearing to completely consume His enemies with fire.

Psalm 22 expresses the feelings of isolation when God seems far away, and we feel completely surrounded and oppressed by our enemies. (Jesus on the cross quotes the first verse of this psalm.) Despite the circumstances, the psalmist praises God and declares that, ultimately, God will triumph.

Psalm 23 describes God as the good shepherd, who leads and guides His sheep. We can know His love and goodness on our journey through life, and His comfort in the most difficult of times. We can live in the sure hope of eternal life in His presence.

Psalm 24 is a psalm of ascent believed to have been sung as the Israelites took the ark of the covenant into Jerusalem. It proclaims the majesty and glory of God. It challenges us to be holy as we seek to enter into the presence of a holy God.

In Psalm 25 David asks God to teach him His ways and to guide him into truth. He acknowledges his sinfulness, and asks God to forgive him. He prays that God will rescue him, and not let his enemies put him to shame.

In Psalm 26 the psalmist asks God to redeem him and have mercy upon him, because he has tried to walk in the ways of righteousness. The psalmist proclaims aloud his praises to God, and declares he loves the house of the Lord.

Psalm 27 is a prayer of confidence and trust in the Lord. No matter who rejects us we can have confidence that the Lord receives and accepts all those who seek Him.

Psalm 28 is a prayer recognising that God is our rock, our shield, our strength and our salvation.

In Psalm 29 we are exhorted to praise and give glory to the Lord. The Lord is enthroned as King for ever. He speaks with authority and power, and what He says is accomplished.

Psalm 30 is a song of thanksgiving. The psalmist thanks God for redeeming him from the pit. God has turned his mourning into dancing and filled him with joy.

Despite all the anguish and sorrow he is experiencing in every part of his being, David, in Psalm 31, continues to choose to put his trust in God. He declares that he is in God's hands, and asks that he not be put to shame.

Psalm 32 is an encouragement to all who have repented before God of their sins and received His forgiveness. When we trust in the Lord we can experience His unfailing love surrounding us.

Psalm 33 is a psalm calling us to praise and worship God. It paints a picture of the God who created all things, who carefully observes all that we do, and who responds to those who walk in righteousness.

Psalm 34 encourages us in the many ways that God helps those who fear Him and walk in righteousness. He brings healing to those who are crushed in spirit, and can deliver us from all our troubles.

In Psalm 35 the psalmist prays to the Lord asking for help in overcoming his enemies. He declares that, when this happens, he will give all the credit and praise to God.

Psalm 36 speaks about the love, faithfulness and righteousness of God. These characteristics of God are there for all who seek to find refuge in them.

In Psalm 37:1-24 we are encouraged to trust in the Lord in all circumstances. We are not to be envious of the wicked, but to wait patiently upon the Lord, and commit all our ways to Him. The Lord blesses those who are totally committed to Him, and He gives them the desire of their hearts.

Psalm 37:25-40 encourages us to walk in righteousness and in the shelter of the Lord. Salvation and deliverance will eventually come to the righteous, and they will inherit the land. The unrighteous, even though they may appear to prosper for a time, will eventually be judged and lose everything.

In Psalm 38 the psalmist expresses how his own sin has affected every part of his being. There is no health in his body, he is tormented by guilt, there is anguish in his heart, he feels that his enemies are triumphing over him and he feels separated from God.

In Psalm 39 the psalmist expresses how he feels that he is under the judgement of God for his sin, and he feels separated from God.

Psalm 40 is a song of thanksgiving to God. The psalmist rejoices that God has heard his cry and lifted him out of the pit. He will not keep this good news to himself, but will share it with others. He has not yet been delivered from his enemies, but is trusting that God will eventually do this.

Psalm 41 is a prayer asking God for healing. The psalmist reminds God of His covenant promise to bless and give health to those who care about the needy. The psalmist acknowledges that his own sin may be contributing to his sickness, but he implies that the betrayal of a friend and the words of his enemies may also be affecting his health.

In Psalm 42 the psalmist expresses his desire for an encounter with God. He longs for the times of intimacy he used to have with the Lord in the past. It is as if his spirit is addressing his soul, which is downcast or depressed, and encouraging it to choose to trust and praise God.

Psalm 43, like Psalm 42, reminds us to praise God, even when we might not feel like it. The psalmist addresses his soul, which is depressed because of what his enemies are doing, and encourages it to choose to trust and worship God.

In Psalm 44 David recognises that it is only through God's help that Israel has been able to take the land and defeat their enemies in the past. In order that his enemies cannot gloat over him now, David calls to mind God's unfailing love, and asks Him for help in the current circumstances.

Psalm 45 is a hymn of praise to a king, presumed to be David, or one of his descendants. It extols the godly virtues of the king and poetically talks about how his bride will be blessed. It recognises that God has established His everlasting throne, and so some of the verses in this psalm can be interpreted as being messianic.

Psalm 46 invites us to put our trust in God whatever the circumstances. Written perhaps to encourage the inhabitants of Jerusalem during a siege, we can take strength and encouragement from the fact that God's kingdom will never fall, and that God will eventually be exalted in all the earth.

Psalm 47 is a call to praise and worship God as King over all the nations. God is on His throne, and He reigns and is to be exalted.

Psalm 48 is a hymn celebrating that Zion (Jerusalem) is the place where God has chosen to dwell among His creation. We can apply this psalm to God's heavenly throne or, in anticipation of Jesus' millennial reign, to the earth.

Psalm 49 is a reminder about our frailty, and that we will all face physical death one day. So we should be concerned about our eternal salvation, and take comfort in it, rather than being jealous or fearful of the ungodly, who seem to be prospering.

Psalm 50 reminds us that God is almighty and the judge of all. He does not need anything from us to sustain Him. Our worship to Him should be out of thankfulness for what He does for us. God hates hypocrisy, and those, who claim to honour God with their lips but not with their hearts, will suffer the consequences.

Psalm 51 is a confessional hymn in which the psalmist acknowledges his sins before the Lord. This psalm is thought to have been written by David after Nathan confronted him about his adultery with Bathsheba and his murder of Uriah. He realises that sin is not simply dealt with by offering a sacrifice to God. God is looking for a change of heart and David asks God to cleanse him and create a pure heart within him.

Psalm 52 is a psalm of encouragement for when we feel surrounded by those who do not fear the Lord and are being used by the enemy to oppress and discourage us. Those who prosper at the expense of others will face everlasting ruin, but the righteous, who trust in God's unfailing love, will spend eternity praising God.

Psalm 53 tells us that it is foolish to deny the existence of God. Denying accountability before God eventually leads to self-centeredness, corruption and persecution of those who do believe in God. God will eventually put such people to shame.

Psalm 54 is both a prayer for help when we feel under attack, and a prayer of thanksgiving in anticipation that God hears and answers prayers, and will deliver us from our enemies.

In Psalm 55 David pours out his heart to the Lord after being betrayed by a close friend. He feels threatened and undermined by what is happening around him, and would just like to run away and hide. He prays that God will confound the speech of those who oppose him. Despite the hurt and pain he feels from the betrayal, David chooses to put his trust in God.

Psalm 56 is a request for help in times of trouble. The psalmist chooses to put his trust in God, rather than be fearful of what man can do to him. The concept of God having a bottle for our tears, or recording our tears, presents a wonderful picture of God being able to empathise with us in our pain and suffering.

In Psalm 57 we are encouraged to worship and praise God despite the circumstances. When we feel as though we are surrounded by wild animals, or about to fall into the trap of the enemy, we can choose to find shelter and refuge in God, and praise Him for His love and faithfulness.

In Psalm 58 the psalmist laments those in leadership who do not govern with justice. He prays that they may be removed from office, and looks forward to the day when the righteous are rewarded.

Psalm 59 is a prayer asking for protection. The psalmist asks for deliverance from his enemies who seek to attack him, although he is innocent of any crime. He recognises that God is his strength, and the fortress in which he can take refuge.

Psalm 60 is a prayer for help during a time of war. The psalmist reminds God that they are His chosen people, but they feel that He has rejected them. They cannot win the battle on their own, but with God's help they can trample down the enemy.

Psalm 61 is a general cry for help written at a time when the psalmist was feeling weak. He recognises that God is his fortress and a strong tower in which he can take refuge. He asks for long life, and that God will protect him with His love and faithfulness.

In Psalm 62, we are encouraged to put our trust in God. God is our rock, our refuge and our salvation. We can pour out our hearts to Him. We are reminded that God is both strong and loving.

Psalm 63 is a song of praise which encourages us to earnestly seek God, even when we are going through difficult times. The psalmist has seen the glory of God in the past, and knows that God will help him again. In this knowledge, he is able to cling on to God and find refuge in the shadow of His wings.

In Psalm 64 David cries for help and protection from the lies of those who plot against him. His enemies encourage each other in their wickedness, and pride themselves in their futile plans. He rejoices that he can take refuge and shelter in God, and that God can deliver him, and turn the words of his enemies against themselves.

In Psalm 65 the psalmist acknowledges that it is God who formed and upholds the universe, and speaks of the future when all men will acknowledge God. We are reminded to thank God for the provision of food, and the blessings that He bestows upon us. The psalmist thanks God for forgiving his transgressions, and for His awesome deeds of righteousness.

Psalm 66 is a call to worship and praise God, and to remember all the good things He has done for us. The psalmist recognises that God has brought him through difficult trials, but that God has sustained him and used these trials to refine Him. God heard his prayer and answered it, because the psalmist (David) did not cherish sin in his heart.

Psalm 67 is a prayer asking that all nations would know God's ways and His salvation, and that all people would praise Him. This prayer will ultimately be fulfilled during the millennial reign of Jesus, when all the world will fear God and enjoy His abundant blessings.

Psalm 68:1-18 is a song of spiritual warfare. The psalmist asks God to arise and defeat His enemies. God's heart is for the orphans and widows, the lonely, and those held in captivity and slavery. In vision, the psalmist sees God leading a great victory parade of His chariots and the spoils of war, as He comes again to reign in Jerusalem.

Psalm 68:19-35 looks forward to Jesus' millennial reign from Jerusalem. God has saved us from death, and will surely defeat all His enemies. The psalmist describes the victory procession of the King into the sanctuary. Envoys from all the nations who have opposed Israel, will submit to Him, and acknowledge the power and majesty of God.

In Psalm 69:1-18 the psalmist likens himself to somebody engulfed by floodwaters, as he cries out to God to rescue him. He feels all of his enemies scorn and mock him because he puts his trust in the Lord. He even feels rejected by his own family, as he asks God in His mercy to help him.

In Psalm 69:19-36 the psalmist continues to pour out his heart to the Lord about how he feels scorned and shamed by the actions of his enemies. Despite his suffering, he determines to praise and thank God, and rejoices that God will save Zion, and that it will be inhabited by those who love God.

Psalm 70 is a short prayer asking God to come and rescue the psalmist from his troubles. It is a reminder to us that we should praise and exalt God, even when we are struggling and in need of encouragement or help.

In Psalm 71 the psalmist declares that God alone is his strong refuge. Despite all the difficulties he has faced, he chooses to put his trust in God, whom he describes as the rock and fortress where he can always go, and who will deliver him from all of his enemies. He determines to always declare the mighty works of God, and to worship and praise God for His faithfulness and His salvation, even though he has not yet fully experienced it.

Psalm 72 (the final psalm attributed to David) is a prophetic psalm looking forward to the rule of the messianic King. His everlasting reign will be one marked by justice and the defeat of all of His enemies. He will rescue and help all those who are weak, or in need, and it will be a time of great prosperity. All the kings of the earth will bow down to Him, and the whole earth will be filled with His glory.

In Psalm 73 the psalmist questions why the arrogant and wicked are often seen to prosper, and wonders if his own seeking after righteousness is in vain. He answers his own questions by recognising that those who do not know God will eventually perish. On the other hand, those who seek after God will know His presence and guidance, and will be taken into glory.

Psalm 74 would appear to have been written after the destruction of the temple in Jerusalem by the Babylonians, in about 586 BC. The psalmist is in despair about what has happened, but declares that God is still sovereign, as he remembers all that God has done in the past. He asks God to remember His covenant, and to rise up to defend His cause, and rescue those who cry out to Him.

In Psalm 75 the psalmist declares that God is sovereign. He upholds the earth and He judges with righteousness. There is a warning not to use power and authority (symbolised as a horn) in ungodly ways. God will ultimately take away the power and authority of the wicked and give it to the righteous.

Psalm 76 is a song of celebration recognising that God triumphs over His enemies. Because God does ultimately bring judgement and pour out His wrath, He should be feared by individuals and by nations.

Psalm 77 is a psalm of encouragement when things are not going well. The psalmist feels rejected by God, who does not seem to be answering his prayers. In his low condition, he chooses to encourage himself by meditating on God's word, and remembering all the miraculous and good things which God did, in leading His people out of captivity.

Psalm 78:1-31 starts with a reminder of the importance of teaching children, the next generation, all that God has said and done in the past, so that they will not become rebellious like their forefathers. The psalmist recounts the miracles that God did in bringing the Israelites out of captivity in Egypt. The Israelites, however, witnessed these miracles, but quickly started to grumble and rebel against God, and put Him to the test despite His faithfulness towards them.

In Psalm 78:32-55 the psalmist continues to recount the miracles God did in bringing the Israelites out of slavery in Egypt. In spite of all these miracles the Israelites were rebellious, and they broke God's covenant and did not keep the law. Their hearts were not loyal to Him. They only turned to God as their rock and deliverer when He disciplined them. God restrained His full anger towards them, led them like a shepherd through the wilderness, and settled them in the promised land.

Psalm 78:56-72 records that, despite having been brought out of captivity and settled in the promised land, the Israelites continued to sin against God. They rebelled against Him and were disobedient. As a consequence, even the ark of the covenant was captured by their enemies. God, however, remained faithful to them, and raised up David as their king. (David was not a descendant of Joseph, but came from the tribe of Judah.)

Psalm 79 is a lament following an invasion of Jerusalem, and a defiling of the temple. It is a prayer asking God to come and help His people, and to preserve those who have been taken prisoner. It is a prayer asking God to deal with the enemies who have defeated them, so that His name will be glorified among the nations.

Psalm 80 is a prayer asking God to restore the nation of Israel. The psalmist reminds God that He brought the Israelites out of Egypt and established them in the land of Israel. The nation has now been ravaged and is mocked by its enemies. The psalmist asks God to make His face shine upon them again, and to save and restore Israel.

Psalm 81 is a call to return to worshipping the true, living God. It is a reminder that God brought the Israelites out of captivity in Egypt and provided for them in the wilderness. The Israelites, however, did not submit to God, but, instead, went their own way, because their hearts were stubborn. If the people worship God alone, He can fully meet their every need, and quickly subdue all their enemies.

Psalm 82 is a prayer for God to act as the righteous judge of the universe and bring true justice to the weak and the oppressed. Men who have been appointed as rulers and judges (gods) on the earth, to act in God's place, have become wicked in their ways. They are reminded that their rule is only for a limited time, and that one day they will die.

Psalm 83 is a prayer to God asking Him to rise up and defeat the Gentile nations who are opposing Israel. It asks God to defeat these enemies as He did in the days of Gideon (Judges 7) and Deborah (Judges 4). It asks that God demonstrates that He is the Sovereign Lord.

Psalm 84 is a song expressing the mounting excitement and joy of a pilgrim going up to the temple at Jerusalem to worship God. The anticipated happiness and joy of meeting with God at the end of their journey enables them to discover blessings, even when passing through the valley of tears (Baca). Those who put their trust in the Lord will know His blessings.

Psalm 85 is a prayer asking God to bring restoration and revival. In it the psalmist reminds God that, in the past, He did relent from His anger and restored fruitfulness to the land. The psalmist declares that love, faithfulness, righteousness and peace are all found in God. These can be experienced again if the people fear God and are willing to listen and be obedient to Him.

Psalm 86 is a prayer written by King David asking God to help him during a time when he feels under attack from his enemies. He acknowledges that God is loving, forgiving, good, faithful, slow to anger and compassionate. David expresses his desire to know more of God's ways, and prays that he might have an undivided heart towards

God.

Psalm 87 exalts Jerusalem as the city of God and His dwelling place on earth, from which the waters of life flow. It declares that a day will come when all the nations who oppose God will acknowledge Him and recognise those who belong to Him. The reference to names being recorded in a register is a reminder that our names are recorded in the Book of Life when we receive Jesus as our Lord and Saviour.

Psalm 88 expresses the heart cry of those who are suffering, grieving or in despair. They feel weak, lonely and fearful and feel that God has turned His face away from them. All they can do is keep crying out to God in the hope that He will answer them.

Psalm 89 1-13 declares that God is the almighty God who created the heavens and the earth. Nothing can compare with Him and His power. He has established an everlasting covenant with His chosen people, which will not be broken, because God is completely faithful in all that He does.

Psalm 89:14-29 declares the faithfulness and righteousness of God, and how He blesses those who acknowledge Him. It continues with a re-affirmation of the Davidic covenant and God's promises that, from the line of David, one will come who will be the most exalted king in all the earth. Although written in praise of David, this psalm ultimately has its fulfilment in Jesus, ruling as King of kings and Lord of lords.

In Psalm 89:30-52 God declares that He will not break His covenant with David and his descendants, even if they rebel against God and He has to discipline them. In verses 38-45 the psalmist records the current situation in which their enemies are being victorious, but then goes on to remind God of His promises and asks Him to act, and reveal His love and faithfulness.

Psalm 90 is a prayer asking God to show His favour on the people, and guide them into their destiny. It acknowledges that God is eternal, and His concept of time is different to ours. The Israelites feel that they have been experiencing God's judgement and wrath because of their iniquities, and they now ask that God will have compassion on them, so that they may know His blessings and joy in their lives.

Psalm 91 describes in vivid terms the security we have when we are fully committed to God and put our trust in Him. When we do this, we come under His covering and protection, and we do not need to fear the work of the enemy. God will send His ministering angels to help us, and we have the authority and power to trample on lions and snakes (Satan).

Psalm 92 is a song of praise and worship exalting God for His goodness towards us. It declares that the righteous will flourish and enjoy the presence of God, but that the wicked will be judged and perish. This psalm is a reminder to us to be continually thanking and praising God for His love and faithfulness.

Psalm 93 is a short psalm declaring that God is eternal and powerful, and that He reigns. God is holy, and what He plans and purposes will be accomplished.

Psalm 94 is a prayer asking God to execute His judgement on the wicked, who crush the people and fail to look after the widows and orphans. It declares that God will never forget His people, and that He helps us, even in the difficult times we experience. The psalmist declares that God has become his fortress and refuge, and that, one day, God will bring judgement and punishment upon the wicked.

Psalm 95 is a call to worship God with thanksgiving and joy. He is the creator God and the almighty shepherd, and we are the flock under His care. In this psalm we are reminded to listen to God, and not harden our hearts and become rebellious. The Israelites did this in the desert after being freed from captivity in Egypt, and, as a consequence, that generation did not enter into the Promised Land.

Psalm 96 is another psalm that encourages us to praise and worship God, declaring who He is and what He has done. We should come before Him and worship Him with reverence and in holiness, acknowledging that He reigns. This psalm looks forward to the day when its words will be completely fulfilled, as Jesus comes again to rule in glory.

Psalm 97 is a song of victory and triumph declaring that God reigns. It is a psalm that sings of the present spiritual reality of God's supremacy over all things, and looks forward to a time of complete fulfilment on the earth, when Jesus comes again.

Psalm 98 is a song calling us to praise and worship God because of His works of salvation. It is a psalm which can be applied to the personal salvation God has already worked in our own individual lives. It can also be applied to those times when God has moved in response to our prayers and, ultimately, it applies when Jesus returns as judge, at the end of time.

Psalm 99 is a call to worship and praise God in His holiness. It is a reminder to us that God reigns, and that He answers prayer. It is also a reminder that, while we have the freedom to come into His presence, we should also have a godly fear and respect of the awesomeness and holiness of God.

Psalm 100 encourages us to enter into the presence of God with songs of praise and thanksgiving. It reminds us that God made us, and loves us with an everlasting love. He is faithful in all that He says and does.

Psalm 101 is a prayer of personal commitment and consecration to the Lord. The psalmist declares that he will praise and worship God, and have nothing to do with those who practise wickedness and evil. Speaking in his role as king (and prophetically about the rule of Jesus), he declares that he will cleanse the land, and not allow evildoers to dwell in his house, or enter into the city of the Lord.

Psalm 102 starts with a cry to the Lord to help the psalmist, who is experiencing distress. The psalmist looks forward to the day when God will act, and all the nations will fear Him and revere His glory. God is eternal and unchanging, and His purposes will be accomplished.

Psalm 103 is a call to worship God, who alone is worthy of our praise. The psalmist encourages himself by declaring who God is, and what He does for us. He is a God of love, compassion and mercy, who has redeemed us from the pit. He is the God who forgives our sins and heals our diseases. Our response should be to praise Him with all of our being.

Psalm 104:1-18 is a call to praise and worship God. It poetically describes how God is both the creator and the sustainer of the universe. We are not living on a planet that came into being by chance. God is the designer who created the universe, and established the laws which sustain it.

Psalm 104:19-35 is a continuation of this poetic psalm, which declares that God created and sustains the universe. Time, seasons and life cycles all ultimately emanate from God. As we discover the beauty and wonders of creation, it should lead us to want to praise and worship God.

Psalm 105:1-15 is a call to thank God, and proclaim all that He has done. The psalmist reminds us that the covenant God made with Abraham, and later confirmed with Jacob and Isaac, regarding the land of Canaan, which God was giving to them, was an everlasting covenant.

In Psalm 105:16-45 the psalmist recalls the history of the Israelites, declaring that God's hand was upon them. Joseph was sold into slavery in Egypt in order that he might prepare the way for his family when the famine came. The psalmist tells of all that God did through Moses to bring His chosen people out of Egypt and into the Promised Land, so that they might keep His commands and obey His law.

Psalm 106:1-23 is a reminder of how the Israelites quickly forgot about all that God had done for them, and rebelled against Him. He did not destroy them, because Moses stood in the breach between them and God. The psalmist acknowledges his own sinfulness, but is able to praise God, because he knows that God can save him and help him.

Psalm 106:24-48 continues to recount how the Israelites rebelled against God in the wilderness and entered into idolatry. When they entered the Promised Land they continued in their disobedience to God, and defiled themselves. As a result, God handed them over to other nations. When they cried out to God in their distress He heard them, and remembered His covenant with them.

Psalm 107:1-22 is a song of praise reminding us that God's love endures for ever, and that He can redeem us, when we turn to Him. It talks of people wandering in the desert, people chained in darkness, and those who have become foolish in their own rebellion. When they cry out to God in their distress God delivers them. Their response should be to thank God for His unfailing love and wonderful deeds.

Psalm 107:23-43 continues to praise God that He redeems those who cry out to Him in their distress. He is able to deliver us from the storms of life. In His great love God can transform us, just as He is able to provide water in a desert and turn it from a wilderness into a place of abundance and fruitfulness. In contrast, the abode of the wicked is turned into a dry and unproductive land.

Psalm 108 is a prayer to God praising His love and faithfulness and asking Him to help overcome enemies. The psalmist reminds God that they are His chosen people, and that He has promised them victory over the Moabites, Edomites and Philistines. He acknowledges that human help is useless, and that they need God's help.

In Psalm 109 the psalmist asks God to bring judgement upon those whom he has tried to befriend, but who have made false accusations against him. (In view of Jesus' teaching to love our enemies, it is perhaps helpful to view the enemy referred to in such psalms as being the spiritual demonic realm operating through these people, rather than the people themselves). The psalmist declares he is poor, wounded and needy and asks God to deliver him.

In Psalm 110 (a messianic psalm) God declares that the Messiah will sit at the right hand of God (the place of greatest honour), and that He will triumph over all of His enemies. In the end times rulers and nations will be judged

Psalm 111 proclaims the unchanging nature of God. He is gracious, compassionate and righteous. He is powerful, and all He does is glorious and majestic. He is faithful, and all His promises are trustworthy. He is holy, and He alone is worthy of eternal praise.

Psalm 112 is a psalm declaring the blessings which come to those who walk in the ways of the Lord. They will conduct their affairs justly, and will be generous to others. Both they and their children will be blessed, and they will live their lives in security and without fear.

Psalm 113 is a psalm declaring that God is the sovereign Lord who is worthy of praise at all times. He is able to help the poor and needy, and He is able to work miracles, to bring life and hope where there is only barrenness and despair.

Psalm 114 is a reminder that God performs miracles to achieve His purposes. When the Israelites came out of Egypt, God parted the Red Sea, so that they could escape from the pursuing Egyptian army. God dried up the River Jordan, so the Israelites could enter the Promised Land. In the wilderness God brought forth water from the rock. When the presence of God is with us anything is possible!

Psalm 115 is an exhortation to trust in God and give Him glory, because of His love and faithfulness. He is not like the idols which cannot see, or hear, or act. God is our help and shield, and He blesses those who fear Him. We should praise Him now and for evermore.

Psalm 116 is a prayer of thanksgiving, praising God for responding to the psalmist's cry for help. His soul was in turmoil, and he felt surrounded by death, and in chains, but God delivered him. He speaks to his own soul to be at peace, and declares that he will fulfil all the vows that he has made to the Lord.

Psalm 117 is an exhortation for everyone, everywhere, to praise the Lord. The Lord's faithfulness endures forever, and He loves us.

Psalm 118 is a victory song proclaiming how God delivered the psalmist from his enemies, when he put his trust in God. The psalmist declares that God has become his strength and his salvation, and that God's love endures forever. The Lord is with him, so he need not be afraid. The psalmist proclaims that he will live and not die, and that he will praise and thank the Lord.

Psalm 119 is an acrostic psalm exalting the word of God. Verses 1-8 proclaim that those who walk in obedience to God's word are blessed. The psalmist experiences conviction, shame and guilt, as he reads God's commandments, and becomes aware that he has not been obedient in following them.

Psalm 119:9-16 proclaims that, in order to lead a pure life, we need to live in accordance with God's word. The psalmist declares that he has hidden God's word in his heart, and that he speaks out God's laws and meditates upon them. He delights in God's laws, and finds joy in following them.

In Psalm 119:17-24, the psalmist asks God to open his spiritual eyes, so he can see all the wonderful truths to be found in God's word. God's word guides and counsels him. Even though others slander him, or treat him with contempt, he is determined to continue living his life in obedience to God's laws.

In Psalm 119:25-32, the psalmist declares that he has chosen to follow God's law, and asks God to continue to teach him and help him understand the word. Because he is trying to walk in obedience, he is confidently able to remind God of His promises to strengthen and preserve the life of those who follow His ways.

In Psalm 119:33-40, the psalmist continues to ask God to teach him His laws, give him understanding, and direct his path. He declares that he wants his heart to be focussed on God's ways, and not on worthless and self-centred things.

In Psalm 119:41-48, the psalmist declares that he loves God's word, and that he puts his hope and trust in it. He declares that he will always seek to obey God's laws, because they give him freedom, and asks that he may know God's unfailing love and salvation.

In Psalm 119:49-56, the psalmist declares that he finds comfort from reading God's word. Obeying God's laws and precepts are central in all that he does. He feels indignant towards the wicked, who have turned away from God's laws, and mock those who seek to follow them.

In Psalm 119:57-64, the psalmist proclaims that he always tries to follow God's laws, and asks that God be gracious towards, as promised in His word. No matter what others may do to him, the psalmist declares that he will continue to keep the law, and be a friend to all who do likewise.

In Psalm 119:65-72, the psalmist acknowledges that he was afflicted when he went astray and disobeyed God's law. He has learnt from his mistakes, and now chooses to follow God's laws, even though his enemies slander him. He considers God's law to be the most precious thing he has.

In Psalm 119:73-80, the psalmist declares that God has formed him, and given him the ability to understand and put his trust in God's word. He prays that he may know more of God's unfailing love, and that he may be found blameless and without shame, as he meditates upon, and follows, God's commands. He prays that he may be a source of encouragement and hope for others who fear God.

In Psalm 119:81-88, the psalmist declares that he has put his hope and trust in God's word, even though he feels surrounded, and in danger of being overthrown by his enemies. He prays that God will comfort him and preserve him, in accordance with the promises of His word.

In Psalm 119:89-96, the psalmist proclaims that God's word and His faithfulness are eternal. He declares that knowing God's laws, and following them, has preserved his life. Even though others are seeking to destroy him, he will continue to follow God's ways.

In Psalm 119:97-104, the psalmist declares that reading God's word gives him insight and understanding. It makes him wiser than his enemies, and keeps him from doing evil. He loves to meditate on God's word, which he likens to sweet honey.

In Psalm 119:105-112 the psalmist declares that the word of God is like a lamp which guides his path through life. He has set his heart on obeying God's law, which he sees as being part of his heritage. He determines to keep God's laws, no matter what his enemies try to do to him.

In Psalm 119:113-120, the psalmist proclaims that God is his refuge and his shield, and that he has put his hope and trust in God's word. He loves God's word, which instils in him a righteous, godly fear. He prays that God will sustain him and deliver him according to His word.

In Psalm 119:121-128, the psalmist prays that God will protect him, and not allow his enemies to triumph over him. He is able to confidently pray this way, because he has kept God's laws, which he knows are right, and which he highly values.

In Psalm 119:129-136, the psalmist declares that God's word is wonderful, and that it gives light and understanding to everyone. He prays God will direct his path and redeem him from his enemies. The psalmist asks God to teach him His law, and mourns that God's laws are being disobeyed.

In Psalm 119:137-144, the psalmist declares that God's laws are righteous and fully trustworthy. God's faithfulness to His promises has stood the test of time. He delights in God's word, and prays that he can have greater understanding of it.

In Psalm 119:145-152, the psalmist cries out to God to save him from his enemies, who devise wicked plans and are disobedient to God's laws. He declares that he meditates on God's word, and tries to keep God's statutes and commands, which he knows are everlasting.

In Psalm 119:153-160, the psalmist declares that God's word is truth, and that His laws are righteous and eternal. Salvation is a long way off for the faithless and wicked, who do not obey God's word. The psalmist prays that God will defend him and redeem him out of the hands of his enemy, in accordance with His (God's) promises.

In Psalm 119:161-168, the psalmist proclaims that he rejoices in God's Word, which gives peace to those who love it. He hates falsehood but loves God's Word, and declares that he will obey all God's statutes and commands, as he waits for his salvation.

In Psalm 119:169-176, the psalmist prays that God will hear and answer his prayers, because he has chosen to follow God's law. He proclaims that he will always praise God for giving him righteous laws and promises, in which he delights.

Psalm 120 is a song of lament. The writer, living outside of Israel, declares that he wants peace, but is surrounded by those who seek war. He prays that God will hear his cry of distress, and rescue him from the deceit and lies of those around him, who will eventually come under God's judgement and be punished.

Psalm 121 is a song of ascent, often sung as pilgrims made their way to worship at the temple in Jerusalem. The psalmist declares that God is the creator and sustainer of all things. God watches over him, and protects him, and will help him in his time of need.

Psalm 122 is another psalm of ascent, sung as the people went to the temple to worship. In this psalm the psalmist declares that they are approaching the throne of God on earth, and he prays for the peace of the city of Jerusalem.

Psalm 123 is a prayer to God on behalf of the Israelites asking for His help and mercy because of the contempt and ridicule they have experienced from the arrogant and proud, who oppose them. In this psalm the psalmist likens Israel to a slave looking to his master, or a maidservant looking to her mistress for protection and help.

Psalm 124 is a prayer of thanksgiving in which the psalmist declares that it was God who delivered them from the hands of their enemies. If God had not been on their side they would have been destroyed.

Psalm 125 is a song encouraging us to trust in the Lord. As we trust in God we are like a mountain which cannot be shaken. The wicked will not rule over the land allotted to the righteous, but will be banished.

Psalm 126 is a song of joy and thankfulness to God for bringing the exiles back to the land of Israel. It is an encouragement to us to sow, even in the difficult times, because eventually there will be a time of harvest and joy.

Psalm 127 declares that human effort is in vain, unless God is involved in what we are doing. Parents should consider their children as a gift and a blessing from the Lord.

Psalm 128 declares that the blessings of a long life and contentment should be the expected norm when we live in fear of the Lord and walk in his ways.

In Psalm 129, the psalmist declares that God has been his protector, and set him free from the oppression of his enemies. He prays that Israel's enemies will wither, and not triumph over Israel.

In Psalm 130, the psalmist cries out to the Lord in the midst of his troubles, declaring that the Lord forgives the repentant sinner and does not hold his sins against him. He prays that the Israelites will put their trust in the Lord, who will redeem them from all their sins.

In Psalm 131, the psalmist declares that he has humbled himself before the Lord, and, as a result, he has peace in his soul. We are encouraged to put our trust in the Lord.

In Psalm 132, the psalmist recalls David's desire to build a temple and resting place for the ark of the covenant. As the people prepare to go to worship God in His temple, he prays that they may find joy, and that the priests serving God in His temple will be righteous. The psalmist also reminds God of His promise to establish an everlasting dynasty for one of David's descendants.

In Psalm 133, the psalmist proclaims the importance of living in harmony with others. It is like the precious sacred anointing oil used for consecrating priests to fulfil God's purposes, and the morning dew which waters the earth and sustains life. He declares that, when there is unity, God is able to pour out His blessings.

Psalm 134 is a call to God's people to praise and worship God, and asks God to pour out His blessings upon them.

Psalm 135 is a psalm encouraging God's people to praise and worship God. The psalmist reminds the people that God is powerful and good, and that He chose the Israelites, delivered them out of Egypt and established them in the land of Israel. The gods of other nations are nothing compared to the living God, who will endure for ever.

Psalm 136 is a call to be thankful to God in view of all that He has done for His people. The psalm reminds us that God is our creator, protector, deliverer and sustainer, and that His love endures for ever.

Psalm 137 is a lament reminding the Israelites of the grief and sadness they experienced during the time when they were in exile in Babylon. The fact that the Israelites' enemies rejoiced when Jerusalem was destroyed is painfully remembered.

In Psalm 138, the psalmist proclaims that he will praise and worship God, because of His love and faithfulness. He declares that the Lord has answered his prayers, preserved his life, and will enable him to fulfil his destiny.

In Psalm 139:1-12, the psalmist declares that God knows every detail about his life, and that He protects and guides him. He sees all that we do, and He knows our thoughts, even before we speak them out. God is omnipresent, and we can know His presence even in the darkest times of our life. His light is able to overcome the darkness.

In Psalm 139:13-14, the psalmist declares the truth that God created us, and that we are fearfully and wonderfully made. Before He created the earth, God knew that, one day, we would be born. God was involved in knitting our body, soul and spirit together in our mother's womb. The psalmist concludes by declaring that he hates anything opposed to God, and asks God to test his heart, and reveal any sin or anxiety in him.

In Psalm 140, the psalmist asks God to rescue him and protect him from his enemies. (We can pray in a similar way about our spiritual enemy the devil.) He prays that the plans of his enemy will fail, and that they will be put to shame. The psalmist concludes by declaring that God will ultimately secure justice for the poor and needy, and that the righteous will praise God, and live in His presence.

In Psalm 141, the psalmist prays that he may be acceptable to God in all that he says, and that his heart be kept from doing evil. He asks that righteous men may correct him if necessary. He prays that his enemies may be defeated, and declares that he is going to keep his eyes on the Lord and take refuge in Him.

Psalm 142 is a prayer asking for God's help in a time of trouble. The psalmist tells God that he feels overwhelmed by the threats of his enemies, and that no one cares for his life. He declares that God is his refuge, and prays that God will set him free from the prison which he feels he is in.

Psalm 143 is a prayer asking that God will demonstrate His faithfulness and righteousness by rescuing the psalmist from his enemies. He feels crushed in his spirit, but determines to hold on to the Lord, and remember all the good things God has done for him in the past. He declares that he is God's servant, and asks that God will silence his enemies.

In Psalm 144, the psalmist praises and thanks God that He is his fortress and deliverer. He asks God to intervene, and help him overcome his foreign enemies, so that the Israelites can prosper, live in peace, and know that they are blessed by the Lord.

Psalm 145 is a worship song, exalting God for who He is and what He has done. God is faithful, gracious, compassionate and slow to anger. He is righteous in all His ways, and is loving towards all He has made. He is near to all who call on Him, and He watches over them. His kingdom is an everlasting kingdom.

Psalm 146 encourages us to rise up in our soul, to choose to praise and worship the Lord, and to put our trust in Him. If we put our trust in man, we will eventually be disappointed. God upholds and sustains the righteous, but frustrates the ways of the wicked.

In Psalm 147, we are encouraged to praise and thank God for all that He does. God is declared to be active in creating and sustaining the world in which we live. The psalmist calls on God's chosen people to praise the Lord, because He has revealed His truth to them.

Psalm 148 is a call to praise and worship God. The psalmist declares that the angels in heaven, all of the physical universe, all the different life forms, and all of mankind should praise the Lord, because He alone is exalted in splendour over all things.

Psalm 149 is a song of praise and victory. The psalmist calls upon the people of Israel to praise and worship God with music and dancing. They are to rejoice and celebrate, because God has equipped them, and enabled them to overcome all their enemies.

Psalm 150 is a call to praise and worship God. We should praise Him not only in the temple, but everywhere in the universe He has created. In this final psalm in the Book of Psalms the psalmist encourages us to praise God with music and dance, and declares that everything which has breath should praise the Lord.

Proverbs

The Book of Proverbs was written to help us to lead a life pleasing to God.

In Proverbs 1:1-19, we read how godly fear of the Lord leads us to wanting to know His plans and purposes for our life. The ungodly ways of the world to achieve wealth appear attractive, but do not be enticed by them. The cost of sinfully gaining wealth at the expense of others will be loss of your own life.

God and His ways are often referred to as 'wisdom' in the Book of Proverbs. In Proverbs 1:20-33, we read that, if we seek God, He will guide us. If we reject Him, calamity will eventually befall us. Living in obedience to God and within the safe boundaries He sets for us, enables us to live in peace and without fear. Those who deliberately reject God's ways will suffer the consequences, and cannot live in the presumption that God will rescue them.

Proverbs 2:1-15 tells us that, if we earnestly seek after God, we will understand Him, and have a rightful fear of Him. We will realise that He is our shield, and ultimately gives victory to the righteous. Seeking after God and His truth instils understanding and wisdom in our hearts. This wisdom will protect and guide us, and stop us following the ways of the wicked.

Proverbs 2:16-22 tells us that godly wisdom will persuade us not to be seduced by the desires of the carnal nature by entering into illicit relationships. But, those who do will find it is a pathway leading to death. In the Bible, ownership of land is very important and is seen as the blessing and provision of God. Those who are righteous will keep the land but those who are unrighteous will be cut off from the land.

Proverbs 3:1-12 reminds us not to forget God's ways and commandments, and instructs us to treat others with love and faithfulness (mercy). We are encouraged to trust in God, and not lean on our own understanding. As a result, we will enjoy good health. The implication is that not trusting in God, and being disobedient, leads to sickness and death. We are encouraged to honour God by giving back to Him the first fruits of that which He gives to us. A consequence (but not the reason we do it) is blessing in our lives. Also, like a good father, God delights in disciplining (training) His children.

Discovering God's wisdom is the best investment anyone can ever make according to Proverbs 3:13-35. Following God's ways brings life, peace and blessings. We are encouraged to exercise sound judgement and discernment. Doing this will take away anxiety and fear, and give us peace. We are instructed to be helpful and charitable towards others, and not to wrongly accuse them or plot against them. Those who walk in righteousness and humility will experience God's blessings. Those who persist in wickedness and perversity will be shamed, and receive cursing into their life.

Solomon, generally credited with writing most of the Book of Proverbs, tells us, in Proverbs 4:1-9, how his father, David, taught him from childhood to seek godly understanding and wisdom, no matter what the cost may be. Such wisdom will protect, and enable one to attain eternal glory.

In Proverbs 4:10-27 we read that walking in God's ways is like walking in the light. If we do this, our feet will not stumble, and we will enjoy long life. Following God's ways brings life and health to our body. We are to guard our heart and not be tempted to walk in the way of sinners.

We are reminded in Proverbs 5:1-6 that temptation and sin generally appear attractive and desirable, but they are deceptive and lead to separation from God and death.

Proverbs 5:7-23 encourages us to keep to the path of righteousness. Those who do not do this will look back on their lives with regret. Not following God's ways is like entering into an adulterous relationship. It is abandoning our first love, and results in us being ensnared by the cords of sin.

Proverbs 6:1-11 tells us to disentangle ourselves from the things we have done which have become a bondage to us, and are stopping us living in freedom, or have put our destiny in the hands of others. We are encouraged to be active and not passive, and to act with purpose and have plans for the future. Passivity and laziness lead to poverty.

Proverbs 6:12-15 is a warning to all who practice deception, or act in under-handed ways. They spread strife and dissension, because their hearts are evil. Disaster will suddenly overtake them, and they will lose the opportunity to repent.

Proverbs 6:16-19 lists things that the Lord hates. They include: murder, lying, bearing false witness, pride and an evil heart which plans wickedness.

In Proverbs 6:20-35, we are encouraged to walk in the way of righteousness. Not following God's ways is like pouring burning coals into our laps. There will be consequences, and we will get burnt. Someone breaking the law, out of necessity or desperation, is still liable to the penalty of the law. So how much more do those who wilfully break the law for self-gratification deserve to be punished?

Proverbs 7:1-27 encourages us to walk in the godly wisdom and understanding which will bring life. Submitting to temptation (illustrated here by a young man being seduced by an adulteress) leads to death.

In Proverbs 8:1-11, godly ways or righteousness are personified as wisdom. The words of wisdom are just and true, and they give understanding to the foolish. They are of more value to us than gold or precious jewels.

Proverbs 8:12-36 tells us that godly wisdom includes fear of the Lord and a hatred of all that is evil. Such wisdom enables kings and those in places of authority to rule with justice, and it leads to enduring wealth and prosperity. Righteousness, personified as wisdom, is a characteristic of God which has always existed. Seeking after, and following godly wisdom in all that one does, leads to life and blessings from God.

In Proverbs 9:1-12, godly wisdom is portrayed as a delightful meal or banquet, which everyone is invited to partake of. A wise or righteous man will listen to good advice or correction, and will grow in understanding. Those who are evil, or mock the things of God, will scorn or hate godly rebuke or correction. The fear of the Lord is the beginning of wisdom, and brings the reward of long life. Mockers, however, will reap punishment upon themselves.

In Proverbs 9:13-18, we read that following the ways of foolishness rather than godly wisdom is tempting, and may give instant pleasure, but, ultimately, it leads to death.

Proverbs 10:1-10 tells us that being hard working, diligent and righteous results in blessings and prosperity. Laziness and foolishness, on the other hand, is likened to wickedness, and results in poverty. We will be blessed if we walk in righteousness, with integrity, and are willing to submit to godly authority. If we cheat, lie and use violence we will eventually come to ruin as our sins are exposed.

In Proverbs 10:11-22, we read that godly wisdom brings discernment, and helps us speak words of life and encouragement to others. The words of the wicked incite violence and hatred and lead to ruin. The righteous will heed godly discipline, which leads to life and blessing. The wicked, who ignore godly correction and lead others astray, will eventually be punished. The righteous are wise in what they say to others to encourage them. Foolish and thoughtless words can be sinful and are of little value.

The message of Proverbs 10:23-32 is that the righteous delight in the knowledge of godly understanding. They are able to withstand the storms of life, and their righteous desires are met. The lazy and the wicked are an irritant to others. What they fear will overtake them in the storms of life. The fear of the Lord leads to righteousness, joy, security, discernment and long life. The wicked speak lies, and their false hopes come to nothing.

In Proverbs 11:1-10, we read that, as Christians, our behaviour should be based on integrity, honesty and humility. This leads to life, and the path we should follow and the decisions we should make will be clear. The wicked operate out of pride and in deceiving ways, which eventually will lead to their downfall.

Proverbs 11:11-18 says that there is rejoicing when the righteous are delivered and rescued from their troubles. Likewise, there is rejoicing when the wicked, who try to destroy others, are trapped by their evil ways and perish. A wise man is careful about what he speaks out, and he listens to guidance. We must not betray confidences and become a gossip. If we are kind-hearted we will be respected by others, and we will be blessed. The wicked become wealthy through deceit, but, ultimately, they only bring trouble upon themselves.

Proverbs 11:19-31 tells us that God delights in the righteous, and they will be free, and have life. The wicked will not go unpunished. The beauty or value of something is nullified by ungodliness. Those who are generous-hearted will prosper and be blessed. Those who are selfish, and do not help others, will be resented and cursed by others, and it will eventually lead to poverty. The righteous who seek what is good will flourish like a healthy plant and enjoy life. Those who do evil bring trouble upon their family, and those who trust in their wealth, will reap the consequences.

Proverbs 12:1-4 advises that only fools despise discipline (training) and correction. The righteous will know the favour of the Lord, and will not easily be uprooted. A virtuous wife brings honour to her husband, but when a wife brings shame to a husband it is as if he has a wasting disease. The righteous make good and just plans. They are able to justify their actions, and others can recognise their wisdom. The wicked are deceitful, and seek to take advantage of others. They are despised by others, and eventually will be overthrown. A righteous person will not exalt himself, and he will be hard working. He will treat others with kindness, and will be rewarded for speaking with honesty and integrity. Those living in unreality and pride, and seeking to gain riches at the expense of others through deceitful means, are building a trap for themselves.

We read, in Proverbs 12:15-28, that it is prudent and wise to seek the advice of others, and not act hastily. Reckless words and lies spoken out to others can be very damaging, and go deep into their spirit. We can bring healing to others through words of truth, kindness and encouragement. The Lord delights in people who are truthful, promote peace, and who are careful about what they speak out to others. God despises the foolishness and lies which come from those who have deceitful hearts, and make trouble for themselves. Those who are diligent will prosper, and not become indebted to others. Righteousness will be rewarded with eternal life. The lazy will not prosper, and will become dependent upon others.

We read, in Proverbs 13:1-12, that a wise person will heed godly advice, and be careful about what he or she speaks out. Those who are diligent will achieve their goals. The lazy person may have many goals, but does not achieve any of them. We should act with integrity, and avoid anything that is false. We should not judge people by outward appearance, as things are not always as they seem. The rich may have to use their wealth to deal with threats, which a poor man does not ever experience. The righteous have inner joy and visible success. They prosper, as they accumulate wealth through honest means. The unrighteous experience inner death. Their pride damages relationships, and wealth obtained by dishonest means is frittered away.

We are reminded, in Proverbs 13:13-25, that we should respect those in authority, and listen to wise advice. Doing this will bring life, and help us to be good ambassadors. It is foolish to disregard advice and act in ignorance, as ultimately it will lead to trouble, and there will be a price to pay. We will be successful in life if we seek the counsel of godly people, and let something of their character rub off on us. We will encounter misfortunes if we ignore godly discipline, mix with fools and do not turn away from anything evil. The righteous will leave a godly inheritance for their descendants. It is a mistake not to discipline (train) children in a godly way. The poor often suffer needlessly because of injustice. The righteous will eat to their heart's content, but the wicked, ultimately, will go hungry.

We read, in Proverbs 14:1-10, that, through wise management, a woman can increase her property and standard of living, but a foolish person can quickly destroy the fruit of many years of work. To obtain a good harvest, achieved by utilising the strength of an ox, you also have to deal with the more unpleasant task of cleaning out the stables. We are encouraged to live in truthfulness, discernment and wisdom. We should examine ourselves, confess our faults and weaknesses, and know we are accepted by God. Those who mock others are fools. They often lie, have no discernment, and live a life marked with self-deception.

Proverbs 14:11-18 tells us that righteousness will ultimately be rewarded, but the faithless will reap destruction. We can be self-deceived, and our own good ideas can lead us away from God. Laughter sometimes masks the pain and grief on the inside. Fear of displeasing God should control all of our actions and help us to make wise and prudent decisions. A foolish and hot tempered person will make reckless decisions, which will lead to their downfall.

We read, in Proverbs 14:19-27, that, ultimately, good will triumph over evil. We will be blessed if we are kind and compassionate to the needy. Those who plot evil are deceived and led astray, but, if we seek to do good, we will discover mercy and truth. Words without action are often meaningless. We should speak truthfully about others and not slander them. Godly fear of the Lord is an important foundation principle upon which to build our lives.

Proverbs 14:28-35 says that, if a king or leader loses the respect of those he leads, he will be unsuccessful. Our bodies can reflect what is happening in our hearts. A sinful heart can be the cause of physical sickness. We honour God by showing compassion and kindness to the needy. The righteous have peace and security, even in the midst of turmoil. Godly wisdom resides in the hearts of the righteous, and will show up the folly of the unrighteous. Nations which act with righteousness will be blessed.

Proverbs 15:1-15 reminds us that the words we speak are important. They can impart life and encourage others, or they can crush others in their spirit. A lack of gentleness in the way we speak can arouse anger in others. The righteous are open to correction. Their actions, prayers and sacrifices are pleasing to God, and they can enjoy their worldly wealth. It is foolish to spurn discipline. God detests the outward appearance of righteousness when the intent of the heart is wickedness. Failure to respond to God's correction and discipline ultimately leads to spiritual death and eternal separation from God. Knowledge of God leads to contentment and a positive attitude to life, which is reflected in a cheerful face.

Proverbs 15:16-23 tells us that a simple life based on love and fear of the Lord is far better than a life of luxury, surrounded by turmoil and hatred. The journey of life with God can be likened to travelling on a highway, but life without God can be likened to passing through a hedge of thorns. We will benefit by honouring and respecting godly parental instruction. Our plans will bring greater success when we are open to the advice of others. We feel joyful in our hearts when we know that our words have helped or encouraged someone.

In Proverbs 15:24-33, we read the path of righteousness leads to eternal life. We stay on this path by maintaining a pure heart and acting with honesty and integrity. When we do this, God is able to bless and protect us. In contrast, a life based on pride, greed and wicked thoughts leads to death. The Lord is close to those who fear Him, are open to correction, and who act with humility. He hears their prayers and will honour them. In contrast, the words of the wicked are evil. They despise themselves, and will reap the consequences of refusing to come under God's discipline.

Proverbs 16:1-8 states that it is the attitude of our heart which matters most to God. We may have lots of good plans and ideas, but to be successful we need to commit all that we do to God, and seek His guidance. Ultimately, God is in control and His purposes will be worked out. In His mercy and faithfulness, He has provided atonement for sin. The wicked will eventually be punished. We should be satisfied with a little, rather than gain wealth through unfair and unjust practices.

In Proverbs 16:9-19, we read that kings (those in leadership and authority) should rule with justice and honesty, in the same way that God deals with each of us. We, likewise, should respect those in authority, and not act deceitfully towards them. We need to be wise in our dealings with those who have power or authority over us. Godly values are superior to those encountered in the world. Pursuit of wisdom and understanding is of more value than the pursuit of worldly possessions. Humility of spirit is better than pride and arrogance, which lead to over-confidence and failure.

Proverbs 16:20-33 says that the words we speak out are important, and should be carefully weighed. Words spoken from a wise and discerning heart can be a source of encouragement and healing to others. We can easily fall into self-deception and justify our selfish and ungodly behaviour. Satisfying our basic needs in life is an incentive for working honestly, and earning an income. Gossip ruins our relationships with others, and our ungodly words can be like a fire, which burns and affects everything it comes into contact with. The wicked will tell lies, and mislead others, in order to achieve their own purposes. The righteous, however, are more likely to live a long life than the unrighteous. The ability to exercise self-control is more important than our actions and deeds.

We are told, in Proverbs 17:1-9, that it is better to live in poverty and peace than to have wealth, if it is accompanied with disunity and strained relationships. It is the purity of our heart which is important to God. We should ignore malicious gossip and not spread it. We honour God by showing compassion towards those less fortunate than ourselves. One's family should be a source of joy and godly pride. The words of a leader or ruler should be truthful and trustworthy. Some people, (wrongly), consider that bribery is the key to achieving their goals. Repeatedly offending someone will ruin even the best of relationships.

In Proverbs 17:10-17, we read that a meaningful rebuke of a wise man is far more effective than a hundred blows given to a fool. Dealing with a fool intent on following his plans can be more difficult than facing an angry, self-protecting animal. An evil person intent on rebellion will not find mercy. If we repay someone's good with evil, we will bring a curse upon ourselves. We should be careful about starting a quarrel with someone. Often they have many stored up issues, which they will bring into the argument. We should seek justice for all; condemning the innocent is as bad as acquitting the guilty. A fool will waste his money on things of no lasting value. Sometimes we can get on better with our friends than our close relatives.

Proverbs 17:18-28 advises that it is unwise to guarantee payment of someone else's debt. Foolish behaviour can bring grief and shame to our family. We make trouble for ourselves if our hearts are corrupt, and we tell lies. It is sinful when, out of pride and arrogance, we insist we are right and quarrel with others. Laughter is good medicine, but crushing of our human spirit can manifest itself as physical sickness. We should think before we speak, and consider the effect our words may have on others. We should always act with fairness, and never accuse the innocent of wrong doing, or condemn someone who has acted with integrity.

We read, in Proverbs 18:1-9, that it is unwise and self-seeking to be independent, and isolate ourselves from others. We need to empathise and understand what others are experiencing, so that our words to them bring life. The wicked have contempt for others, and dishonour them with their self-opinionated words. Allowing wickedness to flourish and not seeking justice for the innocent are both wrong. The words we speak are important, and can become our undoing. It is very tempting to listen to gossip about someone, which then goes deep into our heart, and affects our relationship with them. Being half-hearted or idle in our work will eventually lead to ruin.

Proverbs 18:10-24 exhorts us to find our security in God rather than falsely put our trust in our worldly possessions. The proud, ultimately, will fall, but the humble in heart will be exalted. Our human spirit imparts life to our bodies, but, when our spirit is crushed, we can easily succumb to physical sickness. A wise person will seek understanding and listen to all sides of the argument before making a decision. People are more likely to listen and be open to what we say, if we are generous and kind towards them. In our relationships with others we need to be careful about taking offence, and allowing unresolved differences to become barriers, which prevent reconciliation taking place. Words are powerful, and can bring life or death. Consequently, we need to be very careful about the words we speak out to others. We also need to be careful about who we listen to, and the advice they may give us. We may have many acquaintances, but a true friend will stick with us no matter what happens.

Proverbs 19:1-9 tells us that many people want to be the friend of a rich man, but they quickly desert him, if he becomes poor. We need to seek godly wisdom before we act, rather than act with zealous haste, and then blame God for the consequences of our foolishness. Ultimately, all those who give false testimony, or lie, will be judged and punished. It is a sad reality of life that many people want to be friends with the rich, but those who are poor and in need of help are often deserted by their family and friends.

We read, in Proverbs 19:10-17, that we know that certain situations are not at all right, such as a fool living in luxury, or a slave controlling his masters. We need to exercise patience, and be willing to overlook offences against us. It is a blessing and a source of security when we find favour with those in authority over us. A godly wife, who runs her home well, is a gift from God. The Bible encourages us to be hard working, and not become lazy, which will eventually lead to poverty. God will bless those who give to the poor. Obedience to God's instructions leads to life, but disobedience leads to death.

Proverbs 19:18-25 encourages us to train up our children in the ways of the Lord, and not leave them to their own devices. People have to learn from their own mistakes. If we always cover their mistakes they may never learn. We need to be teachable, in order that we grow in wisdom and understanding. We can have many ideas and plans, but the important thing is to know and follow God's plans. We have a God-given desire to be loved and accepted. A rightful fear of God creates a solid foundation for our lives. The lazy or idle person will not even help themselves. Rebuking a scoffer may have little effect, but a wise person, when disciplined, will learn from his or her mistakes.

Proverbs 19:26-29 tells us that, if we treat our parents wrongly, and do not honour them, we bring shame and disgrace upon ourselves.

If we are unteachable, we become like fools and scoffers, who feed on evil, and eventually have to face the penalties prescribed for breaking the law.

Proverbs 20:1-8 tells us that misuse of alcohol results in our self-control being weakened, and makes us more vulnerable to sinful temptations. Being lazy and failing to plan for the future will result in poverty. If we arouse the anger of those with authority over us, we will reap the consequences. It is wise to avoid engaging in foolish quarrels and arguments. Righteousness in one generation brings blessings into the next generation. The real attitude and plans of someone's heart often need to be carefully drawn out. When we have to give an account for our behaviour our wrong motives and attitudes will be exposed. We can claim we have unfailing love in our hearts, but the true test is whether we are faithful.

When tempted to judge others, Proverbs 20:9-17 reminds us that none of us is perfect. We need to treat people equally and fairly, and not show favouritism. Our actions generally display what is in our heart, but God, who created our eyes and our ears, is the one who truly knows the real attitude of our heart. Laziness eventually leads to poverty. We need to act with honesty and integrity in our business dealings with others. Do not trust someone who gets involved in foolish debts. Making excess profit at the expense of others may appear attractive, but is no different from fraud, which will eventually reap its own reward.

Proverbs 20:18-25 encourages us to seek godly advice from those whom we can trust, and who will not betray our confidence, before making major decisions. To enjoy a long life, honour your parents and respect their godly authority. Becoming independent of them, and ignoring their godly wisdom too early in life, may cause you problems. Allow the Lord to be your defender, and do not plot revenge and judgement towards those who have sinned against you. We hardly understand our own hearts, so consequently our judgement of others will be biased, and like using dishonest scales. Do not hastily makes vows or promises which you will later regret, or be unable to keep.

Proverbs 20:26-30 tells us that, to enjoy a long reign, a wise king will expose and sift out evil from his kingdom, and show love and mercy towards his subjects. God sees the attitudes and motives of our heart. Sinful behaviour and attitudes can change in response to discipline, and the desire to avoid punishment.

We read, in Proverbs 21:1-7, that the Lord is more interested in our heart attitudes and motives, and whether we are doing what is right and just, than in our religious activities. When the heart of an individual (even a king) is open to God, He will lead and direct his or her path to fulfil His purposes. It is sinful to be boastful and arrogant, and to look down on others. Those who resort to violence will be punished. To be successful in what we do, we should plan diligently, and not act in haste. A fortune made by lying will eventually be lost.

Proverbs 21:8-15 tells us that living in isolation can be better than living in an environment where there is constant quarrelling and argument. The wicked crave evil and show no mercy to others. We ourselves can learn when we see others being disciplined for their wrongdoing. A wise person will listen to others, and grow in knowledge. God sees the wicked deeds of men, and will bring them to account. If we do not show mercy to others, God will not show mercy towards us. A secret gift or bribe may bring temporary relief, but, when true justice prevails, the righteous are blessed, and the wicked are punished.

We read, in Proverbs 21:16-23, that, if we focus on enjoying worldly pleasures, we will miss God's plan for our life, and follow a path which leads to death. The wealth of the wicked will eventually be inherited by the righteous. A wise person will make provision for the future, but a foolish person will squander all that he has. It can be more desirable to live in a desert than to live with someone who is argumentative and quarrelsome. If we seek righteousness and justice, we will be honoured by God and receive His mercy and life. To overcome an enemy one needs to destroy the strongholds in which he trusts. By being careful in what we speak, we can avoid creating problems for ourselves.

Proverbs 21:24-31 concludes by saying that the proud and arrogant will look down on others and mock them. The righteous will give generously to others, but those who are selfish and lazy just crave things for themselves. God hates religious hypocrisy, and even more so if there is an evil intention or motive behind it. Those who give false witness will eventually perish, along with all those who listen to them and support them. We can make many plans and preparations but, ultimately, human wisdom and human plans cannot prevail to overcome the plans and purposes of God.

In Proverbs 22:1-8 we find the advice that humility and fear of the Lord are more important than worldly riches. We should not think more highly of ourselves if we have wealth, because, before God, who made us, we are all equal. The wise person will be alert to danger, and take appropriate precautions. We come under the control of those to whom we owe money. If we fail to resist temptation, we become like the wicked, and will reap the consequences. It is important that children are taught good moral principles, so they become responsible adults.

We read, in Proverbs 22:9-21, that those who mock and insult others are a source of division and disharmony. We ourselves feel blessed when we are generous to others. If we have a pure heart and speak with kindness, people will want to befriend us. God preserves the truth of His word, which will ultimately prevail over everything. Those who are lazy sometimes use ridiculous excuses to justify their actions. Foolishness reigns when there is an absence of training and discipline. Oppressing the poor, or only seeking to win the favour of the rich, ultimately leads to eternal poverty. We need to know God's wisdom and truth, and apply it in our own lives. Doing this will help us to trust in God. When we know and understand His word in our hearts, God is able to help us speak it aloud at the appropriate time.

Proverbs 22:22-29 tells us not to take advantage of the poor, or try to exploit them through the legal system, because God will act to defend them, and we will suffer the consequences. It is unwise to choose to associate with angry and argumentative people, because we may start to imitate them and behave like them. If you enter into unwise financial transactions by acting as guarantor for the debts of someone else, you will end up in poverty. Respect the property of others and do not try to acquire it illegally. Your work will be valued and appreciated if you carry it out diligently and skilfully.

In Proverbs 23:1-12 we read various instructions. Exercise self-control and do not be led by greed, when faced with many options. Do not be jealous of what others have. Do not covet worldly wealth and spend your whole life trying to acquire it. Do not be deceived by those who are selfish. Despite their words and flattery, they have their own self-interest at heart. The way you think will ultimately determine how you behave. Be open to receive instruction and knowledge. It is foolish to scorn wise words. Do not deprive someone of their inheritance, or take advantage of the weak, because you will arouse the anger of God, who is their defender.

Proverbs 23:13-25 advises that it is better to train and discipline children, even though it may be painful, rather than to allow them to become rebellious and lose their eternal life. Parents rejoice when they see their children acting righteously and with integrity. Do not envy those who sin and seem to prosper, but rather live a God-centred life, with hope for the future, resting in Him. Seek to live a righteous and self-controlled life. Gluttony and drunkenness eventually lead to poverty. Honour your parents, and learn all you can from them, and from their mistakes. Parents are blessed when they see their children acting righteously.

We read, in Proverbs 23:26-35, keep your heart focussed on God. Sexual temptation and immorality are compared to a criminal waiting for a chance to rob and steal from you. Wrong relationships will not be able to meet your real needs, and they are like a deep pit, which will trap you. Misuse of alcohol can become addictive and life controlling. It causes strife and depression, and brings restlessness, confusion and unreality into your life.

Proverbs 24:1-12 says do not envy or seek to associate with those who rebel against God. Instead, seek wisdom and understanding, so you can build something beautiful and precious. Seeking wisdom and knowledge, and being open to guidance, will help you live a successful and victorious life. The unrighteous scheme and plot out of selfish motives, and act in folly. If you are self-reliant, and unable to draw strength from God, you will struggle in the face of adversities. God knows the motives of your heart and you should not plead ignorance, or be indifferent to the suffering and needs of others.

We are told, in Proverbs 24:13-22, that wisdom is good food for the soul, just as honey is tasty and is nourishing food for the body. Having godly wisdom and understanding gives the righteous hope and strength, which enables them to overcome adversity. We should not be envious of the wicked, who will reap the consequences of their actions one day. We should not gloat or rejoice over the misfortunes of those who have been deceived into sin and led astray by Satan. Instead, we should fear God, and ensure that we ourselves do not join in their rebellious ways.

Proverbs 24:23-34 concludes by saying that we need to act with impartiality and fairness when upholding the law. The guilty must not be wrongly declared innocent, but convicted for their crimes. If we always speak with honesty, we will earn the love and respect of others. We should prioritise what we do, so that the more important things are done in a timely way and are not overlooked. We should not slander or falsely accuse others, or retaliate in a sinful way when others sin against us. We should learn from the mistakes that others have made. If we are lazy, or act unwisely, we will eventually reap the consequences of our actions and have no one to blame except ourselves.

We read, in Proverbs 25:1-10, that men claim glory and honour for discovering the mysteries of nature, but actually the glory should go to God, who is the creator. Just as silver becomes purer as the dross is removed, so will the righteousness of a nation increase, if those in power who are unrighteous are removed from office. If we exalt ourselves, we will be humbled. We should be careful when making judgements based solely on our perception of what we have seen with our own eyes. If we betray the confidences of others, our reputation and character will be irreparably damaged.

Proverbs 25:11-17 advises us that our timely words of encouragement, or even correction, can be very precious to those who receive them. A master is greatly blessed by a servant who is trustworthy, and can accurately express his master's instructions or desires to others. Do not disappoint others by failing to keep your promises. Our goals can often be attained through persuasive words, delivered with gentleness and patience. Too much of a good thing can have harmful results. If we do not respect the boundaries of others, relationships will suffer.

Proverbs 25:18-28 says that bearing false witness against someone is like attacking them with a knife. Unfaithful friends will be unable to help us in our time of need. Be empathetic to the needs of others. When we grant mercy to our enemies, they become convicted of their wrong doing, and we are blessed by God. Being unduly argumentative ruins relationships. Sin and unrighteousness cause good things to become defiled. If we lack self-control, we have no defences, and will easily submit to the temptations of the enemy.

We are instructed in Proverbs 26:1-12 not to honour or imitate the foolish behaviour of others. What they need is godly correction. A curse is ineffective if it is undeserved, and no rights or power have been given to the enemy. Challenge and correct the foolish words of others, so they do not become conceited. Trusting a fool, or appointing him to a position of authority, undermines one's own authority and power, and can be likened to self-inflicted damage. Those who trust in, and boast of, their intellectual understanding, are worse off than fools. A fool will keep repeating the same mistakes, and if you employ such a person they will be a hindrance to you achieving your goals.

Proverbs 26:13-28 says that an unproductive person will often justify their laziness and passivity with unreasonable excuses. They are unable to see the stupidity of what they are doing, and how they are failing to help themselves. Do not excuse the hurt you cause others by claiming that you were only joking. Try to live in peace with others and not be quarrelsome, or a gossiper. Such behaviour can be likened to adding further fuel to a burning fire. Do not simply judge people by their outward appearance and manner. We can be misled and deceived by their words, which mask their real heart attitudes and motives. Lies and flattery will eventually be exposed for what they are.

Proverbs 27:1-11 tells us not to be proud and self-promoting, but rather to allow others to compliment us and speak well of us. Emotional stress, caused by others, can be more tiring and draining than physical work. Jealousy can be a more destructive emotion than anger or hatred. It is better to hear the truth spoken in love by a friend, even though it may be painful, than to be deceived and hurt by the flattery and lies spoken by an enemy. Our circumstances of life greatly influence our attitudes, and our likes and dislikes. Cultivate the friendship of those who welcome you and accept you, and have your best interests at heart. In times of need such friends can offer more support than even your own family members.

Proverbs 27:12-27 advises that the prudent will plan ahead and be careful about standing as a guarantor for the debts or unsecured loans of others. It is difficult to restrain someone who is quarrelsome or contentious by nature, and whose behaviour is very irritating. Our personality and character is developed and refined as we interact with others. Just as a mirror reflects physical characteristics, so heart attitudes reflect the inner person. The praise and affirmation that we receive from others is one way of assessing our character development. It is difficult to change the ways of a fool. Future security and happiness lies in using the talents that God has given us, and being wise stewards of all that is entrusted to us.

We read, in Proverbs 28:1-12, that the unrighteous praise each other, and their lives are often marked with restlessness, as they try to avoid being brought to justice. When the leaders of a nation rebel against God's laws, it eventually leads to a breakdown in authority, and unstable government. It is better to be poor, but righteous, and understand justice, than to be rich, but unrighteous, and to eventually lose one's wealth, and see it given to the poor. The righteous are a credit to their family, whereas the unrighteous bring shame upon their family. Sin is a barrier to effective prayer. If we cause others to sin, we will reap the consequences. If we exercise discernment, we will be able to see through those who lack godly wisdom, and are only wise in their own eyes.

Proverbs 28:13-20 instructs us that, when we acknowledge and repent of unconfessed and hidden sins, (which are always a barrier to spiritual growth), we can receive God's mercy and forgiveness, and keep our hearts from becoming hard. Dictatorial leaders, who lack godly wisdom, trample and crush those who are under their authority. The guilt of sin, which is un-repented of, and unforgiven, leads to a life of torment. The righteous enjoy security and blessing, but the unrighteous face sudden disaster and punishment for their wrong doing. Diligence and hard work bring reward, but living in unreality and fantasy leads to a life of poverty.

We read, in Proverbs 28:21-28, that we should not flatter or show partiality towards others in the hope of obtaining a reward, but confronting in love will reap greater benefits in the long run. Being mean-spirited rather than generous is a pathway to overall poverty. If we declare something to be right, when it is obviously wrong, we are doing the work of Satan. We find peace and security when we trust in God, rather than trusting in our own wisdom and understanding. Those who are generous to the poor, and are not driven by greed, will prosper.

Proverbs 29:1-8 starts by saying that, if we fail to respond to godly correction, we will reap the consequences when disaster comes upon us. The righteous are a source of joy to their family, but the unrighteous squander their wealth and bring shame. A nation will prosper under righteous leadership, but will be unstable and brought down where there is corruption. We make a trap for ourselves and lose our inner joy if we engage in sinful behaviour, or court wrong friendships through flattery. We should care about others being treated justly and not exploited, and seek to defuse angry confrontation.

The advice of Proverbs 29:9-19 is that we should strive to be self-controlled and not give vent to anger, which can damage our relationships with others. The wicked despise the integrity of the righteous. If those in authority listen to lies, their subordinates will become corrupt. All people have in common the fact that God that gives them life. For a kingdom to endure, its ruler must administer justice fairly. Failure to bring godly correction and discipline to children may result in them bringing shame and disgrace upon their family. When there are no clear moral boundaries, wickedness will abound. If you bring your children up under godly discipline, they will be a blessing to you. Words alone, without other corrective measures, may be insufficient to bring about changed behaviour.

Proverbs 29:20-27 concludes by saying that only fools speak out hastily, without considering the consequences of what they say. If we lack self-control and give vent to our anger, we will commit sin, and damage our relationships with others. If we are humble, we will gain honour and respect, but pride will lead to our downfall. The righteous and the unrighteous do not share the same values. If we enter into partnership with the unrighteous, we will be under great pressure to compromise our Christian values. Fear of man undermines our ability to trust in God. We can seek justice from worldly authorities, but ultimately true justice only comes from God.

Proverbs Chapter 30 records the sayings of Agur. In verses 30:1-9 he admits that his understanding and wisdom is limited. Who, he asks, (prophetically pointing to Jesus) has really witnessed the power of God, or understands how He created, and sustains, the universe in which we live? The word of God is without error, and is a shield to those who trust in Him. We should be careful that we do not corrupt it, and we should pray that God will protect us from all deception. We should also pray that God will supply our daily needs, and that our hearts will not become hardened through seeking after riches, or bitter through struggling with poverty.

Proverbs 30:10-23 continues by saying that if you slander others you will eventually reap a consequence. Someone can consider themselves righteous and pure, yet be proud and disdainful of others. Such self-deceived individuals may curse their parents by not honouring them, and through their words and actions may unjustly take advantage of others. We should avoid becoming like leeches and seeking after worldly riches and pleasures which will never satisfy us. Those who dishonour their parents will reap the consequences of their actions. The writer declares that the ways of someone who is in love are often as mysterious to him as the things in nature that he doesn't understand. Individuals, and others involved, can be perturbed and struggle, when the natural or expected order of things is reversed.

In Proverbs 30:24-28, the writer makes observations about animals in the natural world, implying that we can learn from their God-given instinctive wisdom. Some animals make provision for their future food supply. Some act in unity. Some build their homes in a place of security, while others are able to dwell safely in the palace of the king. We need to repent if we have pride, or if we have entertained wrong thoughts. If we stir up the anger of others, it will result in conflict and strife.

In Proverbs 31:1-9, we are encouraged not to spend our life seeking to satisfy the desires of our carnal nature. Instead we are to speak up and defend the rights of the oppressed, the poor and the needy.

Proverbs 31:10-22 describes the character of a godly wife. She is someone who is highly valued by her husband, who has full confidence in her, and provides for her. She always seeks the best for her husband, and ensures that her family are well fed and clothed. She manages her household well, and is kind and generous to the poor and needy.

Proverbs 31:23-31 concludes the character description of a noble wife. She brings honour and respect to her husband, who feels blessed by her and praises her. She is not idle, and manages her household well. She is wise, and plans for the future. She is praised by all, and is known as someone who fears the Lord.

Ecclesiastes

The Book of Ecclesiastes, commonly believed to have been written by Solomon, expresses the meaninglessness of life in the absence of knowledge and understanding of God.

Chapter 1 expresses the opinion that from an earthly perspective our lives are meaningless. Man works and strives to make a living, but anything achieved is quickly forgotten by subsequent generations. Gaining earthly wisdom and understanding is not the answer, as this only raises even more questions.

In Ecclesiastes 2, the writer declares that he has been unsuccessful in finding a meaning to life through seeking pleasure, or through undertaking many great building projects. He has sought wisdom, but, although acknowledging it is better to live as a wise man rather than a fool, ultimately both die, and all they have passes on to someone else. God gives happiness and wisdom to those who please Him, but the wealth and riches accumulated by a sinner are meaningless.

In Ecclesiastes 3, the writer declares that there is a time for every activity that is common to mankind. Although an individual may obtain job satisfaction from what they do, they may not see how it fits into God's eternal purposes, and, on reflection, may see everything they do as meaningless. If someone does not know that their spirit lives on after death, they will see themselves as no different to the animals, and view their earthly existence as meaningless.

In Ecclesiastes 4, the writer declares that he can see no meaning in the lives of those who live under oppression, or those who, out of envy of what others have, spend their lives trying to accumulate wealth. Even the lonely, who have no one to inherit their wealth, can spend their lives in this meaningless way. He finds it meaningless that some people will respect and honour the king's successor and put their trust in him, while others will later come along and be opposed to him.

In Ecclesiastes 5, the writer warns that we should be careful to fulfil any promises which we make to God. He declares that wealth does not equate to happiness. Those who are wealthy often want more, and spend their lives in fear of losing what they have. He reminds us that we can't take our wealth with us when we die. He concludes that God wants us to find happiness, peace and fulfilment in our daily lives, and not to be anxiously striving to gain material possessions.

In Ecclesiastes 6, the writer declares how meaningless life is to those who have material possessions, which fail to give them contentment and happiness, or have children who do not honour or respect them. It is meaningless to live a long life if it is all spent trying to satisfy desires which cannot be met. Outside of God, who or what can give meaning to a person's life?

In Ecclesiastes 7, the writer continues to record his observation on life. It is foolish to live a life of pleasure ignoring the fact that one day we will all die. Wisdom is a good thing and preserves the life of its possessor, but no one can fully understand or attain the wisdom of God. He observes that sometimes the righteous perish and the wicked enjoy a long life, but that does not justify us living in foolishness. He concludes that God created mankind righteous, but that everyone has sinned.

In Ecclesiastes 8, the writer proclaims the pragmatic wisdom of being obedient to the king and not questioning his actions. He declares that, although the wicked often seem to prosper and the righteous suffer, it will go better for those who fear God. He concludes that we cannot comprehend the meaning of life from observation alone, and without reference to God.

In Ecclesiastes 9, the writer declares that the righteous and the wicked share the same destiny of physical death. He observes that no one knows when they will die, and that we ought, therefore, to live life to the full. (Life would indeed be meaningless if death is the end of our existence, and if the way we live our lives on earth has no bearing on our eternal destiny).

In Ecclesiastes 10, the writer exalts the merits of wisdom in contrast to foolishness. If fools are promoted to positions of authority and act out of self-centredness, there will be consequences that affect everyone. There are dangers associated with many activities, but a fool is more likely to expose himself to them. Laziness and idleness result in the erosion of one's wealth and possessions.

In Ecclesiastes 11, the writer proclaims that no one can be certain about what will happen in the future on earth. However, that should not stop any one from working or planning for the future, and enjoying each day as it comes, remembering that we will have to give an account to God for what we have done.

In Ecclesiastes 12, the writer exhorts his readers to be ever mindful of God. In the final verses of this book the writer concludes that, although the whole cycle of earthly life may seem meaningless, God will judge everything that we have done, including those things done in secret. Therefore, we should fear God and obey His commandments.

Song of Songs

Song of Songs is a poem honouring marriage and wedded love. It is in the form of a dialogue between a young maiden and her betrothed lover (personified as being King Solomon), eagerly awaiting the consummation of their marriage. It is generally recognised as an allegory proclaiming God's love for His chosen people, and Christ's love for the Church.

In Chapter 1, the couple poetically express their love for one another, and declare how attractive they find each other.

In Song of Songs 2, the couple express how special they find their partner and how, in their eyes, their partner outshines all their peers. The maiden likens her beloved to a gazelle or young stag on the mountains in springtime, looking for a mate. Her hope and desire is that he will come to her, and invite her to join him. She declares that he has taken her to the banquet table, and that his banner over her is love.

In Song of Songs 3, the maiden, in her dreams, fears losing her lover. She declares that she will search everywhere to find him. When she finds him, she will take him home to introduce him to her mother, and obtain her approval for her choice of partner. She likens the arrival of her lover to King Solomon in his chariot, arrayed in splendour, and escorted by many nobles.

In Song of Song 4, the young man poetically expresses how beautiful and desirable he finds his bride. She is perfect, and without flaw. He likens her to a secret garden filled with fragrant flowers and choice fruits, and declares that she has stolen his heart. She responds by inviting him to come into the garden and enjoy its fruit.

In Song of Songs 5, (interpreted by some as a continuation of the dream of Chapter 3), the couple have consummated the relationship, but now her lover has departed, and she feels desolate and lonely without him. She searches for him, but is unable to find him. She poetically expresses how physically attractive she finds him.

In Song of Songs 6, the maiden expresses the fear that her lover, (personified as the king), has other admirers in his harem. He poetically declares, however, that the maiden is unique amongst all the others in the harem, and is the one he most favours.

In Song of Songs 7, the young man poetically expresses how attractive and desirable he find the maiden, and declares that he wants to make love with her. She responds by declaring that she belongs to him, and desires that he come and make love to her.

In Songs of Songs 8, the maiden wishes that her lover was like ordinary men, so that she could more openly approach him, and declare her love for him. Her love for him is so great that nothing could buy it, or take it away. She concludes by declaring her undying love for her lover (the king). She compares herself to a vineyard, which she could rent out to a tenant farmer, but declares that she wants to give this vineyard as a gift, only for the king.

Isaiah

The Book of Isaiah was written between 740BC and 685BC.

In Isaiah 1, we read that Israel has rebelled against God and become a sinful nation. They have abandoned righteousness, and are not protecting the orphans or widows. Because of their sin, their prayers and sacrifices have become meaningless to God. Unless they repent, God will bring judgement upon them through their enemies, and only a remnant will survive.

Isaiah 2 is a prophecy concerning the end times and the millennial reign of Jesus, when He will rule all the nations from Jerusalem, and there will be a time of peace. The pride and arrogance of man will be humbled, and God will be exalted. There will be great fear among the people, who will try to hide from the splendour of His majesty.

Isaiah 3 is a prophecy about what is going to happen to Judah and Jerusalem. (Judah was the southern kingdom and Israel the northern kingdom, formed when Israel divided, following the death of Solomon.) Their leaders and skilled craftsmen will be taken away, and law and order will fail. The wicked will be judged, the proud women will be humbled, and the armies defeated in battle.

Having said what will happen to Judah and Jerusalem because of her sinfulness and pride, in Isaiah Chapter 3, Isaiah Chapter 4 now gives hope concerning the restoration which will eventually follow. The branch of the Lord (the Messiah) will be glorified in Jerusalem. There will be a cleansing from sin and bloodshed, and Jerusalem will become a place of shelter and refuge.

In Isaiah 5, Judah and Jerusalem are like a vineyard established by God. Because it has failed to produce good fruit, God is allowing the walls of the vineyard to collapse and will use other nations to bring judgement on the people, who have turned away from Him, and rejected His law. Judgement will come upon all who reverse God's order by calling evil good, and darkness light.

Isaiah 6 records Isaiah's commissioning as a prophet. He has a vision of God in His holiness, seated on His throne and surrounded by angels. In the presence of God's holiness, he becomes acutely aware of his own sinfulness. His lips are touched with coals from the fire of God, and he is appointed to bring God's word to the people. He is warned that they will harden their hearts and not understand the message, until destruction has come upon them.

Isaiah 7 records a prophecy to King Ahaz of Judah, who, when invaded by Israel (Ephraim) and Syria, did not trust in God, but made a treaty with the Assyrians. Syria and Israel will be overcome before a child yet to be born is weaned. However, God will use the Assyrians to lay waste the land of Judah. The messianic prophecy of a virgin giving birth will be ultimately fulfilled in Jesus.

In Isaiah 8, Isaiah has a son named 'quick to plunder'. He prophesies that Israel and Syria will be overcome by the Assyrians within one or two years, and that Judah too will be invaded, but God will deliver them. The people should fear God, and not the Assyrians. They should seek God, and not fortune tellers or spiritists. If they do not do this, the people will enter into spiritual darkness.

Isaiah 9 continues to warn about the future for the northern kingdom of Israel. Because the people will not turn to Him, God will remove their leaders, and the false prophets, who lie and mislead them. The people will face famine and distress, and will turn against each other, and Judah. Amid this prophecy of doom there is still hope for the future. God will give them a Messiah, who will be called Wonderful Counsellor, Mighty God, Everlasting Father, Prince of Peace.

Isaiah 10 records that, although God will use the Assyrians to overthrow Israel and invade Judah, He will punish them for their pride and arrogance, because they will boast that they have done everything in their own strength and defeated the God of Israel and Judah. Because there is a remnant in the land who seek God, God will stay the hand of the Assyrians and defeat their invading army.

Isaiah 11 and 12 are a messianic prophecy describing the character of the Messiah and the nature of His kingdom. He will gather the exiles of Israel and Judah from the four quarters of the earth. His kingdom will be based on righteousness and justice. This prophecy paints a glorious picture of the millennial reign of Jesus, when there will be peace throughout the world, and great rejoicing in what God has done.

Isaiah 13 is a prophecy concerning Babylon (one of the world's super-powers at that time). God will raise up the Medes to invade Assyria, and completely destroy her splendour and devastate the land. The invading army will be cruel and merciless, and will have no compassion on those living in Babylonia. This prophecy was fulfilled in about 540 BC, when the Medes invaded Babylon.

In Isaiah 14, God says He will reunite Israel and Judah, and restore them in the land. They will ultimately rule over the nations which oppressed them. The prophecy against Babylon continues, with a taunt against its king. The taunt is not so much against the earthly king, but against the spiritual power beyond his kingdom. This power

(Satan) wanted to exalt itself above God, but has been brought down to the pit (Hell).

In Isaiah 15, we read an oracle, or prophecy, concerning Moab, (a land bordering the eastern side of the dead sea). It speaks of the wealth of the nation being carried away, and the land becoming desolate. There will be much loss of life, and great mourning by the people. The fugitives from Moab, and those remaining in the land, will face further trials, symbolised by a lion coming upon them.

Isaiah 16 is a continuation of the prophecy against Moab. Because of her pride and arrogance, Moab's vineyards will be trampled down, and the Moabites will lose their joy. Fugitives from Moab will seek shelter in Israel to escape from their oppressors. It is prophesied that this initial devastation will come upon Moab within three years. (Fulfilled by the Assyrian invasion of Moab in about 715 BC.)

Isaiah 17 is an oracle, or prophecy, addressed to Damascus, the capital city of Syria, (a country located to the north of Israel). The city will be completely destroyed (fulfilled in about 732BC, following a siege by Assyria). However, there will be a remnant who will turn back to God, and abandon pagan worship. The invading armies will be like a raging river until God rebukes them, and they disappear overnight.

Isaiah 18 is an oracle against Cush (thought to be southern Egypt), and Isaiah 19 is an oracle against Egypt. (Judah was looking to Egypt to defend them against Syria and Assyria.) Both countries will be overrun by a cruel foreign power and their infrastructure devastated. (This was fulfilled with the Assyrians' invasion in about 675 BC). The prophecy concludes by saying that eventually Egypt will return to the Lord along with Assyria.

In Isaiah 20, we read how Isaiah went around stripped and barefooted, following the capture of the city of Ashdod by the Assyrians in about 710 BC. This action by Isaiah was to symbolise that Israel's strategy of forming an alliance with Egypt to protect herself from the Assyrians would ultimately fail.

Isaiah 21 begins with a prophecy that Babylonia, one of Israel's main enemies at that time, will itself be invaded and defeated by a fierce enemy from the south, who will come upon them like a whirlwind. This was fulfilled when the Medes and Persians, (Elam), invaded in about 540 BC. Fugitives from this invasion will flee into Arabia, inhabited by the tribe of Kedar (a descendant of Ishmael), but they too will be decimated by the invasion.

Isaiah 22 is a prophecy addressed to the Valley of Vision

(Israel), and vividly portrays the fall of Jerusalem. The people have trusted in their own defence, and not in God, and thought they were safe. However, their leaders have fled, and the walls of the city are breached. Shebna, the self-exalting steward in charge of the palace, will be replaced by the godly Eliakim, but he too will be unable to save Jerusalem.

Isaiah 23 is a prophecy that the mighty city of Tyre will be destroyed, (fulfilled in about 570 BC, following a siege by Nebuchadnezzar), but eventually restored.

Isaiah 24 talks about the devastation which will come upon the whole earth at the end of the age, because the people have disobeyed God's laws, and broken covenant with Him. Ultimately, however, the spiritual powers will be bound like prisoners in a dungeon, and the Lord Almighty will reign gloriously in Jerusalem.

In Isaiah 25, the prophet praises God for His faithfulness, as he looks forward to the fulfilment of history. He declares that God will swallow up death, and will wipe away every tear, and take away all shame. He will destroy all that stands in opposition to Him, and He will prepare a banquet for His people to enjoy. On that day, all those who have put their trust in the Lord will rejoice.

Isaiah 26 is a continuation of end times prophecy, when peace will be established in the world. The prophet acknowledges that the Israelites have failed to be a light for the world, and have become idolatrous. Judgement will come upon the unrighteous, but we can take encouragement that there will be resurrection and joy for the righteous. In the meantime, we can know God's peace when we put our trust in Him.

Isaiah 27 says that evil, (described here as Leviathan, or a serpent), will be finally overcome. The fortified cities and idolatrous practices of those who have rebelled against God will be brought down. God's kingdom will be established, and it will be like a fruitful vineyard, with God protecting it. Those who have been in exile will return to worship God in Jerusalem.

Isaiah 28 starts by saying that the northern Kingdom, (Ephraim), will be trampled down, because of pride. Judah, and its religious leaders in Jerusalem, are behaving like drunks, and trusting in the treaty with Egypt to save them. They have turned God's covenant into a set of rules. They too will be swept away, until God acts to save them. Using an analogy from farming, Isaiah says that the time of discipline will come to an end, and that God will employ His methods to produce a harvest.

Isaiah 29 is addressed to the city of Ariel (Jerusalem), which will be besieged by the nations of the earth. However, the Lord Almighty will intervene to save the city, and the people will be astonished. At that time spiritual eyes will be opened, and the people will acknowledge the holiness of God. The unrighteous, who think that God does not know what they do, and who treat God with no respect, will be cut down.

Isaiah 30 begins with a rebuke to those who make their own plans, without consulting God. They are ignoring the warnings that God is speaking through the genuine prophets, and are depending on Egypt to protect them from their enemies. Eventually (in the end times), when the people turn back to God and call upon Him, He will respond, and heal their wounds, and bring prosperity to their land. God will come like a consuming fire, and He will judge the nations.

In Isaiah 31 the prophet again brings a rebuke against those who put their trust in others (Egypt), rather than in God. He encourages them to turn back to God. God is faithful to His word, and, in the end times, will rise up to protect Jerusalem, and defeat the enemies of His chosen people. His enemies will recognise that it is the hand of God which is against them, and will be terrified.

Isaiah 32 looks forward to the day when the Messiah King will reign, and His kingdom will bring justice, and a place of refuge from the storm. People's eyes will be opened to understand the deception which has engulfed them. He warns that calamity will soon overtake Israel, but, in the end times, God will pour out His Spirit. There will then be a time of peace and prosperity.

Isaiah 33 initially addresses Assyria, who will break the peace treaty it had with Judah, and will invade and plunder the land of Israel. God will arise and destroy this enemy. This chapter concludes by looking forward to the day, when Jerusalem will be restored, and be inhabited by the righteous remnant. It will be a place of peace and freedom. There will be no sickness, and the people will know their sins have been forgiven.

Isaiah 34 is a prophecy concerning all the nations of the world, as typified by Edom, which oppose Israel. Their armies, and the demonic powers behind them, will be totally defeated by God (the battle of Armageddon). These nations will become like desolate ground, only inhabited by wild animals, and will never rise to power again. This will all happen in accordance with God's word (His scroll).

Isaiah 35 is a glorious prophecy concerning the restoration of Israel as the abode of the redeemed which will reflect the splendour of the Lord. It is described as a place with an abundance of vegetation and water, to be entered by the path of holiness. God will come to exercise His divine judgement, and save His people. The redeemed of the Lord will be filled with joy, and there will be no sorrow, sadness or sickness.

Isaiah 36 records how the Assyrians invaded Judah for the first time in about 700 BC, during the reign of King Hezekiah. The invading army comes to Jerusalem and arrogantly boasts that it is no good relying on Egypt for help, or trusting in God. The Assyrian armies have defeated every nation, and their gods could not help them. The Assyrian army commander appeals to the people to not be misled by Hezekiah.

In Isaiah 37, Hezekiah responds to the challenge and threat of the invading Assyrian army, by seeking God. God responds through a word from Isaiah that the Assyrians will not capture Jerusalem, but will withdraw. Subsequently, an angel of the Lord went through the Assyrian camp, and 185,000 men died. The Assyrian army withdrew, and it was another 120 years before Assyria finally conquered Judah.

In Isaiah 38 we read how Hezekiah became terminally ill, but was granted a further fifteen years' life by God. God confirmed that He would extend Hezekiah's life by causing the shadow of the sun to go backwards.

Isaiah 39 records how Hezekiah shows an envoy from Babylonia all the treasures of Jerusalem. Isaiah prophesies that all these treasures and the descendants of Hezekiah will one day be taken to Babylon.

Isaiah 40 is a chapter of comfort and hope. The prophet declares that God's glory will be revealed. He will come as both the gentle shepherd who comforts His people, and as the sovereign Lord, with power to judge and reward. Nothing is comparable to the everlasting God, who created, and sustains, the universe. He is able to encourage and strengthen all who put their trust and hope in Him.

In Isaiah 41, the prophet reaffirms that God's purposes for Israel will be accomplished, and that God is able to orchestrate events to make this happen. Ultimately, it is God who is in control, and not worthless man-made idols. All who rage against Israel will be put to shame. God originally choose Israel, and will continue to help her. He will re-establish Israel as a prosperous and fertile land, and all nations will become subject to her.

Isaiah 42 prophetically foretells of the character of the Messiah. He will be kind and gentle, and will establish justice in the world. He will open blinded eyes and set the captives free. He will also march out like a mighty warrior, and will triumph over all His enemies.

Isaiah poses the question whether people will learn from their history and listen to Him. The Israelites have sinned by becoming blind and deaf to the things of God, and that is why they have experienced calamities.

In Isaiah 43, we find an assurance from God that Israel is precious in His sight, that God is both her creator and redeemer, and that He will be with her in times of difficulty and trial. Although Israel and Judah were being driven from the land of Israel because of their sin and disobedience, God says He will restore them back to the land. God will do this just as assuredly as He delivered Israel from Egypt, and the army of the Pharaoh.

Isaiah 44 starts with God continuing to declare that He will bless Israel and restore the land, because He is God, and there is no other god like Him. Man's futility in creating idols and worshipping them is satirically described. God is sovereign and overturns the learning of the wise. He will redeem Israel. During the reign of Cyrus, a decree will be made to rebuild Jerusalem and the temple. (This prophecy was fulfilled in about 535 BC.)

In Isaiah 45, God continues to declare that He alone is the sovereign God, and that all that He decrees will come to pass. God will raise up Cyrus (the King of Persia, who, together with King Darius of the Medes, overthrew the Babylonian Empire in about 540 BC), who will release the exiles, and allow them to rebuild Jerusalem. Israel will be saved with an everlasting salvation. All those who worship idols will be put to shame, and every knee will bow to God.

Isaiah 46 continues to contrast the helplessness of idols (specifically mentioning two false gods of the Assyrians - Bel and Nebo), compared to the omnipotence of God. God's purposes will stand. God will provide a way of righteousness and salvation for Israel.

Chapter 47 of Isaiah is a prophecy against the Babylonians. God has used them to discipline Israel, but they are full of pride, and are trusting in witchcraft and wickedness to maintain their power. God declares that they will be suddenly, and quickly, overthrown. (Physically fulfilled when the Medes and Persians defeated the Babylonians in about 540 BC.) Spiritually, Babylon also represents Satan's demonic kingdom, which will ultimately be completely defeated and overthrown by God.

Isaiah 48 is a rebuke to the Israelites, who claim to worship God, but do not operate in truth and righteousness. For the sake of His own name, God has had to discipline them. If they had followed God's instructions, they would have enjoyed righteousness and peace.

God, however, has not finished with them. Just as He redeemed them from Egypt, He will redeem them from the Babylonians.

Isaiah 49 speaks about the everlasting nature of God's covenants. Israel was chosen by God to display His splendour. Even though she has been unfaithful, He cannot simply forget her, because she is engraved on the palms of His hands. God will have compassion on His chosen people, and will restore them back to the land of Israel. She will become a light to the Gentiles. The whole world will witness what the Lord does, and know that He alone is our Saviour and Redeemer.

In Isaiah 50, the Israelites are declared responsible for their captivity and separation from God. What is to happen to them is a consequence of their transgressions and sins. Isaiah, talking about himself and prophetically about Jesus, has put his trust in the Lord, who will be his shield and defender against all who accuse him. It is a reminder that those living in darkness need to turn to God and put their trust in Him, rather than trying to create their own light, which only leads to destruction.

In Isaiah 51, the Israelites are encouraged to return to their roots and the promises made to Abraham. God will bring an everlasting salvation and His righteousness will never fail. God delivered them from Egypt (referred to here as Rahab) and He will act again to restore Jerusalem. The judgement, which has been poured out on them because of their sins and disobedience, will be poured out on the unrighteous, who torment and oppress God's chosen people,

Isaiah 52 proclaims the future glory of Jerusalem. The city, which has been defiled and made desolate, will, one day, be restored. God's servant (Jesus, the Messiah), will bring good news, and a message of peace and salvation. Although He will be disfigured, and many will be appalled by Him, He will be exalted and the kings and nations of the earth will ultimately recognise and acknowledge who He really is.

Isaiah 53, written about 700 years before the birth of Jesus, prophetically speaks of how the Messiah will bring salvation and healing through His suffering. He will be despised and rejected, and will carry the punishment for our sins, even though He Himself will be sinless and blameless. He will be led like a lamb to the slaughter, and many will be justified and saved because of what He willingly endures on their behalf.

Isaiah 54 is a prophecy in which God affirms His commitment to Israel, and declares that she will be restored. No matter what happens, God will have compassion on Israel, and His covenant of peace will not be removed. A time will come when Israel will be re-established, and no weapon forged against her will prevail.

Isaiah 55 is an open invitation for all to seek and find spiritual fulfilment and life for their soul. It is a call for the wicked to forsake their ways, and receive forgiveness. God declares that His ways are not our ways, and that His Word will go forth and accomplish His purposes. The redeemed of the Lord will be filled with joy, and the unproductive land completely restored, as an everlasting sign to the glory of God.

In Isaiah 56, God reminds the Israelites of the importance of being obedient to Him by observing the law and maintaining justice. God declares that salvation is not only for the Jews, but to all those who turn to Him, and hold fast to His covenant. This chapter finishes with a rebuke to the prophets of Israel, who are blind to what is happening. They are self-focussed and are failing in their role as shepherds, to speak out God's truth, and to lead and guide the people.

Isaiah 57 is a continuation of the rebuke of the leaders in Israel. They have rebelled against God, and are worshipping false Gods, both openly and in secret. Instead of turning to God for strength, they have turned to pagan idols and superstitious practices. Although God is angered by what they have done, He declares that He will bring restoration and healing to the repentant, but that He will punish the wicked.

Isaiah 58 is a rebuke to the spiritual leaders, who are being hypocritical. While appearing spiritual on the outside, their hearts are not committed to God. They fast, but they exploit their work force. They argue and fight with each other. God challenges them to seek justice for the oppressed, to feed the hungry, to clothe the naked and not talk maliciously about each other. When they do these things they will know God's guidance and blessing.

In Isaiah 59, the prophet declares that the difficulties they are facing are not because God is too weak to help them, but because their many sins and unrighteousness have separated them from God. They are walking in darkness; justice and truth is lacking in what they do and say. God, however, will graciously intervene, and provide a means of salvation and redemption. He is faithful to his covenant and His words, and His Holy Spirit will not depart from those who accept this salvation.

Isaiah 60 is an end-times prophecy describing how Israel and Jerusalem will be restored and established as a light to all. The nations of the world, who oppose her, will be destroyed. There will be an end to devastation and destruction, and peace will exist within her borders.

She will be blessed by the wealth of the world. All her inhabitants will be righteous, and God Himself will reign amongst them, as an everlasting light.

Isaiah 61 is a wonderful prophecy about the Messiah. At the start of His ministry Jesus read this scripture, and affirmed that it applied to Himself. It proclaims that the Messiah will bring both salvation and healing. Those who mourn will be comforted, and the captives will be set free. The recipients of this salvation and righteousness will themselves go on to bless others.

In Isaiah 62, God continues to express His heart for Israel and Jerusalem. He declares that He will not rest until Jerusalem is established as a beacon of righteousness to the whole world. The city will be no longer called 'forsaken' or 'desolate', but will be called 'sought out', and its inhabitants called 'the redeemed of the Lord'.

In Isaiah 63, we read that God, in His mercy and love, will become the Saviour and Redeemer of His people, as well as the avenger and the judge of all the nations. The prophet reminds God of the way He brought the Israelites out of Egypt. The people, however, rebelled against God and grieved His Holy Spirit. Isaiah asks God to reveal His presence once more to the remnant, as they return to God, and to remember what He did for them in the past.

Isaiah 64 is a continuation of the prayer of confession and repentance to God. Isaiah, praying on behalf of the people, acknowledges that God is their father, and that they are like clay in the hand of the potter. He acknowledges that they have sinned against Him, and even their righteous acts are like filthy rags, compared to God's holiness. Isaiah, feeling as if God has turned His face away from them, asks Him to relent and to help them.

Isaiah 65 records God's response to the Israelites' prayer of repentance. Although He has revealed Himself to His people, they have rebelled. They have entered into idolatry and have broken His laws. They have not responded to His correction, and will have to face the consequences. Those who turn to God, however, will be blessed. There will be a new heaven and a new earth; a place of peace, joy, prosperity and happiness in the presence of God.

Isaiah 66 summarises the main prophetic themes of the book of Isaiah. God is the creator, whose purposes will be accomplished. He reveals Himself to His creation, but the people rebel against Him. There will be a day of judgement, and they will be assigned to eternal punishment. Those who are contrite and humble in spirit, seeking and responding to God, will be rewarded. They will dwell in the new Jerusalem, established in the new heaven and earth, and they will see

God's glory.

Jeremiah

Jeremiah prophesies to the kingdom of Judah, from about 630 BC, until after the Babylonian captivity in 586 BC.

In Jeremiah 1, Jeremiah declares that, even before he was born, God chose him and appointed him to be a prophet to the nations. The Lord shows Jeremiah that He will use kingdoms from the north to bring judgment upon the Israelites. God commands Jeremiah to speak of what He shows him, and not to be afraid of the opposition he will face, because God will protect him.

In Jeremiah 2, the prophet declares that the Israelites have forsaken God, who rescued them from captivity in Egypt, and brought them into the Promised Land. They did not seek God, but, instead, sought other gods of their own creation, and put their trust in Assyria or Egypt to help them. They have rebelled against God, and not responded to His discipline.

In Jeremiah 3, the Israelite's idolatry is likened to adultery and promiscuity. Although God 'divorced' the northern kingdom, allowing her to be over-run by her enemies, the southern kingdom of Judah has not learnt from this, and continues in her idolatry. If they acknowledge their guilt, God will give them shepherds after His own heart.

Jeremiah 4 is a prophecy about the imminent invasion of Judah from the north by the Babylonians. The Israelites have brought this invasion and devastation of the land upon themselves, because they rebelled against God.

Jeremiah 5 is a continuation of the prophecy concerning the invasion of Judah. Neither the people nor the leaders, who should instruct the people, know or follow the way of the Lord. There is no fear of the Lord. The prophets lie, and say that disaster will not befall them, and the priests rule by their own authority. The land will be devastated, and the Israelites taken into captivity in a foreign land.

Jeremiah 6 concludes the prophecy that Judah will be invaded and devastated by an invasion from the north. The invading armies will besiege Jerusalem and destroy it. The prophets and priests are deceitful, and declare that there is peace, when there is no peace. The Israelites refuse to follow the ancient paths, or listen to the warnings given by the watchmen. Because of their rebellious ways, their sacrifices and offerings are unacceptable to God.

Jeremiah 7 is a rebuke to the Israelites for trusting in deceptive words, and believing they are safe, when they are not following the ways of God. They have not learnt any lessons from what happened to

Shiloh. (The original place of worship destroyed by the Philistines in 1050 BC.) The Israelites provoke God's anger by their practice of idolatry and worship of false gods. Because they have not responded to correction, and truth has perished, disaster will come upon them.

In Jeremiah 8, the prophet laments what will happen when Israel is overcome by her enemies. These enemies will be like venomous snakes, who will desecrate the graves of the dead, and take the Israelites into captivity in a distant land, where they will mourn over what has befallen them. Jeremiah declares that the priests and prophets are behaving deceitfully by falsifying the word of God, and not looking after the people. There is no acknowledgement or repentance of sin.

In Jeremiah 9, the prophet weeps over the spiritual condition of the nation. He declares that the Lord will punish, test and refine Israel, because she has forsaken His law. Jerusalem will be destroyed, and the people scattered amongst the nations. The people boast about their own wisdom, strength and wealth, rather than boasting about their relationship with God. Salvation and help does not come through physical circumcision, but through circumcision of the heart.

In Jeremiah 10, the prophet describes the futility of creating and worshipping worthless idols. The Lord who created the heavens and the earth is the only true, living and eternal God. Judgement will come upon Israel because of her idolatry, and the people will be removed from the land. The shepherds are senseless, and have not followed the Lord, and so their flocks will be scattered.

In Jeremiah 11, God rebukes Israel for breaking His covenant with them by not obeying Him, and by returning to the sins of their fore-fathers. As a consequence of their idolatry, disaster will come upon them. Because they are burning incense to Baal, God tells Jeremiah not to even pray for them, and that He will not listen to them. Jeremiah rebukes the men of Anathoth, who were plotting to kill him, and declares that they will all be destroyed.

In Jeremiah 12, the prophet asks God why the wicked seem to prosper, and when judgement will come upon them. God replies that, for a time, He will abandon His inheritance, and give Israel into the hands of her enemies. Israel will become a desolate wasteland, like a trampled down vineyard which bears no fruit. Israel and her neighbours will be uprooted, but God will re-establish them in their lands. However, those nations who do not listen to God will again be uprooted and destroyed.

In Jeremiah 13, the prophet acts out a parable, describing the deterioration and uselessness of a new linen belt, which has been worn, and then exposed to dampness and soil. It is an example of what will happen to Judah because of her pride and wickedness. Because of her stubbornness and many sins, she will be shamefully exposed and taken into exile. Those with whom she has made a peace treaty will rule over her.

In Jeremiah 14, God declares that He will not respond to prayers offered during a time of severe drought, because the nation has turned away from Him, and they only seek help when they want something from Him. The prophets are lying when they tell the people that famine and disaster will not come upon them. Jeremiah repents before God on behalf of Judah, acknowledging the wickedness of both the current and previous generations.

In Jeremiah 15, God responds to the prophet's prayer concerning the drought being experienced in Judah. God declares that He would not even respond to the prayers of Moses or Samuel, because of the sins of Manasseh (who brought idolatry and Baal worship into the temple). The nation will be destroyed, and the people enslaved. Jeremiah is told that he is to be God's spokesmen to the people. The people will reject, and fight against, Jeremiah, but God will protect him.

In Jeremiah 16, God tells Jeremiah not to marry or have children, because of the suffering and death which will come upon the nation during his lifetime. The Israelites will be removed from the land because of their rebellion and idolatry. God declares, however, that they will be restored to the land, coming back from the north and all the other countries where they have been banished. This restoration will be seen to be as great a miracle as their deliverance from Egypt.

In Jeremiah 17, the prophet proclaims that Judah's sin is inscribed on the hearts of the people. Their hearts are deceitful, and God will search their hearts, and reward them according to their deeds. But, blessed is the man who puts his trust in God rather than man. God instructs Jeremiah to go to the gates of Jerusalem and declare that destruction will come upon the city, if the people refuse to obey God, and dishonour Him by breaking the Sabbath regulations, and not keeping the Sabbath day holy.

In Jeremiah 18, the prophet goes to the potter's house and compares the work of the potter to the way in which God shapes and directs the affairs of the nations on earth. Unless Judah turns from her wicked ways and stubbornness of heart, God will bring disaster upon her. Jeremiah asks God to bring judgement on those who have plotted against him and tried to kill him, in order to stop him speaking out the words God has given him.

In Jeremiah 19, the prophet is instructed to go to Ben Hinnom (the place where King Ahaz and King Manasseh had set up an altar and carried out child sacrifices to Molech). There he smashes a clay pot and declares that this is what God will do to Israel, because of her rebellion and sin. An enemy will lay siege against them, and they will be so desperate for food that some will even become cannibalistic.

In Jeremiah 20, Pashhur, the chief priest, has Jeremiah beaten and placed in the stocks, because of what he is prophesying. Jeremiah responds by telling Pashhur that he will be taken into exile and die in a foreign land. Although he faces persecution and ridicule, Jeremiah declares that he is compelled to speak out God's words, which are like a burning fire within him. He gives thanks that God is with him, and will rescue him from his persecutors.

Jeremiah 21 records how King Zedekiah asks Jeremiah for a word from God, when Jerusalem is being attacked by the Babylonians, led by King Nebuchadnezzar. God declares through Jeremiah that Jerusalem will be destroyed by fire. Many will die of starvation or plague, or be killed by the sword of the Babylonians. King Zedekiah, and any of the leaders or people who survive the destruction of the city, will be taken into captivity.

Jeremiah 22 records prophecies about the three kings who succeeded King Josiah. King Jehoahaz (Shallum), who had been taken into captivity in Egypt, will never return. King Jehoiakim, who was more concerned about building himself a palace than seeking justice for the poor and the oppressed, will be disgraced and no one will mourn his death. (He will be deposed by King Nebuchadnezzar and taken to Babylon in chains.) King Jehoiachin will be taken into exile in Babylon.

In Jeremiah 23, God declares that the prophet and priests are failing in their duties, and will be punished. God Himself will gather His scattered sheep, and place caring and faithful shepherds over them. He will raise up a Davidic king to rule over them. God declares that He is against the godless prophets, who claim to be speaking the words of God, but are only speaking out of their own imagination, and lead the people astray by giving them false hope.

Jeremiah 24 records a vision in which the prophet sees two baskets of figs. The good figs represent the good exiles taken into Babylon along with King Jehoiachin. God will watch over them, and they will return to the land. The bad figs represent King Zedekiah and his officials who took over from King Jehoiachin, and became even more unfaithful towards God. God declares that they will be punished by plague, famine and sword, and become an object of ridicule.

Jeremiah 25 records a prophecy given during the reign of King Jehoiakim. For twenty-three years, God's warnings, given through Jeremiah, have been ignored. Therefore, God now declares that He will use the Babylonians and King Nebuchadnezzar to bring judgement and devastation upon Israel and the surrounding nations. These nations will become subject to the Babylonians for seventy years, before the Babylonians themselves are judged and overcome by other nations and great kings.

Jeremiah 26 records another prophecy given during the reign of King Jehoiakim, declaring that the temple and Jerusalem will be destroyed, if the Israelites continue in their disobedience. The priests and the other prophets want to put Jeremiah to death, as they had done to the prophet Uriah. The court officials, however, defend Jeremiah, saying he should not be killed, because he has only spoken out the words which God has given him, just as Micah had done during the reign of Hezekiah.

Jeremiah 27 records how God instructs Jeremiah to wear a yoke around his neck to symbolise what will happen to Israel and the surrounding nations. They will become subject to the rule of the Babylonians. If they resist and listen to the lies of the false prophets, who say this will not happen, their lands will be devastated and the people banished from the land. The prophets of Judah are lying when they say that the articles from the temple, taken by Nebuchadnezzar, will soon be returned.

Jeremiah 28 records how the prophet Hananiah breaks the wooden yoke which God instructed Jeremiah to wear. He declares that God will break the yoke of the King of Babylon, and within two years Jehoiachin and the exiles, who have already been taken into captivity, will return. Jeremiah declares that Hananiah is lying, and that, instead of a wooden yoke, the Babylonian yoke will be a yoke of iron. Jeremiah correctly prophesies that Hananiah will die, because he is preaching rebellion against God.

Jeremiah 29 records a letter sent by Jeremiah to the Israelites who had already been taken into exile in Babylon, during the reign of King Jehoiachin. He tells them not to believe the lies of Shemaiah, and the other prophets, who say they will shortly return to Jerusalem. He declares that, in accordance with God's plans and purposes, they will be in Babylon for seventy years. He further declares that God is about to bring the sword, famine and plague against the land of Judah.

Jeremiah 30 is a prophecy relating to the restoration of Israel. The nations among whom the Israelites will be scattered will eventually be destroyed. God will discipline the people of Israel and

Judah, and, although they will experience difficult times, (described as the time of trouble when there is fear and no peace), God will bring them back to the land He promised their fore-fathers. There they will serve God, and the Davidic king, whom God will raise up.

Jeremiah 31 continues the prophecy relating to the end time restoration of Israel. God proclaims that the descendants of Israel will never cease to be a nation before Him. He will bring back the Israelites from the land of the north, and from the ends of the earth, where they have been scattered. God declares that He will make a new covenant with Israel, and His law will be written on their hearts. They will all know Him, and God will forgive their wickedness, and remember their sin no more.

Jeremiah 32 records how Jeremiah buys some land from his cousin, despite the fact that the Babylonians have surrounded Jerusalem and are about to devastate the city, and take the Israelites into captivity. God declares that these disasters have occurred because of their sins and the sins of their ancestors. God also declares that He will bring the Israelites back, and that they will again buy and sell land. God will make a new everlasting covenant with His people.

Jeremiah 33 records another prophecy, in which God declares that Jerusalem will be devastated by the Babylonians, but that He will bring back Israel and Judah from their captivity, and restore the fortunes of the land. God reaffirms His promise that He will raise up a righteous leader from the line of David who will be called 'The Lord our Righteousness'. God declares that His covenants and promises are as certain and as unchanging as the physical laws that govern the universe.

Jeremiah 34 records a prophecy, given when Judea was being invaded by the Babylonians, in which God declares that Jerusalem will be defeated, and King Zedekiah taken into captivity. God rebukes the Israelites for enslaving fellow Israelites, despite saying they would not do this. They have broken covenant with God, and, as a consequence, they will be handed over to their enemies.

In Jeremiah 35, the Recabites are praised for faithfully following the commands of their fore-fathers to not drink and to lead a nomadic lifestyle. God contrasts their faithfulness to Israel's unfaithfulness in not obeying God, despite the fact that God has spoken to them many times through the prophets.

In Jeremiah 36, God instructs Jeremiah to write on a scroll all the prophecies he has received, concerning the disasters which will come upon Israel. Jeremiah dictates the prophecies to Baruch, who then reads them in the temple. When the temple officials read the scroll to King Jehoiakim, he burns the scroll, and orders that Jeremiah be arrested. Jeremiah, however, who is in hiding, re-writes the scroll, and condemns King Jehoiakim for his actions.

Jeremiah 37 records that, during the reign of King Zedekiah, the Babylonians, who were attacking Jerusalem, withdrew for a time, when the Egyptian army marched against them. Jeremiah, however, prophesies that the Babylonians will return and destroy the city. Jeremiah is accused of trying to desert to the Babylonians, and is arrested, beaten and imprisoned in a dungeon for a long time, before the king allows him to be kept under guard in the prison courtyard.

In Jeremiah 38, Jeremiah is imprisoned in a muddy well for speaking out the words of the Lord that the Babylonians will defeat Jerusalem, and that those who stay in the city will die by the sword, famine or plague. King Zedekiah allows Jeremiah to be rescued. In a secret meeting with the king, Jeremiah tells him that he and his family will be spared, and Jerusalem not destroyed if he surrenders to the Babylonians. The king, however, is too fearful of the Jews to do this.

Jeremiah 39 records how Jerusalem fell to the Babylonians, following a siege which lasted eighteen months. King Zedekiah tries to escape, but is captured. His children are killed, and he is blinded and taken into captivity, along with the people who have stayed in Jerusalem. The Babylonians set fire to the buildings and break down the city walls. Jeremiah is freed by the Babylonians, in accordance with the word of the Lord, because he has put his trust in God.

In Jeremiah 40, Jeremiah is given the choice to either go into exile in Babylon, or to stay in Judah with Gedaliah, whom the Babylonians have appointed as governor. When they hear that the Babylonians have allowed a remnant to stay in the land, some of the Jews, who fled into other nations, return to Judah. Although warned that Ishmael (one of his army officers), is planning to kill him, Gedaliah does not believe it, and takes no action against him.

Jeremiah 41 records how Ishmael assassinates Gedaliah, whom the Babylonians had appointed as governor over Judah. Ishmael also slaughters a number of Jews who have come to worship God, and takes captive the people who are with Gedaliah in Mizpah. Johanan and the other army officers rescue the captives, and decide to flee to Egypt, because they are afraid of what the Babylonians will do, because Gedaliah has been killed. Ishmael and his followers escape, and set out to join the Ammonites.

In Jeremiah 42, the remnant of Judah, led by Johanan, ask Jeremiah to seek guidance from God on their behalf. They are proposing to flee to Egypt, in fear of what the Babylonians will do in response to the assassination of Gedaliah. They claim they will obey whatever God says to them. God declares that they should stay in Judah where he will protect them and build them up. If they flee to Egypt disaster will overtake them and they will die by the sword, famine or plague.

In Jeremiah 43, the remnant, led by Johanan, reject what God has said through Jeremiah, and go to Egypt, taking Jeremiah with them. In Egypt, Jeremiah prophesies that the Babylonians, led by King Nebuchadnezzar, will attack and overcome Egypt, and that many people will die or be taken into captivity.

Jeremiah 44 records how the remnant, who have fled from Judah to Egypt, continue to worship false gods, and burn incense and make offerings to the Queen of Heaven. They refuse to listen to the warnings given them through Jeremiah. God declares that the disasters, which came upon Judah and Jerusalem, will also come upon them, and only a few fugitives will survive. The Pharaoh of Egypt, like King Zedekiah, will be defeated by the Babylonians.

Jeremiah 45 records a short personal prophecy, given through Jeremiah for the prophet Baruch. God encourages Baruch not to despair, even though He is about to bring disaster upon the Israelites. God declares that He will let Baruch escape with his life.

Jeremiah 46 is a prophecy, recorded in about 604 BC, declaring that Egypt will be defeated by the Babylonians, led by King Nebuchadnezzar. (The Babylonians initially attacked Egypt in about 601 BC and subsequently completely defeated Egypt in a later invasion in about 570 BC.) God declares that, although the nations where the Israelites have scattered to will be defeated, He will save the Israelites, and not destroy them.

Jeremiah 47 records a prophecy against the Philistines, who occupy the coastal strip between Judah and the Mediterranean Sea. God declares that they will invaded by a nation from the north (Babylon), and that the major cities of Gaza and Ashkelon will be defeated.

Jeremiah 48 records a prophecy about Moab, a country located to the east of Judah, but separated from Judah by the Dead Sea. (Part of present day Jordan.) Moab and all her fortified towns and cities will be defeated, and her false god, Chemosh, will not be able to save her. This will happen because of Moab's pride and arrogance, and because she ridiculed Israel. In later times God declares that the fortunes of Moab will be restored.

Jeremiah 49 records prophecies concerning a number of the nations which border Judah and Israel. God declares through Jeremiah that Ammon, Edom, Elam, Hazor and Arum (Damascus) will all be invaded and overcome. These nations eventually were all absorbed into the Babylonian empire.

Jeremiah 50 records a prophecy concerning Babylon. Although God has used Babylon as an instrument of judgement upon Israel, Babylon herself will be defeated by a nation from the north, and her gods put to shame. (This prophecy was fulfilled with the invasion and defeat of the Babylonians by the Medes and Persians in about 540BC.) God declares that He will restore the Israelites, who have been taken captive into Babylon, back to their land.

Jeremiah 51 is a continuation of a prophecy against Babylon. God declares that Babylon and the spiritual powers behind her will ultimately be destroyed. We read of this final fulfilment in Revelation 17-19. (Spiritually Babylon can be considered to represent the kingdom of darkness, opposed to God's kingdom. Through sin and idolatry, Israel submitted to the ruling spiritual powers behind Babylon, which led to her eventually being taken into captivity in the physical kingdom of Babylon.)

Jeremiah 52 describes how the Babylonians lay siege to Jerusalem, and eventually defeat the city and take King Zedekiah into captivity. The temple is destroyed by fire and the city walls broken down. The consecrated temple furnishings and utensils, used in the worship of God, are taken away to Babylon. Over 4,600 Israelites are also taken into exile in Babylon. After thirty-seven years in exile King Jehoiachin finds favour with King Evil-Merodach, and is released from prison.

Lamentations

The Book of Lamentations is a series of five poems written by the prophet Jeremiah, expressing grief over the fall of Jerusalem.

In chapter 1, Jerusalem is personified as a destitute widow in mourning. She has been overcome by her enemies, feels abandoned by her friends, all her treasures have been removed, and there is no one to comfort her. The Lord brought this about because of her sin and rebellion, and she has now become unclean, and an object of scorn among the nations.

In Lamentations 2, what has happened to Jerusalem is clearly portrayed as an act of judgement of God against the people of Israel, because of their sin and rebellion. God has removed His protection and allowed her enemies to triumph over her. The surviving citizens of Jerusalem are now in deep mourning and distress, but have no one to comfort them.

In Lamentations 3:1-23, Jeremiah identifies with what has happened to the Israelites, following the fall of Jerusalem. He declares that he has experienced what it is like to feel abandoned by God and depressed. He knows what it is like to feel as though you are walking in darkness. He knows what it is like to endure the ridicule of others. However, he encourages himself by remembering God's compassion and faithfulness, and His desire to bring restoration.

In Lamentations 3:24-66, Jeremiah continues to identify with what has happened to Israel. He declares that he will wait upon the Lord, and put his trust in Him. We have no right to be angry with God when we suffer the consequences of our sins. When we cry out to God, He is able to rescue us, just as he rescued Jeremiah when he was being oppressed by his enemies.

Lamentations 4 records the horrors which have come upon the people of Jerusalem. They were considered rich and of value, but are now destitute. They are starving to the point where some have become cannibalistic. Her princes and rulers are no longer recognisable. Her prophets and priests are defiled, and like blind men. Edom too will be punished. Despite all these calamities, there is hope, and there will be an end to the suffering being experienced by the Israelites.

Lamentations 5 summarises what has happened to the Israelites as a consequence of their sins. Their inheritance has been given over to foreigners, and they have become like orphans. They are like slaves, and the barest necessities of life are difficult to obtain. Their women have been abused, and their leaders humbled. They have lost their joy, and their dancing has turned to mourning. The Book of

Lamentations finishes with a prayer asking God to restore the Israelites to Himself.

Ezekiel

The Book of Ezekiel records the words of the prophet Ezekiel, spoken out during the period 600-570 BC, to the exiles who had been deported to Babylon.

Ezekiel Chapters 1 and 2 record Ezekiel's vision of heaven, and magnificent celestial creatures, surrounding the throne of God. God speaks to Ezekiel, and commissions him as a prophet to the rebellious people. He instructs Ezekiel not to be afraid of the people, and to speak out boldly, whether the people listen or ignore him.

Ezekiel 3 continues the account of God's commissioning of Ezekiel as a prophet. In vision, Ezekiel sees himself feeding on the words of God written on a scroll. The words are sweet to those who obey God, but bitter to those with hardened hearts. Ezekiel is to be a watchman for the house of Israel. If Ezekiel fails to warn them, he will be held responsible, but the people themselves will be held responsible, if they ignore his words. God will open his mouth, and show him what, and when, to speak.

In Ezekiel 4, the prophet is told to act out what will happen to Jerusalem, when the city is attacked. He is to lie on one side for 390 days (representing the 390 years of Israel's rebellion and sinfulness, since the division of Israel, upon the death of King Solomon). He is then to lie on the other side for a further 40 days, (representing the forty years of Solomon's reign, following the death of King David). He is to eat and drink only a limited amount, to represent the famine which will come upon Jerusalem.

In Ezekiel 5, God instructs the prophet to shave his hair and beard. He burns a third of the shavings in a fire, strikes another third with his sword, and a third he scatters into the wind. God declares that is what will happen to the people of Jerusalem, because of their rebellion and idolatry. Jerusalem will become an object of reproach and horror. A third of the people will die of plague and famine, a third will die by the sword, and a third will be scattered into the nations.

Ezekiel 6 is a prophecy rebuking Israel for her idolatry and detestable practices, and declaring that God is about to bring His judgement upon her. Her altars and places of false worship will be destroyed. Her towns will be laid waste. Many of her inhabitants will die of plague or famine, or by the sword, and many will be scattered among the nations. When this happens, the people will know they are experiencing the judgement of God.

Ezekiel 7 is another prophecy declaring that God is about to bring judgement upon Israel, because of her conduct and detestable practices. Calamity and disaster will come upon the nation. People will die by plague, famine and the sword. Their silver and gold will not be able to save them, and they will be plundered by foreigners. Even God's temple will be desecrated, and its treasures stolen. God declares that, when these things happen, the people will know that He is the Lord.

Ezekiel 8 and 9 record a vision in which the prophet is shown why judgement is about to come upon Jerusalem. He is shown an idol which has been placed in the inner court, elders secretly worshipping idols, a woman engaged in the ritual mourning of Tammuz (a Babylonian god), and men worshipping the sun. In vision, he sees those who lament for what is happening being given a mark on their forehead, and death being given rights over all those who don't have such a mark.

In Ezekiel 10, Ezekiel once more sees a vision of the celestial cherubim surrounding the throne and the glory of God. He describes these cherubim as having four faces, and standing next to whirling wheels. A figure in linen is instructed to take fire from amongst the cherubim and scatter it over Jerusalem. As Ezekiel watches, he sees the cherubim and the glory of God slowly leave the temple.

Ezekiel 11 is a continuation of Ezekiel's vision, in which he is shown the leaders of Jerusalem plotting evil and thinking they are safe and secure. In his vision, Ezekiel is told to prophesy to them that they are not safe, that Jerusalem will fall, and they will die or be scattered among the nations. God encourages Ezekiel by saying that He will bring the Israelites back to the land, and give them a new heart of flesh. The vision concludes with God's glory departing from Jerusalem.

In Ezekiel 12, God instructs the prophet to act out what will happen to the inhabitants of Jerusalem as the city falls, and they and their king are taken into exile. The king will be brought to Babylon, but will not see it. (Fulfilled when the Babylonians captured and blinded King Zedekiah.) Through Ezekiel God rebukes those who refuse to heed the warnings, and declares that the many prophecies about what will happen to Israel and Jerusalem are about to be fulfilled.

In Ezekiel 13, God rebukes the prophets who are speaking out of their own imagination and false visions. They are building flimsy walls without foundations, and hiding their frailty by covering them with whitewash. God will destroy these false walls and the prophets who build them. God also rebukes those who practise divination and magic. They bring death to those who listen to their lies. God declares that He is against them, and will save the people from their hands.

In Ezekiel 14, God rebukes those who practise idolatry and detestable practices but claim to be prophets of God, or seek guidance from God. If they do not repent, God will turn His face against them, and allow them to be deluded, and suffer the consequences of their self-deception. If God brings judgement against a country which has sinned against Him, the righteous in that country will not be able to save the unrighteous from God's judgement, even though they themselves may be saved.

In Ezekiel 15, the people of Jerusalem are compared to the wood of the vine. This wood is only suitable for burning, and is no use to the carpenter. If the wood has been partially burnt and charred in a fire, it has even less use. God declares that He is against the people living in Jerusalem, and even those who escape from there will not escape His judgement.

In Ezekiel 16, Israel is compared to an abandoned child, adopted by God and given many gifts. She grows very beautiful, but uses her beauty to attract the surrounding nations. She becomes worse than a prostitute with them, engaging in their idolatrous practices, including child sacrifice. God will bring judgement upon her, and she will become an object of shame and disgrace. Even so God will not cast her away, but will make atonement for her and renew His everlasting covenant with her.

Ezekiel 17 is a prophetic parable. Babylon (a great eagle) takes the top of a great cedar (King Jehoiakim and the first group of exiles) to a new land (Babylon) and plants a new vine (King Zedekiah) in the land. This new vine, however, seeks after another eagle (Egypt). God declares that this rebellion will be punished, and that King Zedekiah will be exiled to Babylon. God declares that He will plant a cutting in Israel which will grow into a great tree, and will be a shelter for all nations.

Ezekiel 18 is a rebuttal of the fatalistic viewpoint that children automatically have to bear the guilt and punishment for the sins of their father. (This chapter refers to bearing the punishment for sins, rather than bearing the consequences of sin.) God declares that the unrighteous will die for their own sins, but those who choose to live in righteousness and repent of any unrighteousness will live. Each individual will be judged on the basis of their own behaviour.

Ezekiel 19 is a lament concerning some of the recent kings of Israel, who are described as lion cubs who become lions. On the death of King Josiah, his son King Jehoahaz only reigns a short time in Jerusalem, before he is dethroned by the King of Egypt. His brother,

King Jehoiakim, becomes king, but is taken into exile in Babylon by King Nebuchadnezzar. King Zedekiah is uprooted, and also taken into a dry and thirsty land (Babylon), and there is now no king to rule over Israel.

In Ezekiel 20, God, through the prophet, recounts to the elders of the exiles in Babylon how He has been faithful towards the Israelites, despite their continual rejection of, and rebellion towards, Him. Even though God revealed Himself to them and led them out of captivity in Egypt, they have continued in their idolatry. God declares that He will re-gather the Israelites from all the nations where they have been scattered, and, through this, will show Himself holy in the sight of all the nations.

Ezekiel 21 is a prophecy against Judah and Jerusalem, in which God's judgement against her is likened to a sharpened sword, which God has drawn from its scabbard. God will use Babylon to wield this sword against both the Israelites and the Ammonites. Jerusalem and her king will come under siege, and be defeated. False visions and lying divinations will not save the Ammonites from God's judgement.

Ezekiel 22 is a prophecy giving the reasons why Jerusalem has brought judgement upon herself. Her inhabitants have engaged in idolatry and immorality. Her leaders have shed innocent blood, and oppressed the weak. Her priests have despised the holy things of God, and desecrated the Sabbaths. Her prophets have whitewashed what is happening with false visions and lying divinations. The house of Israel has become like dross, and God is about to refine her with His fire.

In Ezekiel 23, the idolatrous behaviour of the northern kingdom (Israel) and Judah is likened to two sisters, who become prostitutes and lust after men, from the time they are in captivity in Egypt. Even when one sister (Israel) is handed over to the Assyrians, the other sister (Judah) continues to lust after Assyria and Babylonia, and defiles herself with their idols, to whom she even sacrifices her children. Because of her sins, she will receive the punishment she deserves.

Ezekiel 24 records a prophecy made on the day that the Babylonians lay siege to Jerusalem. Jerusalem is compared to a cooking pot, the contents of which will be boiled and eventually discarded. The pot itself will then be burnt with fire to remove all the encrusted deposits. Ezekiel's wife dies, but God instructs him not to publicly mourn for her, as a sign to the people how they should respond when they hear that Jerusalem has fallen.

Ezekiel 25 is a prophecy against the nations who have been

enemies of Israel. Because the Ammonites and Moabites rejoiced at the demise of Israel, they too will be defeated by the Babylonians. Because the Edomites and Philistines took revenge against Israel, God will bring His vengeance against them, and their lands will be laid waste.

Ezekiel 26 is a prophecy against the highly fortified coastal city of Tyre. Because she boasted that she would prosper as a result of the fall of Jerusalem, she will become plunder for the nations, and be attacked by the Babylonians. Her walls will be pulled down and the city plundered. (The Babylonians captured the city of Tyre in 572 BC, following a siege that lasted thirteen years.)

Ezekiel 27 is a lament for the city of Tyre. Tyre was a great trading port, and is likened to a splendid sailing ship constructed from the finest materials, and trading with all the nations of the world. This ship, however, will be shipwrecked, and all her wealth will be lost. The other nations will be appalled at what happens to Tyre.

Ezekiel 28 is a prophecy proclaiming that Tyre will be destroyed because, in amassing great wealth, she has become proud and declared herself to be like a god. The prophecy addresses the spiritual power behind Tyre (Satan), describing him as a guardian cherub who became proud and corrupt. He was expelled from heaven, and, one day, will be destroyed by fire. God declares that He will gather the Israelites from where they have been scattered, and they will live peacefully in the land.

Ezekiel 29 is a prophecy against Egypt, likening her to a great fish, which God will catch and destroy. Egypt is also likened to a staff made of reed, which broke, and failed to support Israel when she needed help. For forty years the land will be desolate, and Egypt will become a lowly kingdom. (The Babylonians invaded Egypt in about 572 BC.)

Ezekiel 30 records a prophecy against Egypt. God declares that the Babylonians will invade Egypt and the surrounding nations. Egypt will be laid waste, and the people will be scattered among the nations.

Ezekiel 31 is a lament concerning Egypt. Egypt is likened to a splendid tree which will be brought low, just as Assyria was, when attacked and overcome by the Babylonians. (This happened in about 612 BC when the Babylonians besieged and conquered Nineveh.)

Ezekiel 32 is a prophecy in which Egypt is likened to a lion, or a great sea monster. God declares that He will bring about her destruction by bringing the sword of the Babylonians against her. Her fate will be the same as those of all the uncircumcised nations such as Assyria, Edom, Sidon and Elam.

In Ezekiel 33, God declares that, if the watchman (Ezekiel) warns the people, but they ignore the warning, then they will be held accountable. If he fails to warn the people, the watchman will bear responsibility for what happens to them. God declares that the people listen to the prophets, but ignore what they say. Former righteousness will not save someone who becomes rebellious and disobedient, but the unrighteous who repent and turn from their wicked ways will be saved.

Ezekiel 34 starts with a rebuke to the shepherds (leaders and priests), who have been self-centred, and have failed the people by treating them harshly, and not looking after the weak and helpless. God declares that He will become the good shepherd. He will gather the scattered flock, and He will tend them and protect them. He will judge those who abuse and take advantage of others. The people will become the sheep of His pasture, and He will be their God.

Ezekiel 35 is a prophecy against Mount Seir (Edom). Because the Edomites have been hostile towards Israel and coveted the Promised Land for themselves, God declares that many will be killed by the sword, and that their country will become desolate. They will be judged for speaking out contemptible things about Israel and rejoicing in her downfall.

Ezekiel 36 is a prophecy about the restoration of Israel. God declares that He will restore Israel for the sake of His holy name. The surrounding nations who have scorned Israel will themselves become objects of scorn. God will gather the Israelites from all the nations where they have been scattered, and will re-establish them in the land. The desolate land will become fertile and prosperous. The surrounding nations will be amazed, and recognise that God has brought this about.

Ezekiel 37 is a continuation of the end-times prophecy about the restoration of Israel. In vision, Ezekiel sees the sovereign Lord bring a pile of dry bones back to life. God declares that He will bring the Israelites back to the land. He instructs Ezekiel to bind two sticks together to symbolise that the northern (Ephraim) and southern (Judah) tribes of Israel will be reunited as one nation, living in the land of Israel. They will live in peace as God's people, and God will be their shepherd.

Ezekiel 38 is an end-times prophecy declaring that the nations of the world, led by Gog and Magog (barbaric northern nations), will rise up against the restored nation of Israel. They will attack Israel, but God will intervene. The prophecy speaks of a great earthquake occurring, and torrents of rain, hailstones and burning sulphur being poured out upon the enemies of Israel.

Ezekiel 39 is a continuation of the end-times prophecy, relating to the outpouring of God's judgement upon the nations of the world who rise up to attack Israel. Their armies will be completely destroyed, and Israel will spend many months burying the dead. Israel will use the weapons and resources, which have been arrayed against them, as fuel. The restoration of Israel, and the defeat of her enemies, will be a sign of God's sovereignty to the people and nations of the world.

Ezekiel 40 records a vision experienced by Ezekiel, while in exile in Babylon, in which he is shown the details of a new temple. Many commentators consider that the vision describes a temple which should have been built when the exiles returned to Jerusalem. Some commentators consider that this is a vision of a millennial temple, yet to be built.

Ezekiel 41 is a continuation of the prophet's vision of a new temple in Jerusalem. Detailed dimensions of the doors, walls, courtyards and rooms are recorded. The walls are decorated with carvings of cherubim and palms.

In Ezekiel 42, the prophet continues to record detailed dimensions of the new temple, shown to him in vision. The layout and size of the rooms and galleries to be used by the priests are documented.

Ezekiel 43 is a continuation of Ezekiel's vision of the new temple. He records how, in vision, he sees the glory of God return to the temple. (A reversal of what he saw, in vision, before the fall of Jerusalem, recorded in chapters 10 and 11.) Detailed dimensions of the altar are given, together with details of the sacrifices to be offered on the altar, in recognition of man's sinfulness, compared to God's holiness.

Ezekiel 44 continues the record of Ezekiel's vision of the new temple. God declares that the Israelites must not defile the temple by bringing in unbelieving foreigners. The Levites who served false gods are not to be allowed to serve as priests in the new temple. Only the descendants of Zadok the priest, who remained faithful, are to serve in the sanctuary. They are to consecrate themselves to God, and observe various regulations to keep themselves holy, and so avoid defilement.

Ezekiel 45 documents instructions regarding allocation of land to the priests, and details of the worship and sacrifices to be offered in the new temple. The people are to give offerings based on honest and accurate scales. The king of Israel is to provide the sin offerings.

Ezekiel 46 continues to document instructions regarding

worship and sacrifices to be offered in the new temple. (Perhaps these are best viewed as sacrifices to be offered before the coming of the Messiah, or as memorial sacrifices, offered as a reminder of what Jesus did for us at Calvary.)

Ezekiel 47 continues Ezekiel's vision of the new temple, in which he sees a stream of water flowing out from the temple. This stream of water becomes a wide river, feeding into the dead sea, and bringing life and fertility to the land through which it flows.

Ezekiel 48, which is the final chapter of this book, records instructions for the allocation of the land around the new temple to the tribes of Israel and the priests. The Israelites failed to obey God's original covenant, and, as a consequence, were overcome by their enemies and scattered among the nations. God, however, will restore them to the land, and His presence will be with them.

Daniel

The book of Daniel (written in the period 600-530 BC) includes prophecies fulfilled in Daniel's own life time, as well as prophecies covering the whole of history.

Chapter 1 records how a temporary dispensation, enabling Daniel, Shadrach, Meshach and Abednego, (Jewish exiles being trained to serve the king of Babylon), not to defile themselves by eating food from the king's table, is made permanent when they are found to be healthier and better nourished than the other trainees.

Daniel 2 records how King Nebuchadnezzar of Babylon is troubled by a dream, in which he sees a statue, made of four materials, being destroyed by a large rock. God shows this same dream to Daniel, and gives him the interpretation that the rock represents the kingdom of God, which will replace four earthly empires (Assyrian, Persian, Grecian and Roman), represented by the statue. As a result, Daniel, Meshach, Shadrach and Abednego are given high ranks in the Babylonian court.

In Daniel 3, Meshach, Shadrach and Abednego defy King Nebuchadnezzar by refusing to bow down and worship the golden image which he has had made. They tell the king that their God is able to protect them, but, even if they have to die, they will not bow down to false idols. They are thrown into a blazing furnace, but are unharmed. When the king sees this, he issues a decree declaring that anyone who says anything against the God of Israel will be killed.

Daniel 4 records how Daniel interprets King Nebuchnezzar's dream of a messenger from heaven, ordering that a large tree be cut down until only the stump remains. Daniel tells the king that he will lose his kingdom and become like a wild animal. The interpretation is fulfilled when the king, whilst declaring his own greatness and power, has a mental breakdown. King Nebuchnezzar's sanity is only restored after he acknowledges the sovereignty of God.

Daniel 5 records how a hand-written message suddenly appears on the wall, while King Belshazzar (the son of Nebuchadnezzar) is holding a banquet, praising idols and drinking wine from goblets taken from the temple in Jerusalem. Daniel is able to interpret the message, and declares that King Belshazzar has been judged and found wanting, and that his kingdom will be taken away. That same night Belshazzar is killed and Darius the Mede takes over the Babylonian empire.

Daniel 6 records how the leaders in Babylon, who are jealous of Daniel, persuade King Darius to issue an unchangeable decree that worship of anyone other than the king will result in death. Because Daniel continues to worship God, he is thrown into the lion's den, but God protects him and he is unharmed. Darius has the leaders who plotted against Daniel thrown to the lions, (who immediately kill them), and issues a further decree that everyone must fear and reverence the God of Daniel.

Daniel 7 records a vision of four great beasts, and one like the son of man, given all power, authority and an everlasting kingdom. The four beasts, (lion, bear, leopard and a multi-horned beast), represent earthly empires, and the horns refer to kings or kingdoms within these empires. The horn which arises out of the fourth empire, (overthrowing three other horns), and opposes the saints, seems to refer to the end-times, demonically empowered, kingdom of the antichrist, the man of lawlessness.

Daniel 8 records a prophetic vision of a battle between a ram, (representing the Medes and Persians), and a goat, (representing the Greek empire under Alexander the Great which later split into four power blocks), out of which arises an antichrist kingdom. Although this vision can be seen to be fulfilled in 136 BC, when the temple in Jerusalem was desecrated by Antiochus Epiphanes, most commentators consider this prophecy will only be fully fulfilled during the end times, before Jesus returns.

In Daniel 9, we read how the prophet prays to God, confessing the sins of the Israelites in breaking the covenant, and not listening to the prophets. While praying, Daniel is given a message by the angel Gabriel, which talks about two time periods of sixty-nine sevens, (483 years between the decree to rebuild the temple and the coming of the anointed one), and a period of one seven (seven years, during which worship of God is stopped and replaced by some sort of abomination.)

In Daniel 10, Daniel is visited by an angelic messenger. Daniel had been fasting and praying for three weeks before the angelic messenger appeared and declared that he had been delayed by spiritual opposition (the Prince of Persia), until he received help from Michael (an archangel described as Israel's Prince). Daniel is overcome by the presence of the angel, but the angel touches him and encourages him to be strong.

Daniel 11 records the revelation given to Daniel by an angelic messenger. The Grecian empire will eventually divide into four regions. There will be a series of conflicts between the king of the north and king of the south, during which the land of Israel will be occupied. The king of the north will magnify himself over all, and will blaspheme against God. He and his armies will be destroyed between the sea and the holy mountain (Armageddon).

Daniel 12 concludes the prophecy given to Daniel by the angelic messenger. There will be a time of unprecedented turmoil. Daniel's people will be delivered, after which, those who have died will be raised and judged; some to everlasting life, and some to everlasting punishment. The time periods over which these events will happen, and the description of the setting up of the abomination which causes desolation, are similar to those found in the Book of Revelation, but the exact interpretation is unclear.

Hosea

The Book of Hosea, written in about 750-720 BC to the northern kingdom of Israel, likens the apostasy of Israel to spiritual adultery. In Chapter 1, as a prophetic or allegorical message, God instructs Hosea to marry a promiscuous woman named Gomer, who bears him three children. The names given to these children mean 'scattered', 'not loved' and 'not my people'. Eventually Judah and Israel will come together, and the people will be called 'children of the living God'.

In Hosea 2, Israel is likened to an adulteress, who has left God and conceived children, fathered by Baal. She has not acknowledged that God is the one who provides for her, and blesses her. God declares that she will be punished for her actions, but that eventually He will allure her back to Himself. God will renew His covenant with her, and betroth Himself to her forever. She will be planted in the land, enjoy the peace and blessings of the Lord, and know that He is her God.

Hosea 3 records how the prophet was instructed to treat his wife as God would treat Israel, by re-purchasing his wife, who had left him and prostituted herself with other lovers. The Israelites will experience a time without leadership, separated from God, and without the sacrificial system, until they return to the Lord in the last days.

Hosea 4 is a rebuke to the northern kingdom of Israel, declaring there is no acknowledgement of God in the land. The people have turned to idolatry, and are being destroyed for lack of knowledge. They have prostituted themselves to false gods and wooden idols, and, as a result, will bring shame upon themselves, and be swept away. Judah is warned not to join with Israel in her stubbornness and rebellion.

Hosea 5 is another rebuke to the priests and people of the northern kingdom of Israel (sometimes referred to as Ephraim). They have become unfaithful to God, and there is a spirit of prostitution, (idolatry), in their hearts. They have turned to Assyria for help, but she cannot cure them. God will bring judgement on Israel and Judah, until they admit their guilt and turn back to Him, and He is likened to a lion attacking its prey.

Hosea 6 is a call to the people of Israel to turn back to God, who is able to bind up their wounds and heal them. Acknowledging Him, and being merciful to others, is far more important to God than their sacrifices and offerings. They have defiled themselves with prostitution, (idolatry). Like Adam, both Israel and Judah have broken

God's covenants, and been unfaithful to Him.

In Hosea 7, the wickedness of Israel is likened to a burning fire which does not have to be stoked. She is arrogant, full of lies and deceit, and has rebelled against God. Instead of crying out to God, she turns to Egypt and Assyria for help. Israel slanders God, who trained and strengthened her in the past, and, as a result, her leaders will perish by the sword.

In Hosea 8 God declares that, by rebelling against Him, Israel has sown the wind, but will reap the whirlwind. The Israelites have chosen their leaders without consulting God, and have angered Him by making a golden idol in the form of a statue of a calf (1 Kings 12:28). Their places of worship have become places of idolatry and sin. As a consequence, they will be punished, and become as they were before God brought them out of captivity in Egypt.

In Hosea 9, God declares that Israel has been unfaithful to Him, and, as a consequence, will face poverty and famine, and will not remain in the land. Israel has behaved as she did in the wilderness at Baal Peor, where she engaged in immorality and worshipped the Moabite gods. Israel's roots in God have withered, and so she will become unfruitful, barren, and a nomad among the nations.

In Hosea 10, God continues to declare through the prophet that Israel will reap the results of her own wickedness. Instead of reaping the fruit of God's unfailing love, the Israelites have hardened their hearts, and have reaped evil. Israel's places of worship will be destroyed, and her golden idols will be taken by the Assyrians. Because she has trusted in her own strength, her army will be defeated in battle, and her king will be destroyed.

In Hosea 11, God expresses His love and compassion towards His chosen people. He desires to be a father to them, but they have not recognised His divine leading and protection, and have rebelled against Him. God will not completely destroy them. Eventually they will acknowledge Him, and return with trembling, and He will settle them in the land.

In Hosea 12, God declares that Israel has abandoned Him and sought security from earthly kingdoms. Her merchants use dishonest scales and boast about their wealth. Israel has provoked God to anger, and she will reap the consequences. By exiling them from the land, God will cause the Israelites to live in tents, as in the wilderness years, before He brought them into the Promised Land.

In Hosea 13, God declares that Israel will suffer the consequences of her rebellion, idolatry and sin. Her fate is likened to an attack by a ferocious wild animal. The once-proud Israel will become like the disappearing morning mist and dew. The people of Israel will fall by the sword, and their treasures and storehouses will be plundered.

Hosea 14 concludes this book of the Bible with a call to Israel to repent and return to God. When she turns from her idolatry and recognises her need of God, He will freely love and heal her. When Israel walks in the way of righteousness she will flourish and be fruitful.

Joel

The Book of Joel is thought to have been written about 600 BC, probably before the Babylonian invasion of Israel or shortly afterwards.

In Chapter 1, God's judgement is likened to a plague of locusts, completely devouring the crops, and causing famine and ruin. The people will lose their joy, and there will be no offerings to support those who minister to God. Joel calls the people to repent, fast and cry out to the Lord for deliverance from His coming judgement, referred to as the 'day of the Lord'.

Joel 2 declares that the day of the Lord is near. The Lord's army is compared to a raging fire, burning up everything before it, and breaking through every defence it encounters. Joel calls to the Israelites to repent, so God will delay in bringing judgement upon them. If they return to Him, they will prosper, and God will pour His Holy Spirit upon them. When final judgement comes there will be signs in the heavens and on the earth, but all who call on the name of the Lord will be saved.

Joel 3 proclaims what will happen to the nations opposing Israel in his day, and looks ahead to the end times, when all the nations of the world opposed to God and the restored nation of Israel will be judged. (The same demonic powers are operating through these nations). The Lord will be a refuge for believers, and His reign in Israel and Jerusalem will be firmly established. A river of water will flow from Jerusalem, bringing life and prosperity to the land.

Amos

Written in about 760 BC, the book of Amos reminds us of the universal justice of God, requiring that everyone will, one day, be judged by God. In Chapter 1, God declares, through Amos, that He will send judgement (fire) upon Syria, Tyre, Philistia, Ammon and Edom, and upon the cities in these nations. This will happen because they have not been compassionate to other nations, but have treated them with brutality and cruelty.

In Amos 2, the prophet declares that God will judge Moab for the way in which she treated Edom. Judah will be judged, because she has rejected the law of God, and entered into idolatry. Israel will be judged, because she oppresses the poor, and profanes God's name through her immorality. Israel orders God's prophets not to speak, and forces the Nazirites to break their vows, made before God. All will suffer disaster, and will be unable to save themselves from God's wrath.

In Amos 3, the prophet declares that God has given His warnings, and is now about to bring judgement upon Israel. An enemy will overrun the land, overcoming their fortresses and plundering their cities. Their houses will be torn down, and the altar at Bethel, (where King Jeroboam had set up an idol of a golden calf), will be destroyed. Only a remnant of those living in Israel will be spared.

In Amos 4, the prophet continues to decry the actions of the northern kingdom of Israel. The people oppress the poor and needy, yet boast about their tithes and the sacrifices which they make before false idols at Bethel and Gilgal. Although they experienced famines, plagues and war, they did not repent of their sins and return to God. Therefore, declares the prophet, the people need to prepare to face their maker - almighty God.

In Amos 5, God calls the people of Israel to repent, and to abandon their worship of false idols and seek Him, so that they might live. They oppress the poor and deny them justice. They tell lies and take bribes, and are living in evil days. God declares that, because of their unrighteous actions, He hates their false religiosity and meaningless false worship, and that darkness will engulf them. Disaster upon disaster will come upon them, and they will be sent into exile beyond Damascus.

Amos 6 is addressed to the complacent and self-indulgent rich of both Israel and Judah, who enjoy the good life, but ignore the plight of the poor and needy. They ignore the fate which has come upon other nations, and are living in the false security of their own self-righteousness. God declares that disaster will come upon them, and that they will be among the first to be taken into exile.

In Amos 7, the prophet sees, in vision, that God's judgement will be like a plague of locusts, or fire, coming upon the land. God declares that He is about to judge Israel against the plumb line of His truth. Also, Amaziah, the priest, rebukes Amos, and tells him to stop prophesying, to leave Israel, and to earn his living in Judah. Amos responds by saying he is merely a shepherd, obediently speaking out what God has said, and that Amaziah and Israel will be taken into exile.

In Amos 8, God declares, through the prophet, that the people of Israel are like a basket of ripe fruit, ready for inspection. They will be judged, because they have oppressed and cheated the poor, and despised the Sabbath, because it interferes with their goal of gaining wealth at the expense of others. This judgement is likened to darkness covering the earth. Their religious feasts will be turned into mourning, their singing turned into weeping, and there will be a famine of hearing God's word.

In Amos 9, the Lord, speaking through Amos, declares that no one will escape the judgement of God. The sins of Israel will be judged, just as the sins of the other nations. In the final verses of the book of Amos, God declares that, at a future time, He will bring back His exiled people to their own land. They will live in prosperity in the land, and will never be uprooted from it.

Obadiah

Believed to have been written in about 560 BC, the book of Obadiah declares that nations like Edom, who oppose Israel, will be judged, but that God's people will be restored, and inherit the kingdom of God. Edom will be punished for gloating over what has happened to Jerusalem and Judah. She will be completely destroyed, as if she had never existed. The house of Jacob (Israel), however, will be re-established, the returning exiles will possess the land, and the kingdom will be the Lord's.

Jonah

The Book of Jonah, written in about 850 BC, is the account of a reluctant prophet, called to preach to the Assyrians in Nineveh.

Chapter 1 records how Jonah tries to flee to Tarsus, but the boat encounters a violent storm. When it is revealed, by casting lots, that Jonah's presence is the reason for the storm, the sailors eventually agree to throw Jonah overboard. The storm immediately dies down, but the Lord provides a great fish, which swallows Jonah.

In Jonah 2, the prophet, from inside the great fish, thanks God for saving his life. In his moment of crisis, he has called out to God, and God has rescued him. He declares that we forfeit the grace which can be ours when we allow an idol, or our own desires, to come between ourselves and God. At the command of the Lord, the great fish ejects Jonah on to dry land.

Jonah 3 records how God speaks to Jonah a second time and instructs him to go and preach in Nineveh. This time Jonah is obedient, and preaches to the Ninevites that God will bring disaster upon them, because of their violence and evil ways. When the Ninevites repent of their actions, and declare a time of fasting, God, in His compassion, relents from bringing judgement upon them.

In Jonah 4, Jonah becomes angry, because God is showing compassion to the Ninevites, and not treating them as Jonah would. In his anger, he declares that he may as well be dead. He shelters from the heat under a vine, but his anger deepens when the vine withers and dies. God challenges his heart attitude, and his concern about a vine. God reminds Jonah that there are 120,000 people in Nineveh, whom He cares about, even though they do not know right from wrong.

Micah

Written during the period 750-720 BC, the book of Micah is a reminder that God is both the Lord and judge, as well as the shepherd-king who forgives.

In Chapter 1 and 2, the prophet declares that God is going to bring judgement upon His people because of their idolatry, and because they have forsaken His ways. The false prophets are in error when they say this judgement will not happen.

Micah 3 is addressed to the leaders of Judah and Israel, and rebukes them, because they have despised justice, and led the people astray. They have accepted bribes, and have falsely prophesied in exchange for payments of money. When they cry out to the Lord, He will not answer them, and disaster will come upon them. Jerusalem and the temple will be destroyed.

Having prophesied the destruction of Jerusalem, Micah 4 proclaims the restoration of Jerusalem in the end times. Dominion and kingship will be re-established. God will gather the exiles together, and the Lord will rule over the nations from Mount Zion.

Micah 5 is a prophecy about the future Messiah, quoted by the advisors to King Herod, when visited by the Magi, seeking to find the baby Jesus. The prophet declares that the future ruler of Israel will come out of Bethlehem and be of the tribe of Judah. He will shepherd His people, and eventually His greatness will extend to all the nations. In the end times the enemies of Israel, along with their witchcraft and idolatry, will be destroyed.

Micah 6 is a rebuke to the Israelites, declaring that God redeemed them out of Egypt and wants to bless them, but they have turned from following His ways. They have not walked in humility, nor acted with justice and mercy. They have turned to worship false idols, and they lie and cheat in their relationships with one another. As a result, ruin will come upon them. They will eat, but never feel satisfied. They will not enjoy the fruit of their labours, and their wealth will be taken from them.

In Micah 7, the prophet describes the misery and helplessness of living in a society which has rejected God's ways, and is reaping the consequences of its sins. Despite this, the prophet declares that he will watch in hope for the Lord. He declares that a time will come when God will show His mercy and compassion, and restore His people. He will forgive their sins and transgressions, and will fulfil the promises made to Abraham.

Nahum

Written about 640 BC, the book of Nahum proclaims that Nineveh (the capital city of Assyria) will be destroyed.

In Chapter 1, the prophet declares that God is all-powerful, and a refuge for all who face troubles. Although He may appear slow to exercise His wrath, He does not leave the guilty unpunished. God will set His people free from the yoke of Nineveh. He will destroy their idols and carved images, (the spiritual powers behind Nineveh), and Nineveh and her allies will be no more.

In Nahum 2 & 3 the prophet poetically describes the fall of Nineveh, (the capital city of Assyria, which was the superpower at the time of Nahum). The gates of the city are thrown open, the inhabitants are helpless and afraid, and the city is plundered of all her wealth. Like other great cities that have fallen, Nineveh is unable to defend itself, and is likened to a lion's den which has been destroyed. Everyone who hears of her destruction rejoices, because they have all experienced her cruelty.

Habakkuk

Written shortly before the invasion of Judah by the Assyrians, the book of Habakkuk encourages us to wait upon, and trust, the Lord.

In Chapters 1 & 2, the prophet questions God, as to why He does not judge wickedness. God responds by saying that the Assyrians have been given authority to execute judgement on Judah. However, the Assyrians themselves will be judged and punished for their sin, and that, one day, the whole earth will be filled with the knowledge of God.

In Habakkuk 3, the prophet poetically describes how God shakes the nations. He prays that God will be merciful, even when His anger is aroused. The prophet concludes by declaring that God will deliver His chosen people. Even if he experiences hardships and can see no immediate solution, Habakkuk proclaims that he will continue to trust, and rejoice, in God his Saviour.

Zephaniah

Written in about 620 BC, the book of Zephaniah reminds the people of Judah that, when the day of the Lord comes, the righteous will be blessed, but the sinner judged and punished.

In Chapter 1 & 2 God declares that judgement will come upon the whole world, and upon Judah, because of her idolatry and deceit. Her wealth and false gods will not save her. The surrounding nations will become wastelands. Those who seek the Lord will be sheltered, and a remnant will inherit the land.

In Zephaniah 3 God declares that judgement will come upon Jerusalem, because of her disobedience, and her refusal to respond to the warnings of the prophets. In the midst of this prophecy about forthcoming judgement, God gives hope by declaring that a time will come when He will rescue all those who have been scattered. He will bring them back to the land, where they will be given honour and praise before all the people of the world.

Haggai

Written in about 520 BC, the book of Haggai encourages the returning exiles to restore the house of the Lord in Jerusalem.

In Chapter 1, God declares that it is time to rebuild the temple. The returning exiles are experiencing little fruit for their labours, because they are focusing on their own desires, and justifying their selfishness by denying it is time to restore the temple. Zerubbabel, the governor, Joshua, the high priest, and the people, respond by beginning the rebuilding work.

In Haggai 2, God encourages the returning exiles to be strong, and declares that He is with them. He controls the wealth of the world, and that, one day, the glory of the temple will exceed its former glory. The people should take careful note of the day on which the foundations of the temple are laid. From that day forward, they will realise that they are starting to experience prosperity, and God's blessings, whereas, previously, they only faced hardship and insufficiency.

Zechariah

Written in about 520 BC, the book of Zechariah encourages the returning exiles to persevere, and reminds them of God's faithfulness.

In Chapter 1, God reminds the people that the disasters, which have come upon them, are a result of their ancestors turning away from God. Through visions given to Zechariah, God declares that He will show mercy to Zion, and that the temple will be rebuilt. God is angry with the nations who scattered Israel and Judah, and He will bring disasters upon them.

Zechariah 2 is an end-times prophecy, in which Jerusalem is portrayed as a city without physical walls, but protected, instead, by God Himself, as a wall of fire around it. The people are called to return, and escape from the nations where they have been scattered, because God will move against those nations who have touched the apple of His eye. Many other nations will be joined with the Lord in that day, and will become His people, and He will dwell among them.

Zechariah 3 is a vision of the restoration of Israel, represented by Joshua the high priest standing in filthy rags before God, and being condemned and accused by Satan. God rebukes Satan, and replaces Joshua's dirty clothes, (sin and unrighteousness), with clean garments, and a new turban. God declares that He is going to bring forth His servant the branch, (Jesus), represented as a stone, and that He will remove the sin of the land in a single day.

Zechariah 4 records a vision, in which the prophet sees a seven-branched, golden lampstand, and two olive trees. An angel explains that the lampstand represents the eyes, or Spirit of God, watching over the earth, and the olive trees represent His anointed servants, (Zerubbabel, the king, and Joshua, the high priest). The angel declares that the work of rebuilding the temple, started by Zerubbabel, should not be despised, and that it will be completed, not by might nor power, but by the Spirit of God.

In Zechariah 5, the prophet sees a vision of a flying scroll, on which is written God's judgement against those who have stolen and lied, (those who have sided with Satan, whom Jesus described as being a thief and a liar). The prophet also sees, in vision, a woman sitting in a basket, who represents the wickedness and the iniquity of the people. The basket and the woman are carried to Babylonia, (which in biblical symbolism represents those who reject and rebel against God, and side with Satan).

Zechariah 6 describes how, in vision, the prophet sees four chariots, drawn by different-coloured horses, being sent out throughout the earth. (These chariots symbolically represent God pouring out His judgement). In a personal message of encouragement to Joshua the high priest, the prophet is told to take some of the silver and gold, sent by the exiles in Babylonia, and make a crown, and place it upon the head of Joshua, declaring that he will build the temple of the Lord.

In Zechariah 7, the people ask Zechariah whether they should fast in the fifth and seventh months. God's response, given through the prophet, is that God is more concerned about their heart attitude than their fasting. He reminds them to administer justice, and show compassion and mercy, especially to those who are vulnerable, and unable to protect themselves. Their ancestors did not heed God's warnings to do this, and so disaster came upon them.

In Zechariah 8, God declares that He is jealous for Zion. Jerusalem will be restored, and known as the city of truth, and God will dwell there. He will bring back His people from the countries where they were scattered, and they will live in peace and prosperity in the land. Their feasts and festivals will be times of great joy. The people from other nations will come to Jerusalem to seek the Lord, because they will recognise that God is with them.

Zechariah 9 continues the end-times prophecy, relating to the restoration of Israel. The nations surrounding Israel will be overthrown, and God will defend Israel from the attacks of marauding forces. He will raise up an army that He will shield, and which will be victorious. In a prophecy, fulfilled by Jesus, God declares that the future righteous king of Israel will bring salvation, and will be seen coming to them, riding on a donkey.

In Zechariah 10, God declares that He is the sovereign Lord, and that Israel's leaders, (the shepherds), have failed the flock, and allowed them to fall into deceit and idolatry. He will raise up a cornerstone, (the Messiah), from Judah. God declares that He will restore and strengthen the house of Judah and Israel. He will gather the people from the lands where they have been scattered, and they will walk in His name.

Zechariah 11 describes prophetically how the good shepherd, raised up to pasture the flock, ends up being despised and rejected, and only valued as being worth thirty pieces of silver, (the price of a common slave, and the amount received by Judas for betraying Jesus). In a possible reference to the end times 'antichrist', the prophet speaks of the worthless shepherd, who will selfishly use the flock to satisfy his own desires.

In Zechariah 12, the Lord declares, through the prophet, that He will be the guardian of Israel and Jerusalem. When the nations of the world all rise up to oppose Israel, He will destroy them. On that day, the people of Israel will know salvation, and will mourn and repent, because they will realise that, in rejecting Jesus, (the one they have pierced), they rejected the promised Messiah.

Zechariah 13 continues the prophecy that all Israel will be saved and come to know Jesus as their Saviour. On that day, there will be a cleansing from sin, idolatry and impurity. Those who have prophesied, (wrongly interpreted the word of God), will be ashamed of what they have done. The sheep, who were scattered when Jesus was rejected, will be re-gathered. They will be refined and tested. They will call on the name of God, and declare that the Lord is their God.

Zechariah 14 describes how, in the end times, the Lord will descend upon the Mount of Olives, and deliver Jerusalem from the hands of the nations, gathered against her. On that unique day, a great earthquake will cause topographical changes. Rivers will flow from Jerusalem to the Mediterranean and the dead sea. Subsequently, each year, survivors from all the nations will go up to Jerusalem to celebrate the Feast of Tabernacles, and worship the King of kings. Those nations who do not go, will suffer drought.

Malachi

Written in about 460 BC, the book of Malachi encourages us to have a living, active faith, and not to become legalistic and dependent on meaningless religious rituals.

In Chapter 1, the Lord declares His love for Israel, but rebukes the priests for not honouring God as they should. God has chosen Israel, and blessed her abundantly, compared to the other nations. However, the leaders and priests do not fear Him, and place defiled food upon the altar, and offer inferior and blemished sacrifices.

Malachi 2 describes how the priests have broken God's covenant, and, as a result, have opened themselves up to receive cursing. Their teaching is false, and they have caused the people to stumble. They have desecrated the temple by bringing in false idols, and in so doing have divorced themselves from God. They have broken faith with the wives of their marriage covenant. They have wearied God with their weeping, while simultaneously endorsing those who are living un-righteously.

In Malachi 3, God declares that He will send a messenger, (John the Baptist), to prepare the way, before the Messiah comes. The Messiah will purify the priests, and bring judgement against all who practise witchcraft, deceit and immorality, or oppress the poor. God will reward those who fear Him and honour His name. Their names are written on a scroll of remembrance. God declares that the people rob Him by not giving their tithes and offerings, and as a result are under a curse.

In Malachi 4, (the last chapter in the Old Testament, God declares that a day will come when He will bring His judgement, and it will be like fire. The righteous will rejoice, and be like calves released from their stalls. The wicked will be trampled down. He instructs the people to remember His laws and decrees, and declares that, before He comes, He will send one like Elijah, to turn the hearts of the fathers towards their children, and the children's hearts towards their fathers.

Matthew

A central theme of Matthew's Gospel is that Jesus fulfils many prophetic messianic passages, found in the Old Testament.

In Chapter 1, Matthew starts with the genealogy of Joseph, listing the generations from Adam to Joseph. He records how Mary, who is betrothed to Joseph, conceives Jesus by the power of the Holy Spirit, and how He is named in accordance with the instructions given to Joseph in a dream.

Matthew 2:1-12 records the visit of the Magi to the infant Jesus. King Herod is disturbed by their message that one destined to be 'king of the Jews' has been born, and orders them to report to him when they find this king. A star guides the Magi to the place where Jesus is, and they present their gifts of gold, incense and myrrh. Warned in a dream not to report back to Herod, they return home.

Matthew 2:13-23 records how King Herod tries to destroy Jesus by ordering the death of all baby boys under the age of two in the area of Bethlehem. However, Joseph, having been warned in a dream, flees to Egypt with Mary and Jesus, and remains there until Herod dies. The family eventually returns to Israel and settles in Nazareth. Matthew highlights how all these happenings are in fulfilment of Old Testament prophecies.

Matthew 3 records the ministry of John the Baptist. Many are baptised by John as a sign of repentance of their sins. John declares that one greater than himself will come, and will baptise them with the Holy Spirit and fire. Jesus comes to John and submits to water baptism as a sign of how He will identify with the sins of mankind. As He comes out of the water, the Holy Spirit descends upon Jesus in the form of a dove.

In Matthew 4:1-11, Jesus is tempted by Satan in the wilderness. If Jesus submits to these temptations He will be following in the footsteps of the first Adam. Jesus, however, resists the temptations and rebukes Satan with quotations from the book of Deuteronomy.

Matthew 4:12-25 records the calling of the first disciples. When Jesus invites them to follow Him, they immediately respond and leave their nets and boats behind. Jesus travels throughout Galilee, teaching in the synagogues, preaching the good news of the kingdom, and healing every disease. Large crowds follow Him.

Matthew 5:1-16 records the beatitudes, which Jesus teaches to the crowds following Him. Those who mourn will be comforted, those who exercise godly virtues will be rewarded, and those who seek the kingdom of God will find it. Jesus encourages us to be light and salt to those around us, so that others will recognise that God is at work in us.

In Matthew 5:17-48, Jesus says He has not come to change the law, but to fulfil it. The law itself will not pass away before the end of time. Being obedient to God and following His commandments is more than just legalistically following rules; it is all to do with heart attitude and maintaining right relationships with others. Jesus challenges us to love our enemies, and pray for those who persecute us.

In Matthew 6:1-18, we are encouraged that our acts of righteousness, such as praying, fasting or giving, should not be done to impress others and gain their praise, but should be something between us and God. Jesus teaches us how to pray. He stresses that receiving God's forgiveness for our own sins is dependent upon our willingness to forgive those who have sinned against us.

In Matthew 6:19-34, Jesus teaches how 'worldly wealth' can be a hindrance in our walk with the Lord, and a source of worry and anxiety. Jesus tells us that we can't serve two masters. We are encouraged to seek God's kingdom first. As we do this, God is able to meet all our needs.

In Matthew 7:1-14, Jesus teaches us not to judge and become critical of others, but rather to examine ourselves, and treat others as we would want them to treat us. Jesus reminds us to ask our heavenly Father for the things that we need. If earthly fathers know how to give good gifts to their children, how much more will God in heaven answer our prayers.

In Matthew 7:15-29, Jesus warns us about being led astray by false prophets. We need to examine the fruit of their lives, and whether they are truly doing the will of God. There is a stark warning for those giving the appearance of being disciples, but who, in their hearts, are not choosing to be obedient. Jesus illustrates this point with the parable of those who build on sand rather than on strong foundations.

In Matthew 8:1-17, Jesus demonstrates His compassion by touching the man with leprosy and healing him. Jesus commends the faith of the Roman centurion and heals his servant. Jesus heals Peter's mother-in-law, and heals many who were demonised or sick. These healings, says Matthew, were fulfilments of Isaiah's messianic prophecy – 'He took up our infirmities and carried our diseases'.

In Matthew 8:18-9:8, Jesus calms the storm at sea, and delivers the Gadarene demoniacs, allowing the demons to go into some pigs. Jesus then heals a paralytic man, after first speaking out that his sins are forgiven. The reaction of the witnesses of these miracles is varied; the disciples are amazed, the Gadarenes ask Jesus to go away, the teachers of the law accuse Jesus of blasphemy, and the crowds are filled with awe and praise God.

In Matthew 9:9-38, the Pharisees sneer at Jesus for eating with tax collectors and sinners, and accuse Him of operating in the power of Satan when He heals a demonised mute man. Jesus heals a woman with an issue of blood, who reaches out and touches His garment, raises a twelve-year-old girl from the dead and heals two blind men. Matthew records that Jesus went throughout the country, preaching the good news and healing the sick.

In Matthew 10, Jesus sends out the disciples to the lost sheep of Israel, with His authority to preach the Gospel, cast out demons, heal the sick and raise the dead. He warns them that they will face rejection and persecution, even from their own families, but they need not be fearful, as the Holy Spirit will give them the words to speak. Those who acknowledge Jesus before men will be acknowledged by Jesus before His Father in heaven.

In Matthew 11, Jesus commends the ministry of John the Baptist. In response to the question of whether Jesus is the Messiah, He tells them to look at the evidence of His ministry. (Jesus is confirming to John that He is fulfilling the messianic prophecies of Isaiah 61 by healing the sick, raising the dead and preaching the good news). Jesus warns of the future consequences for those who reject Him, but invites the weary and the burdened to come to Him and receive His rest.

In Matthew 12:1-37, the antagonism of the Pharisees towards Jesus increases. They accuse Him of breaking the Sabbath, and plot to kill Him, after He heals a man with a shrivelled hand. They accuse Him of healing a demonised man, who was blind and dumb, by satanic power. Jesus speaks out a very strong warning about the consequences of blaspheming the work of the Holy Spirit, and says that we will have to give an account for every careless word we speak.

In Matthew 12:38-50, Jesus rebukes the Pharisees, who only ask to see miracles, but don't respond to His teaching. He prophesies His own resurrection after three days as being a sign to them, and tells them they will be judged for rejecting Him. Their condition is like someone receiving deliverance, but allowing themselves to be re-demonised. Jesus speaks out that His true family are those who do the will of God.

In Matthew 13:1-23, Jesus explains to the disciples that He speaks to the people in parables because many of them have hardened hearts, and are unable to hear or see the truth. He tells the crowds the parable of the sower, and explains its meaning to His disciples. The seed is the word of God, and the different types of soil, in which the seed lands, represent the different ways that people respond to the Gospel.

In Matthew 13:24-58, Jesus tells a number of parables to explain different aspects about the kingdom of heaven. It is like a field of wheat, where an enemy sows weeds. It is like a mustard seed which grows into a great tree, or yeast which works its way through all the dough. It is like a catch of fish which needs sorting, or a treasure worth giving everything up for. Jesus returns to His home town, but He does few miracles there, because of the people's lack of faith.

In Matthew 14, John the Baptist is killed by King Herod for confronting his sinfulness. A large crowd is miraculously fed with five loaves and a few fish, after Jesus blesses the food, and tells the disciples to distribute it to the people. Jesus walks on the water, and Peter does the same, until He takes His eyes off Jesus. Jesus rescues the sinking Peter, and the wind immediately dies down when Jesus gets into the boat with the disciples.

In Matthew 15, Jesus challenges the Pharisees about their legalism and man-made rules. It's the attitude of our hearts which is important to God. Jesus heals by 'proxy' the daughter of a Canaanite woman, after she addresses Jesus as Lord and master. Jesus amazes the crowd by healing many. Jesus again miraculously feeds a crowd of over 4,000 men, plus women and children.

In Matthew 16, Jesus warns that the teaching of the Pharisees is like yeast, which affects all the bread. Jesus commends Peter's faith, when he declares Jesus is the Messiah, and the Son of the living God. Jesus says that His Church will be built on such faith. He will give authority to the Church to bind and loose on earth that which has been bound and loosed in heaven. Following Jesus involves denying ourselves and being willing to submit to God's plans for our life.

Matthew 17:1-23 records the transfiguration of Jesus when He met with Moses and Elijah on the mountain. He tells the disciples that John the Baptist fulfilled the role of Elijah in preparing the way of the Lord. Jesus heals a boy who is suffering with epileptic fits, and whom the disciples were unable to heal, because of their lack of faith. Jesus explains that He will be betrayed into the hands of men, will be crucified, and will be raised to life on the third day.

In Matthew 17:24-18:14, Jesus miraculously provides the coin to pay the temple tax. Jesus explains the importance of being humble, and having a child-like trust, in order to enter the kingdom. Those who sin against children, or cause children to sin, will be dealt with severely. God's heart is for the lost, and He does not want any to perish. Using a graphic illustration, Jesus encourages us to get rid of anything which causes us to sin.

In Matthew 18:15-35, Jesus encourages us, individually, and as a community of believers, to confront, in a godly way, those who sin against us. Jesus reminds us of the authority we have when believers are in unity. In the parable of the unmerciful servant Jesus teaches us the importance of forgiving others, just as God has forgiven us. If we don't, forgive from the heart, we become tormented and a prisoner of our own un-forgiveness.

In Matthew 19, Jesus confirms that marriage should be a life-time commitment, with spouses willing to forgive each other. (He does not endorse the rabbinical school which taught that divorce was allowed for any reason). Jesus welcomes the children, even though the disciples try to stop them. He tells the rich young man that his possessions are an obstacle to him fully entering into the kingdom. Those who sacrifice everything to follow Jesus will find eternal rewards.

Matthew 20:1-19 is the parable of the workers in the vineyard. The landowner, in his generosity, pays all his workers the same amount, despite the fact that some have worked longer hours than others. Those who have worked longer hours have no basis for being jealous, because they were paid what they were promised. Jesus tells His disciples that He will be betrayed in Jerusalem and crucified, but that He will rise again on the third day.

In Matthew 20:20-34, the mother of James and John upsets the other disciples by asking if her sons can sit at Jesus' right and left hand in heaven. Jesus responds by saying that it is not His decision, but God the Father's. He encourages us to be servant-hearted and follow His example. Jesus shows His compassion by healing two blind men who were shouting out for Him to have mercy on them.

Matthew 21:1-22 records Jesus' triumphant entry into Jerusalem, riding on a donkey, in fulfilment of prophecy. He drives out the traders and money lenders from the temple. (We can surmise from Jesus' words that they were cheating and overcharging the visitors to the temple). In Bethany, Jesus curses a fig tree which has no fruit, and it immediately withers. He uses this to encourage His disciples to have faith when they pray.

In Matthew 21:23-46, Jesus is questioned about His authority. He responds with the parable of the two sons. (The son who initially said no but later obeyed his father is commended). In the parable of the vineyard, the tenants abuse the servants sent by the landowner, and kill the landowner's son. Jesus refers to himself as the capstone rejected by the builders. The chief priests and Pharisees know Jesus is talking about them, but are too afraid to arrest Him.

In Matthew 22, Jesus likens the kingdom of God to a wedding banquet. Many of those invited anger the king by their lame excuses. One person is thrown out of the feast for not wearing the correct clothing (an insult to the host, who would typically provide this clothing). Jesus affirms that we will be resurrected, but that our sexuality will be like that of the angels. Jesus summarises the law as loving God with all of our being, and loving our neighbour as we love ourselves.

In Matthew 23, Jesus teaches about servant leadership, and the need for leaders to act in humility. He strongly condemns the religious leaders who are hypocritical, and who do not practice what they preach. They spiritually abuse the people with their religious legalism, and are a barrier to people meeting with God. Jesus teaches that, at His second coming, He will be welcomed as the Messiah, coming in the name of the Lord.

In Matthew 24:1-35, Jesus teaches about His second coming. He warns us not to be deceived by those falsely claiming to be the anointed one, and even performing great signs and wonders. He warns that there will be a time of great turmoil, including wars and rumours of war, and an increase in famines and earthquakes. Believers will face persecution, and many will fall away. Following a time of great distress, Jesus will come again, and all nations will see Him in His glory.

In Matthew 24:36-51, Jesus teaches that the date of His return is unknown. He says that it will be as in the days of Noah. (Noah was expecting the flood and preparing for it in obedience to God. The rest of mankind were described as wicked and scoffed at what Noah was doing.) We are encouraged and challenged to behave as if Jesus' return is imminent. Would we change what we are doing today, if we knew that Jesus was coming back tomorrow?

In Matthew 25:1-30, Jesus continues to teach about His second coming. In the parable of the foolish virgins He teaches that we need to be preparing ourselves as if His return is imminent, and not assuming we will have time later to prepare, or that we can depend on others to save us. In the parable of the talents Jesus teaches that we will have to answer to God for the way we have used the giftings, (time, material possessions and skills), He has given to each one of us.

In Matthew 25:31-46, Jesus clearly teaches that, one day, there will be a day of judgement, when each individual will either enter into their inheritance in the kingdom of God, or be assigned to a place of eternal punishment. In this very challenging teaching, the basis for the separation is the way individuals have responded to the needs of others. This teaching refutes the argument that God is too loving to send anyone to hell.

Mathew 26:1-35 records how Jesus commends the woman who anoints Him with very expensive perfume, despite the disciples' protest that it is a waste of money. Judas plots with the high priest to betray Jesus. Peter claims he will never disown Jesus, but Jesus tells him that he will deny him three times that very night. Jesus celebrates the Passover meal with His disciples, giving the meaning of this feast a completely new significance.

In Matthew 26:36-75, we read how Jesus, in His humanity, submits to the Father's will, as He prays in the garden of Gethsemane. Jesus allows Himself to be arrested, (He could have easily summoned angelic help), and the disciples all flee. The chief priests accuse Jesus of blasphemy because of His claim to be the Messiah, and they mock, and physically abuse, Him. Peter, as foretold by Jesus, denies three times that he knows Jesus, and then weeps bitterly about what he has done.

In Matthew 27:1-26, we read how Judas, who had betrayed Jesus in accordance with prophecy, is now full of remorse, and commits suicide. Jesus is taken to Pilate, who can find no fault in Him. Jesus makes no attempt to defend Himself, other than to agree that He is the king of the Jews. The crowds call for the release of Barabbas, and for Jesus to be crucified. Pilate washes his hands of the matter, but has Jesus flogged, before handing Him over to be crucified.

In Matthew 27: 27-44, we read how the soldiers mock and abuse Jesus by dressing Him in a scarlet robe, (the colour worn by kings), and place a crown of thorns upon His head. They take him to Golgotha, where they crucify Him. The crowds and the priests taunt, and jeer at Jesus, challenging Him to come down from the cross, if He is the son of God.

Matthew 27:45-61 continues the account of the crucifixion. For three hours there is darkness, and Jesus expresses His feeling of separation from God by quoting from Psalm 22, before giving up His spirit. Immediately there are physical manifestations of what is happening spiritually. There are earthquakes, and people raised to life. The curtain in the temple is torn in two. The Roman centurion speaks out his conviction that Jesus is the Son of God. Jesus' body is placed in a tomb.

Matthew concludes his gospel with an account of the resurrection of Jesus, and His appearance to some of the women. Matthew records how the guards, placed by the tomb to ensure no one stole the body, are bribed to say that this actually happened. Before ascending into heaven, Jesus gives His disciples, (and us), the 'great commission', reminding them that they have His authority, and that His presence will be with them.

Mark

Mark is believed to have been a close companion of Simon Peter, who may well have furnished or suggested much of the material found in this Gospel.

In Mark 1:1-20, Jesus is declared to be the Son of God, and the one for whom John the Baptist was preparing the way. Following His baptism by John, Jesus spends forty days in the desert, being tempted by Satan, before returning to Galilee, and calling his first disciples to follow Him and become fishers of men.

Mark 1:21-45 records how Jesus amazes the congregation in the synagogue in Capernaum by using His authority to set a man free from an evil spirit, (who recognises that Jesus is the Holy One of God). Jesus heals Simon Peter's mother-in-law, and many others, who are brought to Him. Jesus demonstrates His compassion and mercy by reaching out and touching a man with leprosy, declaring that He is willing to heal him.

In Mark 2:1-22, Jesus heals the paralytic, let down through the roof by his friends, who have faith that Jesus can heal him. Jesus declares that the man's sins are forgiven, (something that only God can do), and then heals him, thus demonstrating His power and authority to the Scribes and Pharisees. When they criticise Him for eating with sinners, and not fasting, Jesus declares that He has come to call sinners, and that He is the bridegroom, doing new things among them.

In Mark 2:23-3:12, Jesus challenges the legalistic observance of the Sabbath by declaring that the Sabbath was created for man. He heals a man with a shrivelled hand on the Sabbath, stirring up the anger of the Pharisees, who begin plotting how they can kill Jesus. Large crowds follow Jesus, because He has healed many people. Evil spirits recognise who Jesus is, and cry out that He is the Son of God.

In Mark 3:13-35, Jesus appoints His twelve apostles. Jesus teaches that a kingdom divided against itself will fall, and about the need to bind up, or deal with, the strong man, before one can plunder his kingdom. In response to the accusations of the Pharisees that His authority and power come from Satan, Jesus teaches about the seriousness of blaspheming against the work of the Holy Spirit. Jesus declares that doing His will is evidence of being part of the family of God.

In Mark 4:1-34, Jesus teaches many things about the kingdom of God, using parables. He likens the word of God to seed sown by a farmer. Only the seed falling on good ground produces fruit. The seed falling on shallow ground starts to grow, but then withers and dies. Some seed is stolen away by the birds, and some choked by other plants. The kingdom of God is also like a small mustard seed, which eventually grows to become the largest tree in the garden.

In Mark 4:35-5:20, Jesus calms a storm at sea by ordering the wind and waves to be still. When they reach land, a heavily demonised man, who mutilates himself, and exhibits supernatural strength, approaches Jesus. Jesus delivers him of many demons, allowing the demons to enter a herd of pigs. The man is set completely free, but the pigs react to the demons by throwing themselves into the sea. Instead of rejoicing, the local people are afraid, and ask Jesus to leave the area.

In Mark 5:21-43, Jesus raises the daughter of Jairus from the dead, after being ridiculed by the mourners, whom He has to send away. Jesus heals the woman with the issue of blood who comes up behind Him and reaches out to touch the hem of His garment. (Because her illness makes her 'unclean', she is breaking the law by touching a rabbi). Jesus, realising that power has gone out of Himself, asks the woman to reveal herself, and then commends her for her faith.

In Mark 6:1-29, Jesus is unable to do many miracles in His home town, because of the lack of faith there. Jesus sends out His disciples with His authority to preach the good news, heal the sick and cast out demons. King Herod hears what is happening, and thinks that John the Baptist has been resurrected from the dead. Herod previously had John the Baptist beheaded, because he spoke out against Herod marrying his sister-in-law.

In Mark 6:30-56, the crowds follow Jesus everywhere. Out of His compassion for them, Jesus feeds the crowd with five loaves and two fish, which He blesses, before giving them to the disciples to distribute to the people. After spending time alone in prayer, Jesus amazes the disciples by walking on the water to join them, in a boat, on their way to Bethsaida. When they arrive many people are healed, as they reach out and touch Jesus.

In Mark 7:1-23, Jesus challenges the Pharisees and teachers of the law about their legalism. They are nullifying the word of God, and missing the heart of God, by insisting that people should follow man-made traditions. It is not what we eat which makes us unclean, but rather what comes out of our heart. The words which are spoken, evil and wicked thoughts, and the attitude of the heart are the important things which determine whether a person is clean.

Mark 7:24-37 records the healing of the daughter of the Syrian-

Phoenician woman. Jesus identifies that this woman has faith in Him, even though she is not Jewish, and He sets her daughter free, through deliverance. The people are again amazed when Jesus heals a deaf and dumb man, and proclaim "He has done all things well".

In Mark 8:1-21, Jesus has compassion for the second time on the crowds who are following Him, and miraculously feeds them with seven loaves of bread and a few fish. The Pharisees again come to Jesus and challenge Him to perform miracles, to prove who He is. Jesus refuses, and warns the disciples to beware of the Pharisees and their unbelief, which, like yeast in a batch of dough, will influence all the people.

Mark 8:22-9:1 records the two-stage healing of a blind man. In response to a question from Jesus, Peter declares that Jesus is the Messiah, but later he argues with Jesus about His future suffering and death. Peter's rebuke by Jesus reminds us how easy it is to speak out things which are not of God, but of the enemy. Jesus teaches the importance of fulfilling our destiny in Him, (carrying our cross), and not being ashamed of Him, rather than seeking worldly wealth and forfeiting eternal life.

Mark 9:2-32 records the transfiguration of Jesus, and His meeting with Elijah and Moses, as witnessed by Peter, James and John. Jesus heals a deaf and dumb boy, who experiences epileptic-type fits. He explains to His disciples, who were unable to heal the boy, that healing in this instance involves something more than just exercising spiritual authority over demons. Jesus teaches the disciples about His forthcoming death and resurrection, but they fail to understand Him.

In Mark 9:33-50, Jesus teaches the disciples, who are arguing about who is the greatest, about servant leadership. He talks about the seriousness of sinning against, or causing, a child to sin. It's better to be thrown into the sea, with a millstone around your neck, than to do that. Jesus teaches that it is far better to get rid of anything in this life, (no matter how precious it may be), which is stopping you entering the kingdom of God, than to spend eternity separated from God in hell.

In Mark 10:1-31, Jesus reminds His listeners that God's plan is that marriage should be a life-long relationship. Issuing a certificate of divorce, in order to have a relationship with someone else, is the same as committing adultery. He encourages us to have a child-like (trusting) faith in God. Jesus tests the heart of the rich young ruler, who claims to have kept the law. Jesus challenges him to give away his money to the poor and follow Him as a disciple.

In Mark 10:32-52, Jesus continues to speak prophetically about what will happen to Him in Jerusalem. Jesus again teaches about servant leadership, after James and John upset the other disciples, by asking if they can have the places of honour when Jesus comes in glory. He reminds them that He has come not to be served, but to serve, and to give His life as a ransom for many. On the road to Jericho, Jesus responds to the faith of blind Bartimaeus, and heals him.

In Mark 11:1-26, Jesus enters Jerusalem on a colt, and the people welcome Him saying "Blessed is he who comes in the name of the Lord". Jesus drives out the money changers and traders from the temple, declaring that they have made God's house a den of thieves. On the way to Jerusalem, Jesus curses a fig tree, because it has no fruit, and the next day the tree has withered and died. Jesus uses this to encourage the disciples to have faith in God's ability to answer prayer.

In Mark 11:27-12:17, the Pharisees and teachers of the law test and challenge Jesus about His authority to do what He is doing. Jesus responds by telling the parable of the vineyard and the tenant farmers, who ignore the wishes of the landlord and eventually kill the landlord's son. In a veiled reference to Himself, He reminds them of the scripture which says that the stone that the builders rejected has become the capstone.

In Mark 12:18-34, Jesus responds to a question from the Sadducees, who do not believe in the resurrection of the dead. Jesus affirms that there will indeed be a resurrection, because God is the God of the living, but that, in our resurrected state, we will be like the angels, and not married or given in marriage. Jesus declares that the greatest commandment is to love God with all of our being, and the second commandment is to love our neighbours as we love ourself.

In Mark 12:35-44, Jesus teaches from Scripture that the Messiah is not simply a direct descendant of David, but someone whom David would call Lord. He warns His listeners that the teachers of the law like to be considered important, but much of what they do is pretence, and they fail to look after the widows. Jesus commends a widow for making a sacrificial offering to God, even though she is poor.

In Mark 13, Jesus teaches about His second coming in glory, and with great power. Only the Father knows when this will happen. Jesus warns that, prior to His return, there will be a time of great turmoil, including wars, earthquakes and famines. There will be persecution of believers, but Jesus encourages us not to be anxious about being arrested, because the Holy Spirit will give us the words to speak. Jesus also encourages us to keep watch, and not fall into deception.

In Mark 14:1-26, Jesus commends a woman who pours expensive oil on His head, in response to some of the onlookers, who complain that it is a waste of money. Jesus celebrates the Passover with His disciples in what we might call the first Communion service, and in which Jesus likens the bread and wine to His own body and blood. Jesus declares that one of the twelve disciples will betray Him. (Judas has already been plotting with the priests to do this.)

In Mark 14:27-42, Peter, contradicting what Jesus has said, declares that he will never deny or disown Jesus, even if the other disciples do so. Jesus prays in the garden of Gethsemane that He is willing to submit to the will of the Father. Peter, James and John, who are with Jesus, keep falling asleep and do not know what to say to Jesus, who is deeply distressed and troubled concerning what is about to happen.

In Mark 14:43-72, Jesus is arrested and brought to trial, where they mock Him, beat Him, and spit upon Him. They declare that He is guilty of blasphemy, and condemn Him as worthy of death. Three times Peter denies that he is a follower of Jesus, and swears that he doesn't know the man. When the cock crows, Peter remembers that Jesus prophesied that this would happen, and he breaks down and weeps.

In Mark 15:1-32, Jesus is taken to Pilate. Pilate offers to release Jesus or Barabbas. When the crowd is incited to shout for Barabbas to be freed, and for Jesus be crucified, Pilate has Jesus flogged, and hands Him over to be crucified. The soldiers mock Jesus, place a crown of thorns upon His head, and beat Him, before taking Him to Golgotha, where they crucify Him. The priests, the men crucified with Him, and those passing by, mock Jesus.

In Mark 15:33-47, six hours after being crucified, Jesus cries out the first verse of Psalm 22, (a prophetic Psalm which speaks of the sufferings that Jesus is enduring). Jesus then breaths His last, and the curtain in the temple is torn in two. The centurion who witnesses the crucifixion declares that Jesus truly was the Son of God. Mary Magdalene, and some of the other women, watch as Jesus is taken from the cross, laid in a tomb and a rock placed at its entrance.

Mark 16 tells of the resurrection of Jesus. When the women go to the tomb to anoint the body, they discover that the stone has been rolled away, and inside the tomb an angel declares to them that Jesus is risen. Jesus appears to Mary Magdalene, and later to the disciples, commissioning them to go into the world and preach the good news. He promises that signs, including deliverance and healing, will accompany the preaching of the word.

Luke

Luke states that he has written this gospel, following careful investigation of the reports of eye witnesses, so that we can be certain of what happened. Luke starts his gospel with the account of how the angel Gabriel appears to Zechariah and tells him that his wife will conceive a son, John the Baptist, who will prepare the way for the Lord.

The Angel Gabriel appears to Mary and tells her that she has been chosen to be the mother of Jesus, who will be miraculously conceived in her womb by the power of the Holy Spirit. Mary visits her cousin Elizabeth, rejoicing in what God has done and will do.

Luke1:57-80 records the birth of John the Baptist and the restoration of Zechariah's speech. Zechariah prophesies that John will be a prophet of God, and prepare the way of the Lord.

Luke 2:1-20 records the birth of Jesus in Bethlehem. Lowly shepherds are the first to hear the news that the Saviour has been born. They return from visiting the stable, glorifying and praising God for all they have seen and been told.

Luke 2:21-52 records how Jesus was circumcised on the eighth day. Simeon prophesies over the baby that He is the Saviour. In the Scriptures little is said about the childhood of Jesus, except that, as a twelve-year-old, He amazed everyone by His understanding, as He debated with the teachers of the law in the temple.

In Luke 3:1-20, we read about the ministry of John the Baptist, who preached a baptism of repentance for the forgiveness of sins. He told the crowds, who came to him, that true repentance should result in changed behaviour.

Luke 3:21-38 records the baptism of Jesus, and states that the Holy Spirit came upon Jesus, and a voice from heaven said "this is my beloved son, in whom I am well pleased". Luke then lists the 'earthly' genealogy of Jesus, tracing the line of Joseph back to Adam.

Luke 4:1-13 describes the temptation of Jesus by Satan. Jesus maintains His sinless-ness, by resisting each of the temptations of Satan. He rebukes Satan with scriptures from the book of Deuteronomy.

In Luke 4:14-44, we read how Jesus returns from the desert in the power of the Holy Spirit. In the synagogue in Nazareth, He reads the messianic prophecy from Isaiah 63:1-3, and tells the people that He is fulfilling that prophecy. In Capernaum he confronts a demonised man and sets him free, heals Simon Peter's mother-in-law, and heals many who are brought to Him.

In Luke 5:1-16, we read about the calling of the first disciples, including Simon Peter. Peter's response, on meeting Jesus, is to say: "Go away from me. I am a sinful man". The compassion of Jesus is shown in the way He reaches out and touches a man with leprosy, and restores him to health. Verse 16 reminds us that, despite his busyness and the demands made upon Him, Jesus often withdraws to pray.

Luke 5:17-39 records the healing of the paralytic man, let down through the roof. Note that Jesus first ministers forgiveness of sins, before He ministers healing. Jesus calls a tax collector, named Levi, to follow Him, which arouses the anger of the Pharisees.

In Luke 6:1-16, we find the Pharisees are upset that Jesus does not follow their legalistic interpretation of how to keep the Sabbath. They are furious when Jesus heals a man with a withered hand. Following a night of prayer, Jesus appoints twelve of His disciples to be apostles.

Luke 6:17-49 is a challenge of what it means to live in the kingdom of God. We are to bless and forgive our enemies. We are to be generous and merciful to others, just as God is merciful to us. We need to judge ourselves, before we judge others. If we say Jesus is Lord, but are not obedient to His word, our lives are built on shallow foundations, which will eventually collapse.

In Luke 7:1-17, we read how Jesus heals the servant of the Roman centurion. He commends the man for his faith, saying that this centurion has more faith than He has found in all Israel. At Nain, Jesus raises a widow's son from the dead, and the people are filled with awe.

In Luke 7:18-50, Jesus confirms who He is, by declaring His ministry is the fulfilment of the messianic prophecy of Isaiah 61:1-3. Jesus goes to dinner at the house of Simon the Pharisee, who does not treat him with honour or respect. A sinful woman weeps over Jesus' feet, and wipes them with her hair. Jesus commends her actions, and tells her that her sins are forgiven, and that her faith has saved her.

In Luke 8:1-21, Jesus tells the parable of the sower. He explains to His disciples that what happens to the seed, in the various places where it lands, represents how people respond to God's word, and whether what they have heard produces lasting fruit.

Luke 8:22-56 records the accounts of three dramatic healings. Jesus demonstrates the reality of the demonic realm and His complete authority over Satan by delivering the highly demonised Gadarene demoniac. He demonstrates His authority over sickness by healing the woman with the issue of blood. He demonstrates his authority over death by raising Jairus' daughter.

In Luke 9:1-27, Jesus sends out the twelve disciples, with power and authority, to preach the good news, and heal the sick. Also Jesus miraculously feeds a large crowd with five loaves of bread and two fish. Then Jesus challenges the disciples to deny themselves, take up their cross, and follow Him.

Luke 9:28-62 records how Peter, James and John witness Jesus being transfigured, and meeting with Moses and Elijah. Jesus heals a boy who is afflicted with demonically induced, convulsive fits. Jesus talks about being a disciple, and says that we can't follow Him in a half-hearted way.

In Luke 10:1-24, Jesus sends out the seventy-two disciples. He tells them they will not be accepted everywhere, but whoever rejects them is rejecting Jesus, and will face judgement on account of that. They return with great joy and excitement, because the demons submitted to them. Jesus reminds them that their greatest joy should be on account of their salvation.

Luke 10:25-42 records the parable of the good Samaritan, told by Jesus in response to a question about loving our neighbours. Jesus stays at the home of Mary and Martha, where He commends Mary for spending time listening to Him, and gently rebukes Martha for being distracted and worried about many things.

In Luke 11:1-32, Jesus teaches the disciples how to pray. He encourages us to be bold in asking God to meet our needs, and give us the gift of the Holy Spirit. Jesus amazes the crowd by healing a mute man, by driving out an evil spirit. He teaches about deliverance, saying that it is a sign that the kingdom of God has come. Jesus is critical of those who only want to see miracles, but are not willing to hear God's word, or repent.

In Luke 11:33-54, Jesus encourages us to be light to those around us, and to get rid of all darkness on the inside. Jesus is very critical of the Pharisees, who focus on the external expression of religiosity, but do not have the heart of God. They have become self-important, and lay burdens on others, which stop them entering the kingdom of God.

In Luke 12:1-34, Jesus encourages us to be bold in proclaiming and acknowledging Jesus, and not to live in fear of what others say or think. The Holy Spirit will give us the words to speak. Jesus teaches us not to be focussed on worldly wealth, and the accumulation of possessions. Our hearts should be set on seeking God's kingdom, and building up treasure in heaven, rather than treasure on earth.

In Luke 12:35-59, Jesus encourages us to be faithful in serving God, and to live our lives as if the return of Jesus is imminent, as no one knows when His return will be. Jesus warns His disciples not to expect unity and peace, because the gospel message will bring division, even within families.

In Luke 13:1-30, Jesus heals a woman on the Sabbath who had been crippled by a spirit of infirmity for many years, and the Pharisees are indignant. Jesus likens the kingdom of God to a mustard tree, or yeast working its way into dough. He teaches that many want to be in heaven, but that the entry is through a narrow door. Those killed in tragic accidents, or on the orders of Pilate, were not being punished because they were more sinful than others.

In Luke 13:31-14:35, Jesus heals a man with dropsy, (abnormal body swelling), on the Sabbath. Jesus teaches that we need to be humble, and not exalt ourselves. The kingdom of God is like a king inviting many people to attend a great banquet, but many make lame excuses and do not come. There is a cost in following Jesus, and in being a true disciple. We need to be willing to put Jesus above everything else in our lives.

The parables of the lost sheep, the lost coin and the prodigal son in Luke 15:1-16:18 teach about the nature of God, and how He seeks the lost, and welcomes the repentant sinner with open arms. The parable of the shrewd manager teaches us that our goal should be laying up treasure in heaven. Jesus teaches that the goal of accumulating money and earthly wealth is in conflict with wholeheartedly serving God.

In Luke 16:19-17:10, Jesus teaches that, following death, there is a separation, and an un-crossable chasm created between the unrighteous and the righteous. Jesus teaches that those who cause others to sin will be severely judged. We are encouraged to forgive those who sin against us, exercise faith, and to faithfully serve God without self-exaltation.

In Luke 17:11-37, Jesus heals ten lepers, but only one comes back to give thanks. Jesus teaches about His second coming. It will be unexpected and sudden, and many will be simply going about their normal business. There will be a separation at that time, just as in the days of Noah, and Lot, when some were saved, but many perished.

In Luke 18, Jesus teaches us to be persistent in prayer and to be humble before God. Jesus welcomes the little children, and encourages us to trust, and have 'child-like' faith, when we seek God. He teaches how wealth and riches can be a barrier to entering God's kingdom. (This surprises the disciples, as prosperity was believed to be a sign of God's blessing.) Jesus tells his disciples what will happen to Him in Jerusalem. Jesus heals a blind beggar near Jericho.

In Luke 19, Jesus meets with Zacchaeus, who declares he will make restitution to all those whom he has cheated. Jesus tells the parable of the talents, encouraging us to use our God-given gifts to serve God. Jesus is welcomed by the crowds as He enters Jerusalem on a donkey, and drives out the traders from the temple, before teaching the crowds. The Pharisees want to kill Jesus, but are too frightened to do anything, because of His popularity.

Luke 20:1-26 records how the Pharisees tried to trap Jesus in what He was teaching, in order to have a reason for arresting Him. Jesus tells the parable of the vineyard, in which the tenants of the vineyard kill messengers from the king, (the prophets), and finally the king's son, (Jesus). In an obvious reference to Himself, He asks them the meaning of the phrase 'The stone the builders have rejected has become the capstone'.

In response to a question from the Sadducees, who do not believe in the resurrection, Jesus teaches, in Luke 20:27-21:4, that there will be a resurrection, but that it is only on earth that people marry or are given in marriage. In the hearing of the crowds, Jesus warns the disciples to beware of the teachers of the law, because they are filled with self-importance. Jesus commends the widow for making an offering to the Lord, despite her poverty.

In Luke 21:5-38, Jesus prophesies that the temple will be destroyed, (fulfilled in 70 AD), and talks about the end times. He tells them there will be many false prophets claiming to have the anointing of God, and that believers will be persecuted and betrayed, even by their own families. There will be worldwide turmoil and natural disasters. Jesus will return in the clouds with power and great glory. Heaven and earth will pass away but Jesus' words are eternal.

In Luke 22, Jesus celebrates the Passover meal with His disciples, telling them they must serve one another. Jesus sweats drops of blood, as He anguishes about what is about to happen, but He willingly surrenders to the Father's will. Jesus is betrayed by Judas and arrested. He is mocked and ill-treated by His captors. Jesus' prophecy that Peter will deny Him is fulfilled, and Peter weeps bitterly.

In Luke 23, Jesus is taken before Pilate and King Herod. The crowds shout for the release of Barabbas, and Jesus is handed over to be crucified. On the cross, Jesus tells one of the criminals, being crucified with Him, that he will enter paradise that very day. Jesus prays forgiveness for those who are crucifying Him. He commits His spirit into the Father's hands, before He dies, and is placed in the tomb.

Luke 24 records how the resurrection of Jesus on the third day is announced to the women preparing to anoint His body. He appears to two disciples on the Emmaus Road. Jesus appears to all the disciples and opens their minds to understand the Scriptures and what they have witnessed. Before ascending into heaven, Jesus tells His disciples to wait in Jerusalem, until they have been clothed in power from on high.

John

This Gospel was written by the apostle John, in about 90 AD.

In Chapter 1:1-34, John declares the deity of Jesus, by proclaiming that Jesus is the light of the world, and the Word, through whom all things were created. Jesus is the one for whom John the Baptist prepared the way. Jesus became man in order to reveal what God is really like, and to take away the sins of the world. He was rejected by many, but, to those who choose to believe in Him, He gives the right to become children of God.

In John 1:35-51, John the Baptist describes Jesus as the Lamb of God. Jesus calls Peter, Andrew, Phillip and other disciples to follow Him. Jesus supernaturally knows what Nathanael was doing when Phillip encouraged him to come and meet Jesus, causing Nathanael to declare that Jesus is the Son of God, and the king of Israel. Jesus tells him that he will see much greater miracles than this.

In John 2, Jesus turns water into best quality wine, at the wedding feast in Cana. In Jerusalem, Jesus, filled with zeal for His Father's house, drives out the money changers and the traders from the temple, because they have made it into a market. Jesus tells the Jews, who are asking for a miraculous sign, that if they destroy this temple, (referring to His own body), it will be raised again in three days.

In John 3:1-21, Nicodemus, (a Pharisee), comes to meet with Jesus. Jesus tells him that he needs to be born again of the Spirit, in order to enter into the kingdom of God. He declares that God has given His only Son, so that whoever believes in Him will have eternal life. Jesus has not come to condemn the world, but, those who choose to reject Him, bring condemnation upon themselves. Those who believe in Jesus come out of darkness and into the light of His truth.

John 3:22-36 records John the Baptist's witness, concerning Jesus. Jesus, declares John, is the one who has come from heaven. He is the bridegroom, and John's role is only to prepare the way. John must now become less, and Jesus greater. Everything has been placed into the hands of the Son. Whoever believes in Him will receive eternal life, but God's wrath will remain on all who reject Him.

John 4:1-42 records the encounter between Jesus and the Samaritan woman, who came to draw water at the well. Jesus, referring to the Holy Spirit, tells her that He can give her water which will be like a spring of water, leading to eternal life, before declaring to her that He is the Messiah. She is convinced of this fact when Jesus, through a word of knowledge, tells her about her past. She returns home to tell the other villagers to come and meet Jesus, and many of them become believers.

In John 4:43-5:15, Jesus heals the son of a royal official, who is dying, by simply declaring to his father that the boy will live. At the Pool of Bethesda, in Jerusalem, Jesus heals a man who has been an invalid for thirty-eight years, after first asking him if he wants to be healed. The man's disability appears to be connected to sin issues in his life, because, when Jesus meets him again later, He tells him to stop sinning, or something worse will happen to him.

John 5:16-47 records Jesus' rebuke to the Pharisees, who wanted to kill Him because He was healing on the Sabbath, and calling God His Father. He tells them that the Father and Himself are in unity in all things. What Jesus is doing testifies that He was sent by the Father. The Scriptures, which they study, testify about Jesus, but they refuse to believe them, because they do not have the love of God in their hearts.

In John 6:1-14, Jesus miraculously feeds the 5,000 with just five loaves and two fish. After they finish eating, the leftovers fill twelve baskets. The crowd are amazed by what they have witnessed, and Jesus withdraws to the mountain, because He knows the people want to forcefully make Him their king. Later Jesus walks on the sea of Galilee to join the disciples in their boat.

In John 6:25-71, Jesus describes Himself as the living bread, which has come down from heaven to give life to all who believe in Him. Those who do believe will be raised again on the last day. Unless someone eats His flesh, (acknowledges the deity of Jesus), and drinks His blood, (trusts in His atoning sacrifice), they will have no life in them. The crowds find the teaching hard to accept, and start to desert Jesus. Peter, however, declares "To whom shall we go? You have the words of eternal life".

John 7:1-24 records how Jesus goes up to teach in the temple during the Feast of Tabernacles. The people are amazed at His teaching, and wonder how He has so much learning, without having studied. Jesus replies that His teaching comes from God, who has sent Him, and to whom He has come to give honour. He asks them why are they angry with Him for bringing healing to individuals on the Sabbath, if circumcising a baby is not breaking the Sabbath regulations.

In John 7:25-53, the people are divided because of Jesus. Some believe that He is the Messiah, and put their faith in Him. The Pharisees feel threatened by Him, and want to arrest Him, but the temple guards cannot find any basis for doing this. Jesus, referring to the Holy Spirit who would be available to all believers after Jesus was glorified, stands in the temple, and invites everyone to come to Him and drink, so that streams of living water may flow from within them.

In John 8:1-30, Jesus deals with the woman caught in adultery in a compassionate and loving way. She's been brought to Him by the Pharisees, who are trying to trap Him. Jesus declares to the crowds that He is the light of the world, and that whoever follows Him will never walk in darkness. He has been sent by His Father in heaven, and it is God, (whom the Pharisees do not know), who testifies to who Jesus is.

In John 8:31-59, Jesus proclaims that His disciples are those who are obedient to His teaching, and that they will consequently walk in truth and freedom. They will no longer be slaves to sin. Jesus tells His listeners that, although descended from Abraham, they are not true children, because they do not do what Abraham would do. They are, therefore, children of the devil, who is a liar. Jesus declares that He has come from heaven, and that He existed even before Abraham was born.

John 9 records how Jesus restores the sight of a man born blind, having told the disciples that the blindness is not, in this instance, a consequence of generational sin. The Pharisees try to discredit this miracle in interviews with the man and his parents. Jesus later meets with the man again, and reveals to him that He, (Jesus), is the Son of Man. He declares the spiritual truth that He has come into the world so that the blind will see, and those who see will become blind.

In John 10:1-21, Jesus declares that He is the good shepherd, who lays down His life for the flock. His sheep recognise His voice and they follow him. He is the gate by which the sheep can enter safely into the sheep enclosure and find safe pasture. The thief, (Satan), comes to steal, kill and destroy, but Jesus has come to give abundant life. He has been given the authority to lay down His life, and to take it up again. His flock is not just the Jews, but others who hear His voice and respond.

In John 10:22-42, Jesus declares that He and the Father are one. He proclaims that the miracles He has performed testify to who He is. He gives life to the sheep who follow Him, and nothing can snatch them out of His Father's hand. Jesus escapes those who accuse Him of blasphemy and want to stone Him to death. He returns to the Jordan, where many people come to Him, and believe in Him.

John 11:1-44 records the raising of Lazarus from the dead. Jesus empathises with the pain and grief that Mary and Martha are going through, and weeps with them, even though He is about to raise

Lazarus to life. Jesus declares that He is the resurrection and the life, and that all who believe in Him will enjoy eternal life. He calls Lazarus to come out of the tomb, even though he has been dead four days, and instructs those with Him to remove Lazarus' grave clothes and set him free.

In John 11:45-12:11, following the raising of Lazarus from the dead, the Pharisees and chief priests plot to arrest Jesus and have Him killed. (They are fearful that they will lose out if the people follow Jesus, because it will result in civil unrest, which will provoke a response by the occupying Roman forces.) Jesus is anointed with expensive perfume by Mary at the house of Lazarus. Her actions are commended by Jesus when Judas criticises her for wasting money.

In John 12:12-50, the crowds welcome Jesus to Jerusalem, waving palm branches and proclaiming that He is the king of Israel. Jesus speaks about His coming death, declaring that He will draw all men to Himself when He is lifted up, and the prince of this world is driven out. He likens His death to a seed being planted, which will produce much fruit. He explains that He has come into the world as a light so that no one needs to remain in darkness.

In John 13:1-17, Jesus, knowing that His earthly life was about to end, washes the feet of His disciples as an example to them, and us, of how to love and serve one another. He gently rebukes Peter, who initially refuses to let Jesus wash his feet.

In John 13:18-38, Jesus knows that Judas is about to betray Him, and tells him to do it quickly. Jesus tells the other disciples that He is about to be glorified. He gives them a new command to love one another, just as He loves them. Peter declares that he will lay down his life for Jesus, but Jesus responds by telling Peter that he will disown Him three times before the cock crows.

In John 14, Jesus declares that anyone who has seen Him has seen the Father, and that no one comes to the Father, except through Him. Those who love Him will keep His commands. Jesus explains that the Holy Spirit will live within them, and guide them into the truth, and remind them of all that Jesus had taught them. Finally, Jesus declares that the prince of this world, (Satan), is coming, but that he has no hold or authority over Jesus, (because Jesus was sinless).

In John 15, Jesus declares that He is the true vine, and that we are the branches, and stresses the importance of remaining in Him, (being obedient to Him), and producing fruit. He describes the Father as the gardener, who sometimes prunes the branches, so they are even more fruitful. He again reminds us to love one another, and warns that, because the Holy Spirit is within us, the world may persecute and hate us, just as it persecuted and hated Him.

In John 16, Jesus continues to explain to the disciples that He is about to leave them and return to the Father, but that He will send them the Holy Spirit. The Holy Spirit will guide them into all truth, and will glorify Jesus. Talking about His death and resurrection, Jesus tells them they will grieve when He leaves them, but their grief will turn to joy in a little while, when they see Him again. He encourages the disciples that the Father will give them whatever they ask for, in the name of Jesus.

In John 17, Jesus prays for Himself and for His disciples. He prays that Father God will glorify Him in His presence, with the glory He had before the world began. He prays that God will protect His disciples from the evil one, sanctify them with the truth, and that they will be filled with joy. He prays that believers will be in unity, as a witness to the world that God loves them, and sent Jesus.

John 18:1-27 describes how Judas leads a detachment of soldiers to Jesus, so they can arrest Him. Jesus tells Peter to put his sword away, after Peter tries to protect Jesus from arrest. Jesus is taken to Annas for questioning, and is struck on the face by one of the court officials. Peter, meanwhile, makes his way to the courtyard outside, but, when questioned by servants, on three separate occasions, denies that he knows Jesus.

John 18:28-40 records how the Jewish leaders take Jesus to the Roman governor Pilate, because they do not have the authority to declare a death penalty. Jesus tells Pilate that His kingdom is not of this world. Pilate declares that he can find no fault in Jesus. In accordance with a Passover custom, he offers to set free, either Jesus, or a known criminal named Barabbas. The Jews respond by shouting that they want Barabbas released.

John 19:1-16 records how Pilate has Jesus flogged, and how the soldiers mock Him, and place a crown of thorns upon His head. Although Pilate can find no basis for the charges against Jesus, the Jews insist that He should die for claiming to be the Son of God, and they shout out "crucify Him". When questioned by Pilate, Jesus tells him that he would have no authority over Him, unless it were given by God. Because he is fearful of the Jews, Pilate hands Jesus over to them to be crucified.

John 19:17-42 describes how Jesus is crucified, and a sign placed over Him, declaring that He is the king of the Jews. After asking John to look after His mother, Mary, Jesus declares "it is finished" and gives up His spirit. The soldiers, sent to break the legs of those who have been crucified, discover that Jesus is already dead (confirmed by water and blood flowing out, when they pierce His side). Jesus' body is wrapped in spices and pieces of linen, and placed in a nearby unused tomb.

John 20:1-18 records the events of resurrection day. Peter and John rush to the tomb when Mary Magdalene tells them that she has discovered the stone has been rolled away, and Jesus' body has gone. When John sees the empty grave clothes and the folded head cloth, he believes in the resurrection. Jesus later appears to Mary and tells her to report to the disciples that He is returning to His Father in heaven, who is also their Father and their God.

John 20:19-32 records how Jesus appears to the disciples on resurrection day. He tells them He is sending them into the world just as the Father has sent Him. Preparing them for the coming of the Holy Spirit on the day of Pentecost Jesus breathes on them and tells them to receive the Holy Spirit. He appears to them again a week later, and Thomas, who was not present at his first appearance, and had expressed his lack of faith, now declares Jesus to be His Lord and His God.

In John 21, Jesus appears to Peter and some of the disciples at the Sea of Tiberius, and is identified when there is a miraculous catch of fish. Jesus restores and brings healing to Peter, by asking three times if he loves Him. Jesus responds by telling Peter to feed His lambs, and feed His sheep. John concludes his gospel by declaring that Jesus did many other things, and that if everything was written down, the world could not contain all the books that would need to be written.

Acts

The book of Acts, written by Luke, records the development of the early Church, from the ascension of Jesus to Paul's imprisonment in Rome.

In Chapter 1, Jesus ascends into heaven, after first instructing the disciples to wait in Jerusalem until they receive the gift of the Holy Spirit. Angelic beings declare that Jesus will return again, in the same way that they have witnessed Him ascending. Matthias is chosen to replace Judas as one of the apostles.

In Acts 2, the Holy Spirit comes down upon the disciples as tongues of fire, and a rushing wind. They start to speak in tongues, and begin to boldly preach the good news about Jesus. Peter proclaims to the crowd that Jesus, whom they crucified, has risen from the dead, and is their Lord and Saviour. He invites them to repent, be baptised and receive the Holy Spirit. 3,000 are saved, and begin to meet daily to break bread and praise God. Each day God adds to their number.

Acts 3 records how a man, crippled from birth, is healed at the temple gate, in the name of Jesus. In response to Peter's command to walk, the man jumps to his feet, and enters the temple, praising God. Peter tells the crowds, who are filled with wonder and amazement, that they should not be surprised at what has happened. He proclaims that Jesus is the Messiah that the Scriptures speak about, and they have rejected and crucified Him, but God has raised Him from the dead.

Acts 4:1-22 records how Peter and John are arrested, following the healing of the crippled man. They boldly proclaim to the Sanhedrin that the healing was in the name of Jesus, and that there is no other name under heaven by which we can be saved. The Sanhedrin order them to stop teaching about Jesus, but Peter and John respond that they cannot help speaking about what they have seen and heard, and that they must be obedient to God rather than the Sanhedrin.

In Acts 4:23-5:11, the early Church prays for boldness, signs and miracles, as they preach the gospel. The believers are all in unity, and support each other so that nobody is in need. Ananias and Sapphira sell some property, in order to give the proceeds to the Church. However, they lie about how much money they received, and keep some of it for themselves. When Peter tells them that Satan has filled their heart and that they have lied to God, they fall down dead.

Acts 5:12-42 records how the Church continues to grow, and

that many who are sick, or tormented with evil spirits, are healed. The apostles are arrested, but, during the night, an angel sets them free, and they return to the temple to preach. They are brought before the Sanhedrin, and again proclaim that they have to obey God rather than men. The Sanhedrin orders them to be flogged, but the apostles rejoice that they have been counted worthy of suffering, and continue to preach the good news.

In Acts 6, the first deacons are appointed to handle administrative matters in the Church, so that the apostles can focus on prayer, and ministry of the word. The criteria in selecting these deacons, who include Stephen, are that they must be men filled with the Holy Spirit and wisdom. Stephen, who is performing many miracles and preaching and debating with great wisdom, is arrested and brought before the Sanhedrin, where false witnesses testify against him.

Acts 7:1-29 records Stephen's speech to the Sanhedrin, where he is on trial for blasphemy. In order to show that Jesus is the promised Messiah and the fulfilment of the promises made to the people of Israel, Stephen recounts the history of Israel. He begins with the call of God to Abraham to leave his own country, and to go to the land that God would show him.

Acts 7:30-60 continues the record of Stephen's speech to the Sanhedrin. Stephen recounts the history of Israel, declaring that the Israelites rebelled against God, and throughout their history rejected and persecuted the prophets, raised up by God. Now they have betrayed and murdered the Messiah. The Sanhedrin, filled with anger against Stephen, drag him outside and stone him to death. Stephen, as he lies dying, commits his spirit to God, and asks Him not to hold this sin against them.

In Acts 8:1-25, persecution, led by Saul, breaks out against the Church in Jerusalem. As the Church scatters, they preach the gospel wherever they go. Philip goes to Samaria and many are healed, delivered and saved. Peter and John are sent to Samaria, and the believers there are filled with the Holy Spirit, when they lay hands on them. Peter rebukes Simon the sorcerer for wanting to buy the ability to impart the Holy Spirit to others, declaring that his heart is captive to sin.

Acts 8:26-40 records how Philip, directed by an angel of God, meets an Ethiopian eunuch who is reading about the suffering servant from the book of Isaiah. Philip, starting with that passage, explains to him the good news about Jesus. The Ethiopian immediately becomes a believer, and asks Philip to baptise him, when the chariot they are riding in reaches some water.

In Acts 9:1-19, we read how Saul (Paul), who has been persecuting the Church, meets with Jesus on the Damascus Road, and is temporarily struck blind. He is given a vision that a man named Ananias will pray for him, and he will be healed. Meanwhile, the Lord appears in a vision to a disciple in Damascus, named Ananias, asking him to go and pray for Paul, and allaying his fears that he will be arrested. When Ananias prays for Paul his sight is restored, he is filled with the Holy Spirit, and he is then baptised in water.

Acts 9:20-43 records how Paul begins preaching boldly in Damascus that Jesus is the Messiah. This angers the Jews and he has to flee to Jerusalem. Initially the believers there are too frightened to associate with Paul, but Barnabus convinces the apostles that Paul is a changed man. The Jews in Jerusalem want to kill Paul, so he is sent to Tarsus. Peter, meanwhile, heals a paralytic named Aeneas in the name of Jesus, and Tabitha (Dorcas) is raised from the dead when Peter prays for her.

In Acts 10:1-23, we read that Cornelius, a God-fearing Gentile, has a vision, in which an angel tells him to send for a man named Peter, who can be found in Joppa. Peter also has a vision, in which he is shown that God is able to declare clean and pure those things considered unclean under the Old Covenant. (This would include eating at the house of a Gentile.) In the vision, Peter is told that he should go with the three men who are about to arrive at the house he is staying in.

Acts 10:24-48 records how Peter goes to the house of Cornelius, in response to visions given to himself and Cornelius. As Peter preaches the gospel to them, explaining how Jesus went around doing good, and healing all who were under the power of the devil, his listeners are filled with the Holy Spirit, and start speaking in tongues and praising God. Peter, and the believers with him, are amazed, and declare that there is no reason why these Gentiles cannot be baptised in the name of Jesus.

In Acts 11, Peter returns to Jerusalem and tells the Jewish believers what has happened in Joppa. They all agree that God, by pouring out the Holy Spirit on the household of Cornelius, has confirmed that salvation is not just for the Jews, but for all who put their trust in Jesus. Greeks in Antioch are also responding to the Gospel, and Barnabus is sent to investigate. Barnabus fetches Paul to help him, and many are saved, and begin to refer to themselves as Christians.

Acts 12:1-19 records how King Herod has James put to death,

and arrests Simon Peter, in order to try and gain favour with the Jews. During the night, an angel rescues Peter, who is chained between two guards, and leads him out of the prison. He re-joins the believers, who are so surprised that they initially do not open the door to him, when they hear his voice.

In Acts 12:20-13:12, King Herod receives the adoration from the crowds that he is a god, and so is struck down and dies. Following prayer and fasting, Paul and Barnabus are commissioned and sent out by the Church in Antioch, and arrive in Cyprus. Their work there is opposed and undermined by Elymas, who is a Jewish sorcerer. Paul rebukes him as a child of the devil, and he is struck with blindness. As a result, the proconsul in Cyprus becomes a believer.

In Acts 13:13-52, Paul and Barnabus go to Pisidian Antioch (Turkey), and teach in the synagogue that Jesus is the Messiah about whom the Scriptures speak, and through whom there is forgiveness of sins. The Jewish leaders are jealous, but Paul boldly confronts them, and says that, if they refuse to believe, and reject the message, he will then take it to the Gentiles. The word of God spreads through the region, but the Jews stir up persecution, and have Paul and Barnabus expelled.

Acts 14 records that many in Iconium respond to the preaching of Paul and Barnabus, confirmed by miraculous signs. In Lystra, a crippled man is healed, and the crowds try to honour Paul and Barnabus as gods, come down from heaven. The Jews stir up opposition against Paul, and it appears he is miraculously healed, after the crowds try to stone him to death. They continue to preach throughout the region, before returning to Antioch to report back all that God has done.

In Acts 15:1-35, Paul and Barnabus meet with the disciples in Jerusalem to determine how to treat the Gentile believers, as some were teaching that the Gentiles had to be circumcised and taught to follow all the law of Moses. They all agree that salvation is through the grace of Jesus Christ. Two disciples are chosen to accompany Paul and Barnabus, to instruct the Gentiles that they do not have to be circumcised, but they must avoid idolatry and sexual immorality.

In Acts 15:36-16:15, we read that Barnabus and Mark travel to Cyprus, while Paul and Silas go to Syria, Derbe and Lystra to encourage and strengthen the Church in Asia Minor. Timothy is circumcised, (because he is Jewish; not because he has become a believer), and joins Paul in his travels. Paul receives a vision and call to go to Macedonia and Philippi, and so take the gospel to Greece. While in Philippi, Lydia hears the gospel and becomes a believer, and is baptised.

Acts 16:16-40 records how the leaders and officials in Philippi have Paul and Silas beaten and thrown into jail, because they deliver a fortune teller of a spirit of divination. During the night, as they are praising God, an earthquake occurs, and they are set free. They stop the jailor from killing himself, and he and his family become believers, and are baptised. The local leaders become alarmed when they discover that Paul and Silas are Roman citizens, and try to appease them.

Acts 17:1-15 records how Paul goes to Thessalonica, and tries to present the Gospel to the Jews in the synagogue. Some believe, as do many God-fearing Greeks, but other Jews are jealous, and organise a mob to riot. Paul and Silas have to escape to Berea, where the Jews are more receptive, and diligently study the Scriptures to test the truth of what Paul is teaching. Many are saved, but Paul has to leave Berea when Jews arrive from Thessalonica, and stir up opposition against him.

In Acts 17:16-34, we read how Paul arrives in Athens and discovers that the city is full of idolatry. He debates and reasons with the Jews in the synagogue, and with the philosophers in the marketplace. He preaches the good news about Jesus and His resurrection, and declares that he has come to reveal to them the 'unknown God', to whom one of the altars in Athens is dedicated. A number respond to Paul's preaching, and become believers.

In Acts 18, Paul, helped by Priscilla and Aquila, establishes the Church in Corinth, after being opposed and rejected by the Jews living there. Paul stays in Corinth for over a year, before embarking on another journey to visit the churches in Syria, Galatia and Asia Minor. Meanwhile, Apollos, who has a thorough knowledge of the Scriptures, is being nurtured in the faith by Aquila and Priscilla, and is publicly debating with the Jews to prove that Jesus is the promised Messiah.

In Acts 19:1-22, Paul finds disciples in Ephesus who have never heard of the Holy Spirit. They are then baptised in the name of Jesus, receive the Holy Spirit, and begin speaking in tongues and prophesying. The importance of attempting deliverance only in the authority and power of Jesus is shown when some Jews are severely beaten by a demonised man. Many occultic practitioners repent of their activities and destroy their expensive books.

In Acts 19:23-41, demonically inspired riots, led by those who worship the goddess Artemis, break out in Ephesus. The rioters earn their income from making gold and silver models of this goddess, and are fearful they will lose business as a result of the gospel message being preached by Paul, and its truth being confirmed by miraculous signs and wonders. The civil authorities quell the riots by declaring the believers are not breaking the law in any way.

Acts 20 records how Paul visits and encourages the churches in Greece and Macedonia. At Troas, a young man, who fell from a window and died, is brought back to life when Paul prays for him. Paul says farewell to the elders of the church in Ephesus, expecting never to return, as he has been warned that he will face hardships and sufferings in Jerusalem. He encourages the elders to be faithful overseers, and to be on their guard against those who would try to distort the truth.

Acts 21:1-25 records Paul's return to Jerusalem. Agabus prophesies that Paul will be bound up and handed over to the Gentiles. Paul views this as preparing him for what lies ahead, rather than a warning to not go to Jerusalem. Paul is greeted by the leaders in Jerusalem, who rejoice in all that has happened among the Gentiles. They ask Paul to undergo a purification rite, to counter the false accusation that he teaches believing Jews must abandon all the Jewish customs.

Acts 21:26-22:21 records how the Jews rise up when they see Paul, and assume that he has brought Gentiles into the temple area. A riot ensues, and only the intervention of the Roman guards saves Paul from being killed. Paul addresses the crowds, declaring that he is as zealous for God as they are. He tells them of his encounter with Jesus on the Damascus Road, and his commission to take the gospel to the Gentiles.

In Acts 22:22-23:11, the Roman commander orders Paul to be flogged, but then discovers Paul is a Roman citizen. He decides, instead, to bring Paul before the Sanhedrin to defend himself. Paul tells them that he is on trial because he believes in the resurrection of the dead. This causes a violent dispute between the Pharisees and the Sadducees, and the Roman guards again have to rescue Paul. In the night Jesus appears to Paul and says that he will testify about Him in Rome.

In Acts 23:12-35, the Jews hatch a plot to try and kill Paul when he is being taken to appear before the Sanhedrin in Jerusalem. When the Roman commander hears of the plot, he arranges for Paul to be taken to the Governor, Felix, in Caesarea, and for the Jewish authorities to present their case against Paul under the jurisdiction of Felix.

In Acts 24, we have the trial of Paul before Governor Felix. The

Jews accuse Paul of being a troublemaker, and stirring up riots among the Jews. Paul declares that he has done nothing wrong, and that he agrees with everything written in the books of the law and the prophets. To pacify the Jewish authorities, Felix keeps Paul under arrest for two years, while frequently meeting with him to talk, in the hope that Paul might pay him a bribe.

Acts 25:1-22 records that Governor Festus replaces Governor Felix, who had kept Paul imprisoned in Caesarea. The Jewish authorities again request that Paul be handed over to face trial in Jerusalem and be put to death. Paul denies that he has done anything wrong, and, because he is a Roman citizen, claims that any charge against him should be dealt with by the courts in Rome. Festus discusses the problem with King Agrippa, who agrees to listen to what Paul has to say.

Acts 25:26-26:32 records how Paul defends his actions before King Agrippa. He explains how he was a zealous Pharisee persecuting the followers of Jesus. Jesus, however, revealed Himself to Paul and commissioned him to preach the gospel to the Gentiles. The Jews opposed him because he preached that Jesus was the Messiah and had risen from the dead. King Agrippa declares that Paul is not guilty of any crime, and could have been set free, if he had not appealed to Rome.

Acts 27 tells of Paul's perilous journey from Jerusalem to Rome. Despite Paul's warning, the centurion taking Paul, and other prisoners, to Rome sets sail, and encounters severe storms which threaten to sink the boat. Paul encourages them not to be afraid, because an angel of God has appeared to him in a vision and told him that he will reach Rome safely. Although the boat runs aground and is broken to pieces on the island of Malta, everyone on board reaches land safely.

Acts 28 continues the account of Paul's journey to Rome. Following the shipwreck on Malta, Paul suffers no ill effect after being bitten by a deadly snake. Some of the islanders are healed when Paul prays for them. On reaching Rome, Paul meets with the Jews there, and endeavours to convince them about Jesus. The book of Acts concludes by saying that Paul lived for two years in Rome and, although under guard, was free to boldly preach about Jesus and the kingdom of God.

Romans

In the book of Romans Paul explains our need for a Saviour, and how justification and salvation comes through faith in Jesus. He is writing to a church in which there will be Gentiles from a pagan background as well as believers from a Jewish background.

In verses 1:1-17, Paul greets the believers in Rome and shares his desire to visit them and share with them the good news of the gospel.

In Romans 1:18-32, Paul tells us that the eternal nature and power of God are clearly reflected in all that He has created. Those who rebel, reject God and involve themselves in all kinds of wickedness are without excuse, and deserve the judgement that will come upon them.

In Romans 2, Paul stresses the need for obedience in walking in the truth that we have received. Addressing those of his readers who are Jewish, Paul rebukes those who know the law, but do not keep it. It is circumcision of the heart that God is looking for.

In Romans 3, Paul clearly tells us that righteousness comes through faith in Jesus and not by our actions. We have all sinned, whether we are Jews, trying to live by the law, or Gentiles. The law serves to show us that we are all sinners in need of a Saviour.

Using the example of Abraham, Paul argues in Romans 4 that Abraham's righteousness came through faith. It was his belief in God that made him righteous, not his physical circumcision. Abraham is not just the father of the Jewish nation, but is the father of all who believe.

In Romans 5, Paul tells us we are justified by faith. Jesus has died in our place. Sin and death entered into the human race through one man, Adam, and righteousness, and escape from the consequences of sin into eternal life, are now available through the one man, Jesus.

In Romans 6, Paul answers the question; "As we are saved by grace can we ignore the law and continue in sin?" Paul answers and says we must die to sin, and no longer be slaves to sin, which leads to death. Instead, we are to become slaves of righteousness, seeking to be obedient to God.

In Romans 7, Paul explains that the law exposes our sinfulness. As Christians, we face a continual battle between our carnal nature, which wants to continue in sin, and the desires of our spirit, now alive to God and indwelt by the Holy Spirit.

Having talked about the struggle with sin in Romans Chapter 7, Paul talks about the victory we can have when we are led by the Spirit in Romans 8:1-17. The Spirit within us gives us life, and testifies that we are God's children, and His heirs.

In Romans 8:18-39, Paul tells us that all of creation is waiting for redemption. In the meantime, the Spirit helps us in our weakness, and Jesus is at the Father's side interceding for us. Nothing in all creation, says Paul, can separate us from the love of God that is in Jesus.

In Romans 9, Paul continues his argument that salvation is through faith, and not through merely observing the law. Although the Gentiles are receiving righteousness, and entering into the promises of God by faith, Israel is not yet receiving righteousness, because it is seeking righteousness by works.

In Romans 10, Paul continues to stress that salvation is obtained through faith in Jesus, and what He has done for us. This is true for both Jew and Gentile, and all need to hear this message of good news, so that they can respond and make Jesus Lord of their life.

In Romans 11:1-24, Paul asks the question whether God has rejected Israel. His answer is a definite "No!" The Gentiles ('a wild olive shoot') have been grafted into the roots of the cultivated 'olive tree' (Israel), but Israel has not stumbled beyond recovery. Although some branches have been broken off through unbelief, it will be much easier for God to graft them back in at some future point, because they are the natural branches of the olive tree.

In Romans 11:25-36, Paul concludes his argument that God has not yet finished with Israel. Israel is experiencing a hardening of heart until the full number of Gentiles comes in. Then, Paul says, all Israel will be saved, because God's gifts and promises are irrevocable.

In Romans 12, Paul tells us that we should be living sacrifices, and change our earthly way of thinking, so we can know God's will for our life. Paul encourages us to use the giftings we have been given to bless others. We are to act in love and humility towards others, and leave revenge and judgement in God's hands.

In Romans 13, Paul continues to exhort us to behave with love to others. He tells us to respect those in authority, and not rebel against them. We are to clothe ourselves in Jesus, and not follow the desires of our carnal nature.

In Romans 14, Paul encourages us not to become judgemental of the spirituality of others, and not to put stumbling blocks, or obstacles, in their path. This passage is not endorsing liberalism, or compromise with regard to moral law or sin, (which is unchanging).

Rather, it is saying that, as Christians, we need to allow the Holy Spirit to convict, lead and guide others, and not to dogmatically impose our understanding or ways upon them.

In Romans 15, Paul encourages the believers in Rome to seek unity, and to recognise that the gospel is for both Jews and Gentiles. Paul shares that his desire is to keep preaching the gospel of Christ, accompanied by signs and miracles, and that he hopes to visit Rome on the way to Spain, after he has visited Jerusalem.

In Romans 16, Paul completes his letter with some personal greetings. He again urges unity, and urges his readers not to tolerate those who want to bring division. He concludes with a blessing, giving glory to God through Jesus Christ.

1 Corinthians

1 Corinthians is written by Paul to the church he established in Corinth. It addresses various problematic issues affecting the church.

In 1 Corinthians 1:1-17, Paul thanks God for the church in Corinth, and encourages them that God will keep them strong and blameless. He urges them to be in unity, because he has heard that there are quarrels in the church, with groups claiming to follow different teachings.

In 1 Corinthians 1:18-31, Paul tells us that the message of the cross is a stumbling block to Jews, and appears foolish to the world, but it is the power of God for those who are being saved. God chooses to confound earthly wisdom, and use the weak to shame the strong.

In 1 Corinthians 2, Paul continues to explain that the message he preaches is not based on worldly wisdom, but on God's wisdom, demonstrated with the Spirit's power. It is the Spirit within us that enables us to understand and accept the deep things of God.

In 1 Corinthians 3, Paul rebukes the believers in Corinth for following after men, (including himself), rather than God. God has to be the one we look to, not the individuals God chooses to use, or speak through. Jesus is the foundation on which we all must build. What we build on that foundation will be tested, and will be the basis for our heavenly reward.

In Corinthians 4, Paul continues to rebuke his readers, saying that some of them have become arrogant, and wise in their own eyes, and are judging others, including himself. Paul tells them his conscience is clear, but it is only God who can really judge our attitudes and motives.

In Corinthians 5, Paul continues to chastise his readers, and says that they are tolerating ungodly behaviour within the church, and not dealing with it. Those who claim to be believers, but are living sinful lifestyles, should be disciplined and expelled.

In 1 Corinthians 6, Paul tells his readers that they shouldn't be taking other believers to court, and having non-believers act as judge between them. Paul addresses the question of sexual immorality, and teaches that we become one with those we have sex with. He reminds us that our bodies are temples of the Holy Spirit, and that we should flee all immorality, and honour God with our bodies.

In 1 Corinthians 7:1-16, Paul addresses various issues relating to marriage. Paul promotes monogamous marriage for those who have not been called, and gifted, to remain single. God's ideal is that couples should not divorce, but that both partners should be willing to be reconciled. Believers should not divorce their spouses just because they are unbelievers. However, if a non-believer divorces their partner because they have become a believer, the believer is free to re-marry.

In 1 Corinthians 7:17-40, Paul encourages us to be a Christian 'where we are'. Paul then addresses those who are single, and suggests they don't marry, because of the 'current situation', but says the choice is up to each individual. (Some commentators consider Paul was addressing those who were entering into 'marriage relationships' with the intent of not consummating them.) Christians who re-marry after their spouse dies should only marry a Christian.

In 1 Corinthians 8, Paul says that the food offered to idols is not in itself defiled, but our belief system about such food could cause problems for ourselves or others. In our actions we should not undermine the faith of immature believers.

In 1 Corinthians 9, Paul says he makes an effort to identify with his listeners, so he can tell them the gospel. He encourages us to live our Christian lives with purpose, so we can attain our heavenly reward.

In 1 Corinthians 10, Paul reminds us that the Israelites escaped from Egypt and knew God's blessings, but this did not stop them sinning, and, as a result, they suffered the consequences. As believers we are not free to do anything we like, we must resist temptation. When we are tempted, there is always a way out; by making a godly choice. Paul tells us that idolatry involves participation with demons, and must be avoided.

In 1 Corinthians 10:23-11:16, Paul says he will eat all food with thanksgiving, (something we should all do), but will not eat the food if the hosts make the point that the meat is an offering to idols. Paul talks about headship roles. Men should not cover their heads, (as the pagans did when worshipping idols), and married women should wear something, (a head covering), as a sign of being married, and under their husband's spiritual cover.

In 1 Corinthians 11:17-34, Paul gives guidance on how to celebrate the Lord's Supper, or Communion. This should be done in a reverent way, recognising the significance and symbolism of what we are doing. Paul encourages us to examine ourselves, and deal with any sin issues in our life. Some, he says, have become sick, or have died, because they failed to do this.

In 1 Corinthians 12, Paul talks about the gifts of the Holy Spirit, and compares the Church to a body. He lists the various gifts of the Spirit, and ministry roles within the Church. We all have different gifts and roles, and all of us are important to the functioning of the

Church as a whole. We need to recognise the gifts that God has given to others, and not ignore, or elevate, one gift in favour of another, and so bring division into the Church.

1 Corinthians 13 has often been called the love chapter. In it, Paul says we need to act in love in everything we do. If we do things out of any other motive, we nullify what we do. Love is patient and kind. It is not self-centred or proud, but will protect and seek to build up, rather than pull down. Love enables us to forgive others. Love is eternal, and will never fail.

In 1 Corinthians 14, Paul talks about how to use the gifts of the Spirit in an orderly way, without quenching the Spirit, or causing confusion. He commends the use of speaking in tongues in our private devotions, but, when spoken out in a public meeting, there should be an interpretation. Prophecy needs to be tested and weighed. Paul's instruction that women should be silent appears to be addressing an issue of disruptions, caused by their behaviour in the church.

In 1 Corinthians 15, Paul explains the significance of Christ's resurrection, which was witnessed by the disciples, and many others, including Paul. It is the proof that we too will be raised from the dead with new, imperishable bodies. Death came through Adam, but eternal life now comes through Jesus. Jesus will destroy all dominion, authority and power, before handing over the kingdom to the Father.

In 1 Corinthians 16, Paul encourages the Corinthians to put aside a proportion of their income to help support God's people. He explains his future plans, and hopes that Timothy and Apollos will visit them. He encourages them to stand firm, and be strong in the faith. Paul finishes his letter with personal greetings.

2 Corinthians

Paul opens his second letter to the Corinthians by praising God, who comforts us, so that we can comfort others. He shares that he has faced difficult times in Asia, but that God has helped him, in response to the prayers of many. Paul explains why he has been unable to visit the church in Corinth. It would appear, from the way he writes, that some in the church have been openly critical of him.

In 2 Corinthians 2:5-3:6, Paul delegates a discipline issue to the Corinthian Church. (In his previous letter Paul rebuked them for not disciplining those who are living in sin.) Paul has been preaching the gospel in Troas and Macedonia. He explains he does not need letters of recommendation, but that his ministry is validated by the evidence of lives being transformed by the Holy Spirit.

In 2 Corinthians 3:7-18, Paul compares the glory of the Old Covenant to the surpassing glory which comes through the New Covenant. Unlike Moses, we do not need to cover our faces, for the veil has been removed. The transformation which is taking place within us, as we move into freedom, and become more like Jesus, should be visible to all.

In 2 Corinthians 4, Paul writes that he does not distort God's word, but presents truth, and proclaims that Jesus is Lord. The God of this age (Satan) has blinded the minds of unbelievers. Although hard pressed and persecuted, and realising that his mortal body will die, Paul is not in despair. He encourages us to have our eyes on what is unseen, and the eternal glory which is yet to come.

In 2 Corinthians 5, we are reminded that everyone must appear before the judgement seat of Christ. Therefore, we should seek to live lives which are pleasing to Him. We have been reconciled to God through Jesus, who became sin for us. Therefore, we should endeavour to be ambassadors for Christ, and tell others of this message of reconciliation.

Paul starts 2 Corinthians 6 by sharing both the difficulties and joys of being a witness for Jesus. Paul tells us that we should avoid being yoked with unbelievers. There cannot be harmony between the kingdom of light and the kingdom of darkness and, therefore, we need to separate ourselves from all ungodly activities. Paul reminds us that God is our heavenly Father, and that we are His children.

2 Corinthians 7 reminds us to be holy in all that we do, out of reverence to God. Paul speaks of his first letter to the Corinthians, and commends them for responding positively to some of the harsh things he said to them. He is encouraged by the report brought to him by

Titus.

In 2 Corinthians 8:1-15, Paul talks about the need to give generously to support others. He praises the Macedonian church for their generosity, and asks the Corinthians to also be generous. Paul understands the pressures they are under, and says he is not trying to put a further burden upon them, but is seeking equality, as other parts of the Church are suffering even greater hardships.

In 2 Corinthians 8:16-9:5, Paul tells the Corinthian church that he is sending Titus and another brother to help them organise the collection of the offerings, which they have already promised to make. Pauls tells them that this will ensure that the offerings will be handled with integrity.

In 2 Corinthians 9:6-15, Paul continues to encourage the Corinthians to give generously to support the needs of God's people. Their giving should be out of thankful hearts. As they bless others, God will bless them, and meet all their needs.

In 2 Corinthians 10, Paul reminds us that the spiritual weapons we have at our disposal can demolish strongholds. He encourages us to reject all thoughts which Jesus would not agree with. Paul defends his right to speak into the issues confronting the church at Corinth. He is not commending himself, or boasting, but simply fulfilling his role as the founding apostle of the Corinthian church.

In 2 Corinthians 11:1-15, Paul continues to defend his right to address issues in the Corinthian church, and to ask them to financially support the work of God's people. He warns them about false teachers, or apostles who will seek to undermine his authority, and lead them astray. The false apostles may look fine on the outside, but, he reminds them, even Satan masquerades as an angel of light.

In 2 Corinthians 11:16-33, Paul feels the need to counter the boasting of those who seem to be undermining his authority, and trying to lead the Corinthians astray. Paul details the cost he has had to pay, in terms of personal trials, difficulties and persecution in preaching the gospel.

In 2 Corinthians 12:1-10, Paul continues the defence of his ministry, by saying that he experienced a divine revelation of the heavenly realms. But, he writes, he also suffers from a thorn in the flesh, or a weakness, (Paul calls it an affliction from Satan), which serves to keep him humble, and stops him from boasting about his spirituality. When we are weak we have to depend on God, and His power is made perfect in our weakness.

In 2 Corinthians 12:11-21, Paul reminds the Corinthians of the signs and wonders worked in their midst, which authenticate his ministry. He has not been a burden to them, or tried to exploit them, and he is willingly to spend himself for them. He is concerned that, when he visits them, he will find them behaving in sinful ways towards each other, and that they will not have repented of the ungodly sexual sin in which they have indulged.

In 2 Corinthians 13, Paul writes that this will be his third visit to them, and that he will not hesitate to exercise his authority to bring godly discipline, and to build them up. We are reminded that the test of our salvation is whether we have Jesus living in us. Paul concludes his letter by reminding the Corinthians to live in love and peace, and prays a Trinitarian blessing, that they may know the grace, love and fellowship that come from God.

Galatians

The letter to the church in Galatia, a province in Asia Minor, was written by the apostle Paul in about 50 AD.

In Chapter 1, Paul says he is concerned that deception and confusion have entered the Galatian church, and that they are believing a different gospel from the one that he received by divine revelation from God. Following his conversion, the believers in Judah were amazed that Paul, who had formerly persecuted them, was now preaching the gospel.

In Galatians 2, Paul tells the Galatians about his meetings with the Jewish believers, including Peter, James and John, concerning the issue of whether Gentile believers need to undergo physical circumcision. Paul argues that righteousness comes from faith in Jesus, and not by keeping the law. If righteousness can be obtained through observing the law, the sacrifice of Jesus is meaningless.

In Galatians 3:1-25, Paul rebukes the Galatians for attempting the impossible task of trying to obtain righteousness by observing the law, rather than by faith in Jesus. The promises to Abraham, who was declared righteous through faith, were made many years before the law was given. Gentile believers become sons of Abraham through faith, and inherit these same promises. Jesus, through His death, paid the penalty for our inability to obtain righteousness by observing the law.

In Galatians 3:26-4:20, Paul encourages us that, all who put their faith in Jesus, are one, and that there are no distinctions between those of different races or gender. We have become full heirs through Jesus, and we are no longer slaves, subject to the principles of this world, but we are free to be led by God's Holy Spirit. Zealousness for God is good, but when it becomes religiosity, aimed at earning man's approval, it is meaningless, and we lose our joy.

In Galatians 4:21-31, Paul continues his argument that righteousness comes through faith in Jesus, and not by observing the law. Just as Isaac was a fulfilment of a promise of God, and received the promises made to Abraham, we too enter into the promises of God through Jesus. When we strive to obtain righteousness through observing the law, we become like Ishmael, the son of a slave girl who, unlike Isaac, did not inherit the promises made to Abraham.

In Galatians 5, we are encouraged, by Paul, to be led by the Spirit, rather than by our carnal nature, which needs to be crucified. When we do this, the fruit of the Holy Spirit should be evident in our lives. We are set free from trying to obtain righteousness through observing the law, but that does not mean that we are free to indulge in the desires of our sinful nature. Our freedom in Christ should lead us into wanting to love and serve one another.

In Galatians 6, Paul encourages us to examine ourselves, but not take pride in comparing ourselves to others. He reminds us of the very important spiritual principle of sowing and reaping. Our actions are not without consequences. Righteousness leads to life, but unrighteousness leads to death and destruction. He concludes by stressing that circumcision or uncircumcision mean nothing. What matters is that we become a new creation, through faith in Jesus.

Ephesians

Ephesus was a major city located in Asia Minor (Turkey).

In Ephesians 1 Paul reminds us of all the spiritual blessings that come to us because we are in Christ. We have forgiveness of sin, redemption, adoption as sons and the seal of the Holy Spirit through God's predestined plan of salvation. Paul prays that believers may know God better, and know that power, by which God raised Jesus from the dead, and seated Him in the place of authority over all things.

In Ephesians 2, we are reminded that we have become alive to Christ, and are no longer dead in our sins, and under the ruler of this world. Jesus came to reconcile both the Gentiles and the Jews to God, through the cross. We have been saved by grace, through faith in what Jesus has done for us, and not through anything that we ourselves have done. We are now joined to Him. We are His workmanship, and He has a plan and purpose for our lives.

In Ephesians 3:1-13, Paul reminds us that the Gentiles and the Jews are members of one body, and share the same inheritance. These divine mysteries were not given to Paul by other men, but by a direct revelation of God. The Church, moving in the power of the Holy Spirit, is a demonstration of the wisdom of God to the powers and authorities in the heavenly realms. We can approach God with freedom and confidence.

In Ephesians 3:14-4:16, Paul prays that his readers may be strengthened in their spirits by the power of God, and fully grasp the extent of God's love for them. He explains that God has given apostles, pastors, teachers, prophets, and evangelists to prepare God's people for works of service, so that the body of Christ can be built up to maturity, in love and unity.

In Ephesians 4:17-32, we are reminded not to live like non-believers. We are to put off our old self, and to get rid of impurity, deceitful desires, bitterness, slander, and unwholesome talk. We need to be changed in the attitude of our minds, and the way in which we think. We are to be compassionate and kind to others, and walk in forgiveness. Pauls tells us that, when we sin, we give the enemy a foothold in our lives.

In Ephesians 5, Paul continues to remind us how we should live. There should be no sexual immorality, greed, bad language, or coarse joking. We are to walk in the light, in mutual submission to one another, and be filled with God's Holy Spirit. The marriage relationship should reflect Jesus' relationship with His Church. A wife should respect and submit to her husband as head of the marriage, and a husband should love his wife as himself, and lay down his life for her.

In Ephesians 6, Paul tells us that children should obey their parents, and slaves should obey their masters. Parents should train their children, and masters should treat their slaves well. Our battle is not against people, but against spiritual powers in the heavenly realms. Paul compares our spiritual armour to the armour of a soldier. We need to protect our heart and mind, and use our faith to extinguish the lies of the enemy. We need to pray continually, and walk in peace and truth, using God's word as a sword.

Philippians

The letter to the Philippians, written in about 60 AD, is to the church in Macedonia founded by Paul, which we read about in Acts 16:16-40.

In Philippians 1:1-11, Paul warmly greets the church and reminds them that God will complete the work He has started in them. He prays that they will be filled with the love of God, grow in their understanding, and that they will be able to discern God's plan for their lives.

In Philippians 1:12-30, Paul writes that his imprisonment has served to advance the proclamation of the gospel, even though some are preaching the good news from wrong motives. Paul realises that he might die for his faith, but rejoices that, if he dies, he will be with Jesus. He encourages the church to stand firm, even if they have to face persecution.

In Philippians 2:1-18, we are encouraged to be more like Jesus. Jesus was willing to lay aside all His power and majesty, and humble Himself, for our sake. As a result, He has been exalted to the highest place, and is Lord over everything. We are encouraged to work out our salvation in humility, with a godly fear. We should seek to allow God to work through us, without complaining, and in a unity of purpose and love with other believers.

In Philippians 2:19-3:11, Paul writes concerning Timothy, and commends Epaphroditus, who nearly died serving the Lord. He warns the Philippians not to be lead astray by those teaching that salvation comes through circumcision, and following the law. Paul has zealously followed the law, but says he knows his righteousness comes totally through faith in what Jesus has done for him, and not his own actions. He encourages us to want to know Jesus more.

Philippians 3:12-4:1 is an encouragement to persevere in our Christian walk, and to do all that Jesus has called us to do. Paul likens it to an athlete setting his mind on winning a prize, and focussing on the finishing line. We need to keep our mind on heavenly things, and not earthly things. Our citizenship is in heaven, and we can look forward to Jesus coming again, when our bodies will be like His glorious body.

Paul concludes his letter to the Philippians in 4:2-23 by asking for unity in the church, and thanking them for the gifts they have sent him. We are encouraged to constantly rejoice in the Lord, and not to be anxious about anything, but to present our requests to God, who is able to meet all our needs, and to strengthen us. Paul encourages us to think about good and wholesome things, which will lead to peace of mind.

Colossians

The Epistle to the Church at Colosse, (a city in Asia Minor - modern day Turkey), was written from Rome in about 60 AD.

In Colossians 1:1-14, Paul greets his readers, giving thanks that they have received the gospel, which is bearing fruit all over the world. He prays that they may be filled and strengthened with the love and knowledge of God, reminding them that they have been rescued from the dominion of darkness, and brought into God's kingdom, through the forgiveness of sin.

In Colossians 1:15-2:5, Paul writes that the fullness of God dwelt in Jesus, who created, and sustains, both the visible (physical) and invisible (spiritual) realms. Through the cross, we have been reconciled to God, and will be presented to Him, without blemish and accusation, if we continue in the faith. Paul writes that he gladly endures suffering, so he can fulfil his commission to preach the glorious mystery of the gospel to the Gentiles, and help them avoid being deceived.

Colossians 2:6-23, is a warning to not be deceived by worldly philosophy, or religious legalism, whereby we start to trust in our own actions and strength to overcome sin and somehow obtain salvation. Salvation comes through Jesus, who is over all powers and principalities, having triumphed over Satan at the cross. We, who were dead, have been made alive through faith in Jesus, as we have been joined to Him in His death and resurrection, and our sins have been forgiven.

In Colossians 3:1-17, we are encouraged to put off our old sinful nature and live as children of God. We are to put to death sexual immorality, impurity and greed, and to get rid of anger, lying, malice and bad language. We are to clothe ourselves with compassion, humility and gentleness, and to bear with, and forgive, each other. We are to study God's word, and be filled with His peace, as we live our lives in thankfulness for all that God has done for us.

In Colossians 3:18-4:1, Paul addresses the subject of relationships. Husbands should love their wives, and not treat them harshly. Wives should be in submission to their husbands. Parents should encourage rather than exasperate their children, who should respect, and be obedient, to their parents. Masters (employers) should treat their slaves (employees) fairly, and slaves (employees) should work with sincerity and integrity, as if working for the Lord.

Paul concludes his letter to the Colossians in 4:2-18 with a reminder to be prayerful and thankful. He reminds us to be wise in how we talk to non-believers, but to take advantage of every opportunity to be salt and light to them. There are greetings from various people, including Luke, and Onesimus, who is described as a faithful brother. Paul gives instructions that this letter should also be read to the nearby Laodicean church.

1 Thessalonians

This letter was written by Paul in about 50 AD, to the church in Thessalonica (located in Greece), which he founded during his first missionary journey.

In Chapter 1, he commends their endurance, reminding them how the gospel came to them in power, with the Holy Spirit, and with deep conviction, causing them to turn from idols, to serve the living God. Their faith is a model to others in Greece and Macedonia.

In 1 Thessalonians 2:1-16, Paul reminds his readers how he originally brought the gospel to them. He worked hard not to be a burden to them, and comforted and encouraged them, in the way a father should treat his own children. He gives thanks that they received the gospel as the word of God, and were willing to face persecution from their Jewish countrymen.

In 1 Thessalonians 2:17-3:5, Paul explains why he is writing this letter to them. He had to leave Thessalonica because of the hostility of the Jews (Acts 17:1-10), but subsequently sent Timothy to visit Thessalonica, to encourage the believers in the persecution they were facing there. Paul was concerned that Satan might have tempted them, and nullified his efforts among them. Timothy, however, has now reported back that they are doing well, and growing in their faith and love.

In 1 Thessalonians 3:6-4:12, Paul gives thanks for the good report he received about the Thessalonians, and prays that God will strengthen them, and increase their love for one another. He reminds them of the importance of living holy lives, and avoiding all sexual immorality. He encourages them to lead quiet lives, and to work diligently, so they are not dependent on others, and they win the respect of non-believers.

In 1 Thessalonians 4:13-5:11, Paul encourages us that those who have died will not be at a disadvantage to those living, when Jesus returns. Those who have died in Christ will be resurrected, and return with Jesus, and those living at that time will meet with them in the air. (The so-called 'rapture'.) The timing of the 'day of the Lord' is unknown. To unbelievers it will come unexpectedly, but, as believers, we should be alert and watchful, and live our lives in faith, hope, and with self-control.

Paul concludes his letter to the Thessalonians in 5:12-28 by encouraging us to persevere in our Christian walk, forgiving others and being joyful and thankful in all circumstances. We are reminded to not quench the work of the Holy Spirit, and to respect our Christian leaders. We are encouraged to avoid evil, testing all things, and holding on to what is good. As we do this, God, in His faithfulness, is able to sanctify us, and bring wholeness to our body, soul and spirit.

2 Thessalonians

2 Thessalonians is written by Paul to correct misunderstandings which have arisen, concerning the second coming of Jesus.

In Chapter 1, Paul gives thanks for the believers in Thessalonica, who are growing in their faith and love for one another, despite the persecution they are experiencing. He reminds them that, when Jesus returns, those who persecute them (and who do not know God, and who disobey the gospel), will be punished with everlasting destruction.

In 2 Thessalonians 2:1-12, Paul counters the false teaching that Jesus has already returned, by declaring that Jesus will not return before the rebellion occurs, and the man of lawlessness, (who will proclaim that he is God), is revealed. The coming of this lawless one will be marked by counterfeit signs and wonders, which will lead people into deception.

In 2 Thessalonians 2:13-3:5, Paul encourages his readers to hold fast to the truth they have received. Paul asks for prayer for himself, because of the opposition he faces from wicked and evil men. He encourages the Thessalonians that God is faithful, and that He will strengthen them, and protect them from the evil one.

In 2 Thessalonians 3:6-18, Paul concludes his letter by instructing the Thessalonians not to be idle. Apparently, some of the believers were expecting other believers to provide for their needs. They are not to associate with those who are idle, or who do not live according to the teaching they have received. He prays that his readers might know the peace of God in all circumstances.

1 Timothy

This letter is written by Paul to Timothy, the young pastor in Ephesus, who accompanied Paul on his second missionary journey (Acts 16:1-3).

In 1 Timothy 1:1-11, Paul stresses the importance of teaching sound doctrine, and not being distracted by meaningless talk. He warns Timothy not to tolerate those who are preaching false doctrine, and using the law to bring legalism into the church. The law shows the need for righteousness, but righteousness itself only comes through Jesus.

In 1 Timothy 1:12-20, Paul gives thanks that he can now serve Jesus, although he previously was a sinner who was persecuting and blaspheming God. The changes which God, in His mercy, has made in Paul are a testimony to others of what God can also do for them. He has written this letter to give instructions to Timothy, so that Timothy can be effective in his work, and not be led astray, and his faith shipwrecked.

In 1 Timothy 2 Paul stresses the importance of prayer, and God's desire that everyone should come to know Him. He encourages women to dress modestly, and be in submission. Writing at a time before the New Testament had been compiled, and at a time when only the men formally studied and debated the Old Testament Scripture, Paul says he does not allow women to teach, and to dominate and control men.

In 1 Timothy 3, Paul lays out the necessary characteristics for those who seek to be in leadership roles within the church. They should be men of integrity, who are respected by others, and able to manage their own families well. They should be mature in the faith, and not be self-indulgent, or have more than one wife. Their wife should be someone who is respected and trustworthy. Those seeking to be overseers should be able to teach others, and be gentle and self-controlled.

In 1 Timothy 4, Paul warns about false teaching, which he says is demonic in origin. Such false teaching includes telling people what they cannot eat, and forbidding people to marry. He encourages Timothy to devote himself to public reading of the Scriptures, preaching and teaching, and not to allow people to look down on him because of his age. His life should be an example of godliness for others to follow, and he should always watch his doctrine carefully.

In 1 Timothy 5:1-16, Paul encourages Timothy to treat his congregations as he would his own family, and with impartiality. He offers practical advice as to who the church should be helping. Only those widows with real needs, and who are of good character, should be supported by the church. Some widows should be cared for by their relatives, and others encouraged to re-marry.

In 1 Timothy 5:17-6:2, Paul gives instructions regarding elders and slaves. Elders should be honoured, and any accusation against them needs to be substantiated by more than one witness. If guilty of sin, they should be rebuked publicly. People should not be appointed too quickly into positions of authority in the church. Slaves should treat their masters with respect. If their master is a believer, it does not allow them to treat him less respectfully.

Paul concludes his letter in 1 Timothy 6:3-16 by returning to the subject of false teachers, who promote godliness, as a means of obtaining their own wealth. Paul declares that the love of money is the root of much evil. Believers should not arrogantly put their trust in their wealth, but put their trust in God, focus on their eternal life, and generously share their financial blessing with others. Finally, Paul appeals to Timothy to guard all that has been entrusted to him, and not be side-tracked.

2 Timothy

The second letter to Timothy is the last letter written by Paul from Rome where he is imprisoned and facing death.

In 2 Timothy 1, Paul greets Timothy, and thanks God for Timothy's faith and ministry. He encourages Timothy to boldly preach the gospel of grace received through Jesus, in the power, love and self-discipline which comes from the Holy Spirit. Paul feels abandoned, but gives thanks for Onesiphorus, who has refreshed him, and is not ashamed of him being in prison.

In 2 Timothy 2, Paul encourages Timothy to use the word of God correctly, and not be drawn into meaningless arguments. He reminds us that, as believers, we died with Christ, and that we will live with Him, if we endure. God is faithful, even if we are faithless. We should pursue righteousness, love, faith and peace. We are encouraged to be kind to others, and gently instruct those who oppose us, in the hope that they might understand the truth, and escape from the trap of the enemy.

In 2 Timothy 3, Paul warns about apostasy in the end time Church. People will be self-seeking, and trying to satisfy the desires of their carnal nature, while still claiming to adhere to a form of godliness. They will be lovers of self, and not living in accordance with biblical principles. Their teaching will be deceptive, and needs to be countered by the truth of God's word, which is God-breathed, and can be used for teaching, correcting, rebuking, and training in righteousness.

In 2 Timothy 4, Paul instructs Timothy to always preach the word carefully, and with patience. He is to correct all false teaching, and rebuke those who ignore sound doctrine in favour of what their ears want to hear. Paul acknowledges that he is reaching the end of his life, and will soon receive the crown of righteousness, which is awaiting him. Paul concludes his letter with personal greetings, and asking Timothy to visit him as soon as he can, and bring with him Paul's scrolls and parchments.

Titus

This letter was written in about 65 AD to Titus; a close companion of Paul, who was pioneering the church in Crete.

In Chapter 1:1-9, Paul declares that he is a servant of God, and an apostle of Jesus, living in the hope of eternal life. He instructs Titus to appoint elders and overseers in every town. These men should be of good character, self-disciplined, have only one wife, and their families well behaved. They must hold firmly to the truth they have received, and be able to defend it.

In Titus 1:10-16, Paul encourages Titus to strongly rebuke those who teach false doctrine, and especially those insisting that circumcision is necessary for salvation. Paul describes these false teachers as rebellious deceivers, who are seeking dishonest gain. They claim to know God, but their actions prove otherwise. Their minds and consciences are corrupted, and they are unable to appreciate that which is good and pure.

In Titus 2, Paul encourages Titus to be an example to others in the way he lives and teaches. He should teach men to persevere in their faith, and encourage older women to teach younger women how to be good wives and mothers. Slaves should be honest and respect their masters. Paul stresses the need for self-discipline. Jesus came to redeem us from all wickedness, so that we are able to say no to worldly passions and temptations, and live self-controlled lives.

In Titus 3, we are reminded to be respectful of leaders and those in authority over us, and to operate out of humility and kindness. We have been saved by grace, through the washing of rebirth, and renewal by the Holy Spirit. As a result, we should be doing good, avoiding foolish controversies and arguments, and leading productive lives. Paul concludes his letter by instructing Titus to warn divisive people twice, and then to have nothing more to do with them.

Philemon

This very personal letter was written in about 62 AD to Philemon who is described as a friend and co-worker.

Paul writes to commend a slave, named Onesimus, who appears to have run away from Philemon, and probably has stolen from him. He has now become a believer, and so Paul is sending him back to his rightful master, asking that Philemon accept him, and charge to Paul's account any debt Onesimus may owe Philemon.

Hebrews

The author of the book of Hebrews, (written before the fall of Jerusalem in 70 AD), is unknown, although it may have been the apostle Paul.

Hebrews 1 declares that Jesus is God, the Son. He is the exact representation of God in Heaven, and through Him the world was created, and is sustained. Jesus is superior to all the angels, who are described as ministering spirits, sent to help those who inherit salvation, and Jesus will rule eternally, with all His enemies under His feet.

Hebrews 2 explains that Jesus is higher than all the angels. He took on flesh and blood in order that He might identify with mankind. Through His death, He made atonement for sin, and provided a means of salvation. He has now been crowned with glory, and everything is subject to Him. Through His death, Jesus defeated Satan, and is able to free all those who are held in fear of death. Because He faced and resisted temptation, He is able to help us when we face temptation.

In Hebrews 3, we are encouraged to keep our thoughts on Jesus, who is faithful, and worthy of greater honour than Moses. We are encouraged not to harden our hearts towards God, as the Israelites did, after their escape from Egypt. As a result, they failed to enter the Promised Land and perished in the wilderness. We are to seek to hear God's voice, and to encourage one another.

In Hebrews 4:1-13, we are encouraged to walk in faith and obedience to God's word, so we may enter into God's rest. Some, who have heard the gospel, but have disobeyed it, will not enter into God's rest. We are reminded that the word of God is a sure plumb line, which tests our thoughts, attitudes and actions, which all of us will have to give account for to God, one day.

Hebrews 4:14-5:10 declares that Jesus is the great high priest, who made the perfect sacrifice, because He was without sin. God ordained that Jesus would take this role of high priest, and that through His obedience and perfect sacrifice He would made eternal salvation available to us. Consequently, we can approach Him with confidence, to receive His mercy and help in times of need.

Hebrews 5:11-6:12 encourages us to grow to maturity in our Christian walk, and produce fruit. We are reminded that the basics of our faith include repentance of sin, the need to walk in obedience to God, (because everyone will be raised from the dead to face judgement), baptism in water, baptism in the Holy Spirit, and healing and anointing for service. There is a stern warning for those who, having understood these basics, turn away and reject the salvation offered through Jesus.

Hebrews 6:13-7:10 declares that, when God makes an oath or covenant, He will not violate it. God demonstrates this in the way He fulfilled His promises to Abraham. God's faithfulness to His word is a firm and sure anchor for our faith. Jesus is a high priest who is much greater than Melchizedek, whom Abraham honoured as worthy of receiving a tithe, even before the Levitical priesthood was established.

Hebrews 7:11-28 explains that Jesus fulfils the role of high priest, and is the mediator and guarantor of a new and better covenant, whereby the way in which the law is fulfilled has changed. His death has become the perfect sacrifice for our sins, and does not need to be repeated. Because of His sinless-ness Jesus does not need to make sacrifices for His own sins, as earthly high priests have to, but is eternally able to intercede for us in the presence of the Father.

Hebrews 8 continues to declare that Jesus has established a new and better covenant which has made the Old Covenant, and its ceremonial and sacrificial rules and regulations, obsolete. The tabernacle, built by Moses, was merely a shadow, or copy, of the heavenly tabernacle where Jesus, as high priest, ministers this new covenant. In this new covenant God states that He will put His laws in our minds and on our hearts.

In Hebrews 9:1-10, we are reminded about the earthly tabernacle, built by Moses, in accordance with God's instructions. This tabernacle had an outer room and an inner room called the most holy place, containing the ark of the covenant and the commandments, written on two tablets of stone. Only the high priest could enter the most holy place, and, before doing so, blood sacrifices had to be made on behalf of his own sins, and the sins of the people.

Hebrews 9:11-28 explains that Jesus, as high priest, entered into the most holy place, through the once and for all shedding of His own blood on behalf of the people, thus redeeming them from their sins. Under the Old Covenant everything had to be cleansed with blood from the animal sacrifices. Under the New Covenant we are cleansed by the blood of Jesus. Jesus will appear again, not to bear our sins, but to lead all who are waiting for Him into eternal salvation.

Hebrews 10:1-18 continues to say that Jesus became the one perfect sacrifice, through which we can have forgiveness of sin. The blood sacrifices of animals served to remind the people of their sinfulness, but could not take away sins. Jesus, submitting to the will of God, sets aside the Old Covenant and replaces it with the New Covenant, through which we are made righteous and holy.

Hebrews 19:19-39 encourages us to draw near to God in confidence because of what Jesus has done for us, and to persevere, and not lose heart. There is a stern warning for those who continue to deliberately sin after they have come into the knowledge of the truth, because they nullify Jesus' sacrifice for them. We are exhorted to encourage one another, and live in faith about God's promise that Jesus will return.

In Hebrews 11:1-28, we read that faith is being sure and certain of things that we cannot yet see. Throughout the old testament we have examples of individuals who responded in faith to the promises of God. They were willing to open themselves up to ridicule, make great personal sacrifices, and risk everything they had, in their desire and determination to be obedient to God.

Hebrews 11:29-39 continues to give examples of those who are commended for living their lives by faith in God. They stepped out in faith, and acted in obedience to God. They were willing to face opposition, persecution, and even death. They acted in faith, and with the certainty that they were doing God's will, and were willing to trust the outcome to God.

In Hebrews 12:1-13, we are encouraged to draw encouragement from the lives of those who lived by faith. We are encouraged to fix our eyes on Jesus, and persevere in the plans and purposes that God has for us. If we face hardship or persecution, we should consider it as 'discipline' (training), through which we can grow in our Christian faith, and in holiness, and so produce a harvest of righteousness.

In Hebrews 12:14-29, we are reminded to live holy lives, living in peace with others, avoiding immorality, and not making bitter judgements against others. When God met with the Israelites at Mount Hebron the people were forbidden to touch the mountain, and they were very afraid, because they knew He could easily destroy them. Through Jesus, we are able to come right into the presence of God, but we still need to treat Him with reverent fear, and listen to His voice.

In Hebrews 13, we are encouraged to live godly, righteous lives, helping those less fortunate than ourselves, and not being lovers of money. We are to pray for our leaders, and not be a burden to them. We are warned to avoid deceptive false teaching. The way to God is through Jesus, who does not change, and it is not through the temple sacrifices. The letter to the Hebrews concludes with a prayer that God will equip them with everything they need to fulfil His purposes for them.

James

This book, focussing on the good works and behaviour which should accompany genuine faith, is thought to have been written by James, the half-brother of Jesus.

In Chapter 1:1-18, we are encouraged to persevere with joy in the face of trials which bring our faith to maturity. If we lack wisdom, we should ask God, from whom every good and perfect gift comes. When tempted, we should not blame God, but recognise that we are being led astray by our carnal nature.

In James 1:19-27, we are encouraged to be careful about what we say. Our religion is meaningless if we can't control our tongue. True relationship with God will result in a desire to help others, and to avoid being defiled by the world in which we live. James encourages us to not merely read the word of God, but to obey it. Failure to obey God's word is likened to looking into a mirror, and doing nothing to correct any faults in our appearance that the mirror reflects back to us.

In James 2:1-13, we are encouraged not to show favouritism based on an individual's wealth, or outward appearance. Doing this is not following Jesus' instruction, 'love your neighbour as yourself'. If we fail to keep just one of God's commands, we are law breakers. If we are not merciful to others, we will be judged accordingly.

James 2:14-26 challenges us to be active as a result of our faith. Good deeds and helping others should be the natural outworking of our faith. The absence of such fruit indicates that a person's faith is dead. Saying one believes in God is not enough, (even the demons believe in God). Righteous actions and deeds should accompany faith, just as they did for Abraham and Rahab.

James 3 declares that those who teach will be judged more strictly. We are warned to be careful about what we speak. Our tongue is likened to a rudder controlling a large ship, or a small spark igniting a large fire. One minute we can be praising God, and the next speaking words of discouragement or curse. Bitterness, envy and selfish ambition are described as works of the devil. Wisdom from heaven is pure, compassionate, merciful and peace-loving, and produces a harvest of righteousness.

James 4 declares that fighting and quarrelling are the fruits of worldly pleasures and selfish ambition. God is unable to answer our prayer when we pray from such worldly or selfish motives. God opposes the proud, but when we submit to God we can resist the devil, and he will flee from us. We should not slander someone, and then speak out judgement against them. We should not boast about what we are going to do in our own strength, but rather seek God's will for our life.

James 5 rebukes those who have sought after wealth at the expense of others. It encourages us to wait patiently for the Lord's return, and not grumble about others. Finally, we are encouraged to pray in faith when we are sick. We can ask others to pray and anoint us with oil. We should confess our sins to one another, so our prayers can be righteous, and we can receive God's healing. Those who have wandered from the faith can be restored when they repent and turn back to God.

1 Peter

Peter's first letter, written in about 65 AD, encourages believers to have hope in the face of persecution and suffering.

In Chapter 1:1-12, Peter reminds us that we have a new birth into a living hope through Jesus. We are chosen by God, sanctified by the Holy Spirit and have an inheritance which can never perish. The prophets of old searched for, and longed, to know the things which have now been revealed to us. Trials and sufferings are an opportunity to test the genuineness of our faith.

1 Peter 1:18-19 encourages us to be active and self-controlled, as we work out our faith. We should live lives in holiness and reverent fear of God, who will, one day, judge us. We have been redeemed through the precious blood of Jesus, and our faith and hope arc in God, who raised Him from the dead. Because we have been born again through the enduring and living word of God, we need to get rid of all hypocrisy, malice, slander and deceit, and crave pure, spiritual milk.

1 Peter 2:4-12 declares that we are living stones, being built into a spiritual house, in which Jesus is the cornerstone. We are a chosen people, and a royal priesthood, called out of darkness into God's wonderful light, so we can praise and worship Him. If we trust in Him, we will never be put to shame. As people who have received mercy, we should resist evil desires, and endeavour to lead lives which are a witness to others, even those who persecute and accuse us.

1 Peter 2:13-3:7 encourages us to respect others, and to submit to the authorities placed over us. We are to live as free men, but not use this freedom as an excuse to sin. If we are unjustly punished or persecuted, we should follow the example of Jesus. He did not retaliate, but entrusted Himself to God. Wives should be of a gentle and quiet spirit, and willing to submit to their husbands in a godly way. Husbands should respect their wives, and be considerate towards them.

1 Peter 3:8-22 encourages us to be humble and compassionate, and to live in harmony. We should consider it a blessing if we have to suffer for doing what is right, and not repay evil with evil. Instead we should make Jesus Lord of our lives, and always be prepared to witness to others about Him. Through the once-for-all sacrifice of Jesus we are made alive in our spirit. Just as Noah was saved from the waters of the flood, water baptism is a symbol of our salvation to eternal life.

1 Peter 4 encourages us to use our giftings to serve others in the strength God give us, and without grumbling. Our words should be the very words of God. We should not be surprised if, as believers, we face persecution and suffering, because it is the Spirit of God within us which others find offensive. We should not be ashamed of having to suffer, but should rejoice in the knowledge that we will be overjoyed when Jesus comes again in His glory.

In 1 Peter 5, elders are encouraged to be good shepherds, willingly serving the flock, and not lording it over them. We are all encouraged to act with humility, and be self-controlled and alert, because the enemy is always looking for someone to devour. We need to resist him, and stand against him. Because God cares about each one of us, we should cast all our anxieties and concerns on Him. Finally, Peter prays that God will restore and strengthen his readers, and that they may know His peace.

2 Peter

2 Peter was written to Jewish believers in about 65 AD, warning them about false teachers.

In chapter 1:1-11 we are reminded that God's divine power has given us everything we need for life. Therefore, we should seek to grow in faith, goodness, knowledge, perseverance, self-control, godliness and love. These qualities will help us to be effective and productive in our Christian life, so we will receive a rich welcome into the eternal kingdom of Jesus our Saviour.

Knowing he will soon die, Peter explains in 2 Peter 1:12-21 that he is writing this letter so that his readers will not forget the things he has already told them. He has not been telling them cleverly invented stories, but declares that he was a personal witness to the power and glory displayed in Jesus. What he has witnessed is attested to in the Scriptures. The prophecy of Scripture did not originate with man, but is the inspired word, given under the leading of the Holy Spirit.

2 Peter 2 warns us that there will be false teachers, just as there were false prophets in the past. These false teachers exploit others by introducing heresies, appealing to the carnal nature of their followers and bringing the truth into disrepute. They will be harshly judged, because they slander and blaspheme against God. If someone, who has escaped the corruption of this world by knowing Jesus, becomes entangled in it again and overcome, they are worse off than when they started.

2 Peter 3 encourages us to be patient as we await the return of Jesus. Scoffers will follow their own evil desires and ignore the promises and truth of God's word. The day of judgement, however, will eventually come. The existing heavens and earth will be burnt up by fire, and there will be a new heaven and a new earth, in which righteousness reigns. In view of this, we need to be on our guard against false teaching, and we need to keep growing in the knowledge and grace of Jesus our Saviour.

1 John

The book of 1 John, written by the apostle John in about 85 AD, encourages us to live our lives in joy and in the security of knowing the love of Jesus and our eternal destiny in Him.

In chapter 1, John declares that he is a personal witness to the life of Jesus. When we choose to walk in the light of Jesus, and not in darkness, we are purified by the blood of Jesus. John proclaims that we have all sinned, but that if we confess our sins, God forgives our sins and cleanses us from all unrighteousness.

1 John 2:1-14 encourages us to walk in the light, and in obedience to Jesus. John reminds us that Jesus atoned for our sins, and that, if we do get it wrong and sin, we can ask His forgiveness. However, if we continue to knowingly walk in a sinful lifestyle, or refuse to forgive those who have hurt us, can we truthfully say that we know Jesus? Because our sins have been forgiven, we can know God as Father, and we can overcome the evil one.

1 John 2:15-27 is a warning about being led astray by our carnal nature and seeking after worldly pleasures. John warns about the 'antichrist spirit', which denies who Jesus really is, and promotes other things in the place of Jesus. (This spirit was operating through the false teachers who were claiming to be believers, but were not teaching the truth.) We are reminded that, as Christians, we have eternal life, and that we have the anointing of the Holy Spirit, who teaches us all things.

1 John 2:28-3:10 reminds us that, if we have invited Jesus into our lives, we can call ourselves children of God, because that is what we are. Jesus came to destroy the work of the devil. When Jesus returns we will be made like Him. Because we have been born of God, we should not want to continue walking in sin. This desire to walk in righteousness is a sign of whether someone really has been born again and become a child of God.

In 1 John 3:11-4:6, we are encouraged to love one another, not just with words, but with actions. We know what love is, because Jesus laid down His life in love for us. John encourages us to test every spirit. Any spirit, which does not acknowledge Jesus, is not from God. As believers, we have within us the Holy Spirit, who is greater than any other spirit operating in the world.

1 John 4:7-21 encourages us to love one another. God has shown His love for us by sending Jesus to be an atoning sacrifice for our sins, so we might have life. Our response to what God has done for us should be to love others. We are enabled to do this by the Holy

Spirit, whom God has given to all who put their trust in Jesus. In this way God's love is made complete in us, and His perfect love drives out all fear, because we no longer have to fear death or punishment.

In 1 John 5, we are reminded that the evidence of becoming a child of God is that we love God, and walk in obedience to His commands. In Jesus we overcome the world, which is under the control of Satan. We can have assurance of our eternal salvation, because the Holy Spirit, living within us, confirms that Jesus is the Son of God, as proclaimed by the Father at Jesus' water baptism, and that Jesus redeemed us by His death, and the shedding of His blood on the cross.

2 John

2 John is a short letter, written by the apostle John in about 85 AD, to encourage a group of believers to continue to love one another and walk in obedience to God's commands. John warns them about false teachers, operating under a spirit of antichrist, who are denying that Jesus was truly God made man. He describes such false teachers as deceivers and tells his readers to have nothing to do with them.

3 John

3 John is a short personal letter written by the apostle John in about 95AD to his friend Gaius. He commends Gaius for his faithfulness and for showing hospitality to travelling Christian workers. The behaviour of Gaius and Demetrius is very different to that of Diotrephes, who is driven by selfish ambition, and wants nothing to do with John, or the missionaries that he sends out. John concludes the letter with personal greetings.

Jude

This epistle is believed to have been written in about 67 AD by Jude, the brother of James. Jude warns about false teachers, who deny the lordship of Jesus, and are self-seeking, who slander angelic beings, and who indulge in immorality. He likens them to the angels who rebelled with Satan, Cain, and the inhabitants of Sodom and Gomorrah. They do not have the Spirit, and will ultimately be judged. Jude concludes by encouraging his readers to remain in God's love,band show mercy to others.

Revelation

The book of Revelation was written in about 95 AD by the apostle John, and records a series of visions relating to the current spiritual reality, and prophetically to what would happen in the future.

In Revelation 1, John records how he receives a vision of the Lord Jesus while he was on the Island of Patmos. Jesus declares that He is the living one, who was dead, but now is alive, and holds the keys of Death and Hades. He instructs John to write down what is now, and what is yet to come.

Revelation 2:1-11 records letters to the churches of Ephesus and Smyrna, given to John by Jesus. Jesus praises the Ephesians for their actions, hard work and perseverance, and for not tolerating false teaching, but rebukes them for forsaking their first love. Jesus praises the Smyrneans, who are spiritually rich, despite their afflictions and poverty, and their future persecution, which will be stirred up by Satan. Those who overcome will not be subject to the second death, but will receive a crown of life.

Revelation 2:12-17 records the letter from Jesus to the church in Pergamum. Jesus describes Pergamum as being a place where Satan has a throne, and praises the believers for standing firm, despite persecution. He rebukes them for tolerating the Nicolaitans, (probably a gnostic sect who abused the doctrine of grace to allow sexual licentiousness). If they do not repent Jesus will bring judgement against them. Jesus promises to give a new name to those who overcome.

Revelation 2:18-29 records the letter from Jesus to the church in Thyatira. Jesus commends them for love, faith and perseverance. He rebukes them for tolerating a woman, named Jezebel, who claimed to be a prophetess, but whose teaching was leading them into idolatry and immorality. Those who overcome and do God's will, will be given authority over nations.

Revelation 3:1-6 records the letter from Jesus to the church in Sardis. Jesus tells them that, although they have a reputation of being a live church, they are actually dead. They are called to wake up and repent. Those who respond, and overcome, will be dressed in white, and never have their names blotted out from the book of life.

Revelation 3:7-13 records the letter from Jesus to the church in Philadelphia. Jesus commends them for enduring patiently, keeping His word, and not denying His name, despite their lack of strength. Jesus declares that no one can shut the doors which He opens, and no one can open the doors which He shuts. Jesus will give a new name to those who overcome.

Revelation 3:14-22 records the final letter from Jesus to the seven churches. This letter is addressed to the church in Laodicea, and in it Jesus rebukes them for being lukewarm. He tells them that they are materially rich, but spiritually poor, and that He will spit them out of His mouth if they do not change. Jesus says He is standing at the door and waiting to be invited inside. Those who overcome will rule with Jesus.

In Revelation 4 John describes how, in vision, he enters the throne room of heaven. He sees the four living creatures, who continually praise God and proclaim His holiness. Around the throne there are twenty-four elders, who worship God and lay their crowns before Him, declaring that He creates, and sustains, all things, and that He is worthy to receive glory, honour and power.

Revelation 5 continues John's vision of the throne room of God. God is holding a sealed scroll, which records what is yet to happen. No one is worthy to open the seals except Jesus. He is described as the 'Lion of Judah' and the 'Lamb who was slain, and, with His blood, purchased men for God'. All the creatures in heaven, the elders, and the millions of angels praise and worship Jesus, and bow down before Him.

In Revelation 6 Jesus opens the seals on the scroll recording future events. On opening the first four seals, horsemen of different colours are released, which appear to represent the rise of antichrist, war, famine, death and disease. When the fifth seal is broken John sees those who have been killed for the faith waiting in heaven for God to avenge their death. The breaking of the sixth seal is accompanied by great tribulation as God prepares to bring judgement on the world.

Revelation 7 continues to describe what happens when the sixth seal is broken, and just before God brings His judgement upon the world. We read that 144,000 people from the tribes of Israel are sealed as servants of God. In vision John also sees a great multitude from every nation dressed in white and worshipping God. They are described as those who have been redeemed by the blood of the Lamb. God will wipe away all their tears, and Jesus will be their shepherd.

In Revelation 8, we read of a period of silence in heaven after the seventh seal is opened. In vision, John sees the prayers of the saints on earth going up to God, before seven trumpets are sounded to herald judgement upon the earth. At the blowing of the first four trumpets catastrophic events, (possibly a nuclear war), take place, affecting a third of the earth, and resulting in devastation to land and sea, contamination of water supplies, major atmospheric pollution, and many deaths.

In Revelation 9, at the blowing of the sixth trumpet, demonic hordes are released. They torment mankind by inflicting physical pain upon them, but not causing death. The leader of these demonic hordes has the name 'Destroyer'. At the blowing of the seventh trumpet two hundred million troops are released, and they cause death to a third of the earth's inhabitants. Despite what is happening, the people do not repent, but continue in their immorality and idolatry.

Revelation 10 records that, in vision, John sees an angel (Jesus) holding a small scroll in His hand and announcing there will be no further delays, and that the mysteries of God will be accomplished when the seventh trumpet is blown. John is instructed to take the scroll and eat it. This scroll is probably the one referred to in Daniel 12, describing events in the end times, which Daniel was told to seal.

In Revelation 11:1-14, it is revealed that the Gentiles will trample on the holy city for forty-two months. (This probably relates to the three-and-a-half-year time period mentioned in Daniel 9:27, following the abomination being set up in the temple.) Two witnesses, operating with miraculous powers like those demonstrated by Elijah and Moses, will prophesy during this time. Eventually they are killed by Satan, but then they are resurrected and taken up to heaven, after which a massive earthquake occurs in Jerusalem.

Revelation 11:15-19 brings the sounding of the seventh trumpet, and the declaration that the kingdoms of the world have become the kingdoms of the Christ, and that He will reign for ever and ever. The elders fall down before the throne, praising and thanking God that the time for judgement has arrived.

Revelation 12 describes the appearance in heaven of a woman (about to give birth to a child) and a great dragon, and would seem to be an overview of what has already happened. The woman appears to represent Israel (although some might say the Church). The dragon (obviously Satan) is defeated by the angel Michael and thrown down to earth, together with a third of the angelic beings. Unable to destroy the woman, Satan makes war against all who hold to the testimony of Jesus.

Revelation 13:1-10 describes a beast (a person or kingdom) coming out of the sea (humanity), and being given authority and power by Satan. (The animals that this beast is described as being like, and his various heads and horns, are thought to refer to preceding earthly kingdoms or nations from which he arises.) Referred to as the antichrist, he is worshipped by all whose names have not been written in the Lamb's book of life. He blasphemes against God, and makes war against believers.

Revelation 13:11-18 describes the false prophet, (this could be an individual, or possibly a false religion), who exercises demonic power, and deceives the world into following after the antichrist. He is given authority to set up an image of the antichrist, and all who do not worship this image are killed. The false prophet forces everyone to receive the mark of the antichrist, and those who do not have this mark are unable to trade.

Revelation 14 describes how, in vision, John sees Jesus standing on Mount Zion with the 144,000 Jews, (previously sealed for protection in Revelation Chapter 7), who are righteous, and have now been redeemed from the earth. It seems they are being used to proclaim the gospel, and warn of the coming wrath of God. The chapter concludes with angels being instructed to take their sickles and reap, because the time for harvest, and judgement, has arrived.

Revelation 15 continues to describe John's vision of heaven, and what will happen in the last days. He sees those who have been victorious over the beast and his image, praising and worshipping God, and holding harps given to them by God. He also sees seven angels leaving the heavenly temple, carrying the seven plagues of God's wrath in bowls, which are about to be poured out upon the earth.

Revelation 16 records the pouring out of the seven plagues of God's judgement. These plagues cause the seas and rivers to turn to blood, and painful sores to break out on those who worship the antichrist. The power of the sun increases, causing scorching upon the earth, before the kingdoms of Satan and the antichrist are engulfed in darkness. Demonic spirits incite the kings of the earth to gather at Armageddon. Earthquakes and hailstones (nuclear war?) destroy cities, and change the landscape.

Revelation 17 personifies the spiritual forces behind the financial and political systems of the world as the great prostitute, or Babylon. She has led people into idolatry and immorality, and encouraged the persecution of those who stand for righteousness. She is portrayed as riding a beast, (the antichrist of Chapter 13) representing the kingdoms of the earth who have been seduced by her and have embraced her. These kingdoms make war against the Lamb but are overcome.

Revelation 18:1-8 records John's vision of an angel announcing that the city of Babylon has fallen. Babylon is described as the home of demons, with whom the kings of the earth commit adultery, and the merchants of the world grow rich. Babylon, therefore, could be said to represent the greed for power and wealth, controlling the financial and political systems of the world. God is about to bring judgement upon them.

Revelation 18:9-24 continues the description of the fall of Babylon, representing the financial and political systems of the world, and the spiritual forces behind them. These world systems will be torn down, never to be re-established, and the kings and merchants of the world will mourn that this has happened.

Revelation 19:1-10 describes the rejoicing in heaven, because Babylon has fallen. The multitudes declare that God reigns, that His judgements are true and just, and that the blood of the saints has been avenged. The wedding feast of the Lamb has come, and the bride has made herself ready.

Revelation 19:11-21 describes John's wonderful and powerful vision of Jesus leading the armies of heaven into battle. Jesus is seated on a white horse, and on His robe is written 'King of kings and Lord of lords'. The antichrist and his false prophet are captured and thrown into the lake of burning sulphur.

Revelation 20:1-6 describes how Satan will be bound for a thousand years. Those who have died for their faith and not worshipped the beast are resurrected to life. The second death has no power over them, and they will be priests of God and of Christ, and reign with Him.

Revelation 20:7-15 describes how, at the end of the thousand years, Satan is released, and leads the nations of the earth to rebel against God, and to attack Jerusalem. They are defeated, and Satan is thrown into the lake of fire, along with Death and Hades, where they will be eternally tormented. Then all the dead are judged before the great white throne. All those whose names are not recorded in the book of life are also thrown into the lake of fire.

In Revelation 21, John sees, in vision, a new heaven and earth, and a new city of Jerusalem, in which God will dwell with the righteous. This city, described as the bride of the Lamb, is made of gold, is adorned with precious jewels, and shines with the glory of God. It is a city in which there will be no death, or sorrow, or sadness, and a city into which nothing impure can ever enter.

Revelation 22 concludes John's vision of the new Jerusalem. The water of life flows from the throne of God and of the Lamb. The tree of life bears twelve crops of fruit, and its leaves are for the healing of the nations. Jesus invites all who are thirsty to come and take the free gift of life, and issues a solemn warning against those who change the words of this book. He declares that He is the Alpha and the Omega, the beginning and the end, and that He will be coming soon.

Printed in Great Britain
by Amazon